Super Sport SUZUKI 250 MODEL T20
X·6 HUSTLER
SUZUKI HUSTLER
FORGET YOUR TROUBLES, GET ON SUZUKI
ALL NEW MODE
handful of dynamite
SUZUKI-380
のオートバイ！
コレタ セルツイン
コレタ125 SK・SL
現金正価 ¥63,000 ¥70,000
SUZUKI
WHEELING ALONG IN FIFTH, THE GT-550 TRIPLE IS SO QUIET YOU ALMOST FORGET HOW POWERFUL IT IS— UNTIL YOU TWIST THE THROTTLE.
80
SUZUKI
With a new 3-cylinder GT series.
鈴木自動車工業株式会社
スズキで大地へ挑戦！
Take off to the Country
スズキ・ヘルメット・サービス
安全への願いをこめておくる。
GT 250
GT 350
GT 500
GT 750

SUZUKI MOTORCYCLES

The Classic Two-stroke Era 1955 to 1978

Brian Long

General
BMW Boxer Twins 1970-1995 Bible, The (Falloon)
BMW Cafe Racers (Cloesen)
BMW Custom Motorcycles – Choppers, Cruisers, Bobbers, Trikes & Quads (Cloesen)
Bonjour – Is this Italy? (Turner)
British 250cc Racing Motorcycles (Pereira)
British Café Racers (Cloesen)
British Custom Motorcycles – The Brit Chop – choppers, cruisers, bobbers & trikes (Cloesen)
BSA Bantam Bible, The (Henshaw)
BSA Motorcycles – the final evolution (Jones)
Ducati 750 Bible, The (Falloon)
Ducati 750 SS 'round-case' 1974, The Book of the (Falloon)
Ducati 860, 900 and Mille Bible, The (Falloon)
Ducati Monster Bible (New Updated & Revised Edition), The (Falloon)
Ducati Story, The – 6th Edition (Falloon)
Ducati 916 (updated edition) (Falloon)
Fine Art of the Motorcycle Engine, The (Peirce)
Franklin's Indians (Sucher/Pickering/Diamond/Havelin)
From Crystal Palace to Red Square – A Hapless Biker's Road to Russia (Turner)
Italian Cafe Racers (Cloesen)
Italian Custom Motorcycles (Cloesen)
Kawasaki Triples Bible, The (Walker)
Kawasaki Z1 Story, The (Sheehan)
Moto Guzzi Sport & Le Mans Bible, The (Falloon)
The Moto Guzzi Story – 3rd Edition (Falloon)
Motorcycle Apprentice (Cakebread)
Motorcycle GP Racing in the 1960s (Pereira)
Motorcycle Racing with the Continental Circus 1920-1970 (Pereira)
Motorcycle Road & Racing Chassis Designs (Noakes)
Motorcycling in the '50s (Clew)
MV Agusta Fours, The book of the classic (Falloon)
Norton Commando Bible – All models 1968 to 1978 (Henshaw)
Off-Road Giants! (Volume 1) – Heroes of 1960s Motorcycle Sport (Westlake)
Off-Road Giants! (Volume 2) – Heroes of 1960s Motorcycle Sport (Westlake)
Off-Road Giants! (Volume 3) – Heroes of 1960s Motorcycle Sport (Westlake)
Racing Line – British motorcycle racing in the golden age of the big single (Guntrip)
The Red Baron's Ultimate Ducati Desmo Manual (Cabrera Choclán)
Scooter Lifestyle (Grainger)
Scooter Mania! – Recollections of the Isle of Man International Scooter Rally (Jackson)
Triumph Bonneville Bible (59-83) (Henshaw)
Triumph Bonneville!, Save the – The inside story of the Meriden Workers' Co-op (Rosamond)
Triumph Motorcycles & the Meriden Factory (Hancox)
Triumph Speed Twin & Thunderbird Bible (Woolridge)
Triumph Tiger Cub Bible (Estall)
Triumph Trophy Bible (Woolridge)
TT Talking – The TT's most exciting era – As seen by Manx Radio TT's lead commentator 2004-2012 (Lambert)
Velocette Motorcycles – MSS to Thruxton – Third Edition (Burris)
Vincent Motorcycles: The Untold Story since 1946 (Guyony & Parker)

Enthusiast's Restoration Manual Series
Ducati Bevel Twins 1971 to 1986 (Falloon)
How to restore Honda CX500 & CX650 – YOUR step-by-step colour illustrated guide to complete restoration (Burns)
How to restore Honda Fours – YOUR step-by-step colour illustrated guide to complete restoration (Burns)
Kawazaki Z1, Z/KZ900 &Z/KZ1000 (Rooke)
Triumph Trident T150/T160 & BSA Rocket III, How to Restore (Rooke)

Essential Buyer's Guide Series
BMW Boxer Twins (Henshaw)
BMW GS (Henshaw)
BSA 350, 441 & 500 Singles (Henshaw)
BSA 500 & 650 Twins (Henshaw)
BSA Bantam (Henshaw)
Ducati Bevel Twins (Falloon)
Ducati Desmodue Twins (Falloon)
Ducati Desmoquattro Twins – 851, 888, 916, 996, 998, ST4 1988 to 2004 (Falloon)
Hinckley Triumph triples & fours 750, 900, 955, 1000, 1050, 1200 – 1991-2009 (Henshaw)
Honda CBR FireBlade (Henshaw)
Honda CBR600 Hurricane (Henshaw)
Honda SOHC Fours 1969-1984 (Henshaw)
Kawasaki Z1 & Z900 (Orritt)
Moto Guzzi 2-valve big twins (Falloon)
Norton Commando (Henshaw)
Triumph 350 & 500 Twins (Henshaw)
Triumph Bonneville (Henshaw)
Triumph Thunderbird, Trophy & Tiger (Henshaw)
Velocette 350 & 500 Singles 1946 to 1970 (Henshaw)

Biographies
Chris Carter at Large – Stories from a lifetime in motorcycle racing (Carter & Skelton)
Jim Redman – 6 Times World Motorcycle Champion: The Autobiography (Redman)
'Sox' – Gary Hocking – the forgotten World Motorcycle Champion (Hughes)

www.veloce.co.uk

First published in July 2018 by Veloce Publishing Limited, Veloce House, Parkway Farm Business Park, Middle Farm Way, Poundbury, Dorchester DT1 3AR, England. Tel +44 (0)1305 260068 / Fax 01305 250479 / e-mail info@veloce.co.uk / web www.veloce.co.uk or www.velocebooks.com.
ISBN: 978-1-787112-12-4 UPC: 6-36847-01212-0.
© 2018 Brian Long and Veloce Publishing. All rights reserved. With the exception of quoting brief passages for the purpose of review, no part of this publication may be recorded, reproduced or transmitted by any means, including photocopying, without the written permission of Veloce Publishing Ltd. Throughout this book logos, model names and designations, etc, have been used for the purposes of identification, illustration and decoration. Such names are the property of the trademark holder as this is not an official publication. Readers with ideas for automotive books, or books on other transport or related hobby subjects, are invited to write to the editorial director of Veloce Publishing at the above address. British Library Cataloguing in Publication Data – A catalogue record for this book is available from the British Library. Typesetting, design and page make-up all by Veloce Publishing Ltd on Apple Mac. Printed in India by Replika Press.

SUZUKI MOTORCYCLES

The Classic Two-stroke Era 1955 to 1978

Brian Long

VELOCE PUBLISHING
THE PUBLISHER OF FINE AUTOMOTIVE BOOKS

Dedicated to Kiyo-san, with whom I can share my love of horses and all things mechanical, and my good friends at Suzuki Station in Chishirodai, Chiba, who keep me mobile, and continually provide a level of service far beyond the norm.

Contents

Introduction..6
Acknowledgements..7

1 Birth Of The Marque..8
2 The Fabulous Fifties...16
3 The Early Sixties...32
4 The Late Sixties..62
5 The Sizzling Seventies..98
6 End Of An Era..141

Index..174

Introduction

The author has owned four Suzuki cars in recent years – a Swift for town work, and three Escudos, as they suit the family lifestyle, which tends to revolve around horses, very well indeed. What most folks will have failed to notice is the registration plate on each – a single number seven, not because it's considered lucky out here, but my way of paying homage to an old hero of mine, Barry Sheene. Like many race enthusiasts of my generation, the image of Suzuki and the smiling cockney go hand-in-hand. For many of us, it was our first real exposure to the brand, but what an introduction!

As time goes by, one comes to realise that Suzuki has made some superb road bikes – a fact the Americans learnt much quicker than the Europeans, who were too busy defending home-grown marques to appreciate what the Hamamatsu-based manufacturer had to offer. It was exactly the same in the car world, of course, with the likes of Toyota and Datsun being looked down on for years, until they proved their worth through reliable use and their results in motorsport.

Most people will know me as a car guy. But my love of old bikes is very real – the racing side I've already mentioned, but they are in my blood, too, and the only reason I haven't owned a ton of them is simply down to timing and funds. I was so into cars as a kid that I never had a penny to spare for anything else. Add in the fact that the kind of bikes I wanted required big money (and even bigger money to insure), and one can see why my enthusiasm remained largely on an academic level. As for the DNA bit, I was the first in the main family line to own a car – everyone before me had a wide range of British motorcycles for as far back as anyone can remember, and even my mother can ride a racer and help strip an engine! Her aspirations of being an engineer were soon halted by my grandfather, however, despite most of the family working on aero-engines and so on. He thought an engineer was no job for a lady, but the fact that every other old photo of her is on a different bike speaks volumes. In addition, my father was a Harley man until a bad accident made him opt for four-wheel transport, and his brother (who taught me the basics of mechanical engineering and bodywork, for which I will forever be grateful) used to race a lot in his younger days. Anyway, it's fair to say I have more than a passing interest in the subject ...

I guess that DNA has surfaced of late, for I started looking for a nice classic bike to restore. This had happened many times before, but never as seriously as this, and having fallen madly in love with the unique lines of the Colleda Seltwin SB, this is what started this project in motion – the same thirst for knowledge that's kicked off many a car book, and even the odd camera

The bike that kicked off a complex (and expensive!) but extremely enjoyable project, challenging yet fun in much the same way as the most difficult of jigsaw puzzles. With luck, the Seltwin will be in perfect condition by the time Tokyo hosts the 2020 Olympics.

tome. Of course, I have an unfair advantage living in Japan with a wife who can translate original material day and night, but hopefully this, not least combined with the full co-operation of the factory, will result in a volume that will satisfy even the most ardent of Suzuki fans.

So, here we go with a long overdue history of the Suzuki (and Colleda) two-stroke models of the classic era, touching on the company history and contemporary mopeds along the way (I hope you will forgive me for this, but I figure the full-blooded mopeds and playthings like RV bikes are a different subject, and prefer to dedicate what space we have to the more exciting machines that hardly ever get covered with information being so hard to come by – even a famous Japanese journalist once wrote "the early Suzukis are a complete mystery"), and, of course, the varied racers fielded by the works team that put the Suzuki name up in lights for so many of us.

Acknowledgements

No book can be completed without the help of others, and in projects like this, my wife Miho is always an invaluable part of the equation. Research always manages to bring up discrepancies. There are still those that question who the designer of the Nissan Fairlady Z is, or the true story behind the Daimler SP engine and its links with the Rootes Group, despite me presenting overwhelming facts that prove what has been written before is wrong, but such is the life of an author and historian. Within my tally of 80 books, never have I come across so many wild statements, brought about through rapid changes and a model range that more often than not don't tie-up from country to country (at least not at specific dates, as one would expect, even when the bikes were the same type, and there's no consistency on who takes the lead on introducing new lines either), but hopefully our ability to cross-check original material and speak to those involved in their native language will put any myths to bed.

Ultimately, despite all sorts of archive material being lost over the years (and many organisations you would expect to have stuff, such as the Motorcycle Federation of Japan, simply not bothering to record events if the lengthy but fruitless phone call made by my wife is anything to go by, with others being the typical and sadly all too common Japanese 'name and shape only' places that give selected retired folks a cushy number), it's the very real enthusiasm of those at the Hamamatsu factory that has allowed this project to blossom, and kept me going whilst getting fed up of hitting brick walls and adding up the cost of buying increasingly rare material by the truckload in order to try and do a good job. I think I have spent more on this project than the last ten put together!

Notwithstanding, there are many people to thank, in particular Satoru Makoshi, Shunsuke Ikeda and Kenichi Oshima at the head office in Hamamatsu, as well as Alun Parry at Suzuki GB, Marina Ogawa and Takaaki Matsuo at Yaesu Publishing, Takahara Books, dozens of sellers on auction sites across the world, and Ken Kobayashi at Miki Press, who always has his finger on the pulse. I also have to thank the various racers and engineers I've spoken to over the years, as it has helped put a lot of things into perspective, and Rod Grainger for having faith in me, allowing me to tackle something outside my regular line of work for Veloce in a manner that has taken up a lot more pages than he'd have liked. Now all that remains to be said is that I sincerely hope you will find the end result enjoyable, useful and worthwhile …

Brian Long
Chiba City, Japan

"An excellent buy, sir ... but if you are married, it's as well if you don't talk in your sleep"

1 Birth Of The Marque

To discover the history of the Suzuki brand as we know it, one needs to go back to October 1909, and the foundation of the Suzuki Loom Works by Michio Suzuki in Hamamatsu, located in Shizuoka prefecture on Japan's main Honshu island. Sitting about halfway between Tokyo and Osaka, and close to the established merchant city of Nagoya, Hamamatsu quickly became the equivalent of places such as Coventry in England, with numerous companies moving from the cloth and weaving business into cycles, before ultimately taking on the challenge of other motorised transport and specialised forms of engineering.

Famous for its textile making since the mid-1800s, as well as Suzuki, Yamaha can also trace its roots back to Hamamatsu, and a certain Soichiro Honda was born there, too, establishing firms that had links with Toyota (based in the neighbouring Aichi prefecture) and Yamaha before he set out on his own path with a company bearing his name.

Although you may be wondering why this is important, it serves to illustrate that the area was already well-known for its engineering base and the skilled workforce that came with it, even after a huge earthquake followed by relentless waves of B-29 bombers during the Second World War did their best to break the spirit of the community.

Michio Suzuki pictured with a bust that was presented to him by dealers selling the Diamond Free after the Second World War.

Michio Suzuki was born in a village a stone's throw from this bustling environment on February 18, 1887. He worked from an early age, picking cotton and helping on the family farm, before he started building floor looms alongside his mentor, Kotaro Imamura. Suzuki duly put his experience and undoubted talent to work in creating his own loom as soon as he finished his apprenticeship. Eventually, the loom he created for his mother allowed her to weave almost ten times faster than before, and word quickly spread. By 1909, he'd secured enough orders to justify the establishment of his own loom works, originally based in an old silkworm house on land rented to him by his uncle.

The first Suzuki factory, situated in what is today's Nakajimacho, in the Naka area of Hamamatsu. It was soon remodelled into something a little grander, with a small display area at the front, but there's no doubt that the Suzuki empire was built on humble beginnings.

Suzuki moved with the times, talking to users about their wants and needs, producing the machines they needed to create the types of cloth that fashion demanded at a reasonable price. In 1911, he was employing ten people, but his workforce had already increased to 60 by the end of the Great War thanks to a number of large orders from domestic textile and weaving companies.

With electricity becoming widely available in the area, Suzuki developed power looms as well, allowing him to cater for clients of all sizes. The firm's growth allowed it to be registered as the Suzuki Loom Manufacturing Co – a joint-stock company – on March 15, 1920. The timing could have been better, as Japan's economy took a nosedive in the spring of that year, and was made even worse after the huge earthquake that struck the Kanto area in 1923.

Fortunately, Suzuki's business was able to survive thanks to its ability to manufacture looms of a specialist nature (as opposed to those making simple white cloth), and with further refinements, a new machine was patented in 1930 that allowed sarongs to be produced with ease. Exports of Suzuki looms began all over south-east Asia straight after, their huge popularity in countries like Indonesia more than making up for the shortfall in home sales, and expansion followed via the takeover of a number of smaller concerns. Only after Japan walked out of the League of Nations due to a quarrel over Manchuria's occupation did trade slow down, but nothing would deter Suzuki from looking forward.

A four-wheeled excursion

Ironically, the reliability and longevity of the Suzuki looms meant that repeat sales were few and far between. Suzuki concluded that if the company was to survive long-term, a line of consumable products was needed, and what better than an automobile – a new and fashionable item as far as Japan was concerned, with the potential for a decent profit margin.

One will remember that Toyota (then Toyoda Automatic Loom Works) had the same idea, but while the AA was based on the technology of large American machines, Suzuki decided to go in the opposite direction and chose the frugal Austin Seven as the starting point for its car. Britain's little Austin Seven was actually adopted by several companies, ranging from BMW in Germany, Rosengart in France, and Nissan in Japan, the owner of the Datsun brand.

Research started in August 1936, with a reference car being bought in 1937, and a few 13bhp Suzuki prototypes were duly

One of the prototype Suzuki cars built before war production dominated activities at the huge Aioicho factory, which opened in September 1922. The head office was moved there in 1926.

built before the project was ultimately scrapped in 1940. Given the huge cost of automobiles in relation to Japanese wages at the time (meaning that only 75,700 motorised passenger vehicles were registered in 1937, mostly US models, despite a population of around 70,000,000!), dropping the car project was probably the right move, even if outside factors were the main cause behind its demise.

In any case, thoughts of motor vehicles were quickly put on hold by a huge stream of military orders that came about due to the Second Sino-Japanese War. In the end, a massive new factory had to be built (at the site of today's head office) to keep up with demand. Duly completed in September 1939, Saburo Suzuki, the husband of one of Michio's daughters (known as mukoyōshi, it was quite common in Japan for husbands to take over the family name of their wife, in particular in farming or business arenas) and an engineer by trade, was put in charge of it. At least the factory was related to cars in a small way, producing crankshafts and pistons for wartime Isuzus.

Interestingly, Saburo Suzuki had started looking at motorcycle engines at the same time as the car research, leading to a prototype being constructed in the autumn of 1937. However, this project was also abandoned, as the factory had trouble keeping pace with its current orders let alone cope with a new product line.

Suzuki was kept busy making things like hoses, tyre

SUZUKI MOTORCYCLES: THE CLASSIC TWO-STROKE ERA

The Takatsuka factory pictured before it was damaged during the war. Completed in 1939, this was much the same size as the Aioicho one at that time, showing just how successful Suzuki had become within a very short period.

reinforcements and sails for ships before moving on to armaments and ammunition from 1938 onwards. As the war raged on in Manchuria, orders came in for items as diverse as machine parts and aircraft bomb sights. By the end of 1941, when the war in the Pacific kicked off, Suzuki was employing over 6000 people, with 12-hour shifts the norm and just two days a month for rest. Wartime production, especially given the distinct lack of metals and other raw materials, as well as supplies of oil being blocked, was truly staggering. As a result, the company's share capital had increased more than fourfold since the start of WWII.

We mentioned Coventry as a European equivalent of Hamamatsu earlier, and that industrial base unfortunately meant both suffered a similar fate during the war. In reality, both were legitimate targets for heavy bombing due to their concentrated engineering-based activities, and, as a result, both cities were hard to recognize come 1945.

Anyway, the massive M8.1 earthquake of December 1944 coincided with the first of the bombing raids, and the following April saw 70 B-29s attack Hamamatsu, adding to the overall misery. Plans to build another factory were basically brought to an end after another raid involving no less than 200 planes took place in the middle of May. As far as Suzuki was concerned, the war was effectively over, three months before Emperor Hirohito announced Japan's surrender over the radio. Still the bombs kept coming, though, with 95 per cent of the main factory destroyed in the end.

Postwar recovery

One cannot really appreciate the state Japan was left in after VJ Day without seeing contemporary pictures – the Americans had used tons of incendiary devices during their air raids, wiping out huge swathes of wooden housing, while regular bombs saw to what was left, knocking out sturdier structures and roads. Tokyo, Nagoya and Osaka were in ruins, with over 8,000,000 homeless on the streets, food was in short supply, and the trains left running were packed with folks trying to trade their last belongings, as their cash was basically worthless. Transport was desperately needed to get the country mobile again, but it had to be cheap to buy, frugal and tough.

Such was the devastation, followed by a tight grip on material supply and usage imposed by GHQ that lasted until the Allied forces (led by General Douglas MacArthur for most of the occupation, with General Matthew Ridgway eventually taking his place) finally pulled out of Tokyo in 1952, that even though there was a definite requirement for motor vehicles, few were in a position to fill the gap in the market.

In the eyes of MacArthur, with so many left with nothing after the conflict, exports were always going to be the key to postwar recovery, so the production of smaller, high-value items like cameras was encouraged, bringing much-needed foreign currency into the country. This seemed like a reasonable idea, and indeed, one only needs to look at the success of companies like Nikon and Canon to see there was mileage in it, but, somewhat ironically, it was US military orders for the Korean War effort that got the auto makers rolling again – another war helping to repair the damage from an earlier one. Toyota's boss, Eiji Toyoda, even went so far as to say: "The orders were Toyota's salvation."

A handful of motorcycle manufacturers, such as Meguro, Showa, Rikuo and Miyata (who had all been furnished with military contracts for their bikes, incidentally), gingerly went back to what they knew best, while the Nakajima Aircraft Co. (later Fuji Heavy Industries) and Mitsubishi started making scooters. At the other end of the scale, Soichiro Honda decided to use some war surplus two-stroke 50cc generator engines to power bicycles as a cheap form of transport. This Type A model evolved into the Type B and Type C before the legendary Type D 'Dream' was launched in August 1949. The 'Dream' was a proper motorcycle with a 98cc engine integrated into the frame, and was, as such, a major advance over its predecessors. It was probably the 1952 Cub that put Honda on the map, though, its huge success prompting Honda to build a massive new factory in Saitama, close to Tokyo.

Meanwhile, Suzuki had dismissed all its workers at the end of August 1945, with only a skeleton administrative staff kept on to keep the company alive. With permission from GHQ,

BIRTH OF THE MARQUE

plans were put in place to revive loom manufacture for cloth production within the works, along with a loom repair service, with the reborn business centred at the Takatsuka site only. There was also an order from the national railway operator for repairs to locomotives and rolling stock, so the old staff members were slowly brought back into the fold as soon as the factory was rebuilt, albeit at numbers in the hundreds rather than the thousands at this stage.

In reality, though, while the long-term vision was there, to survive on a day-to-day basis, the company turned its hand to anything that would bring money in, including shovels and farm tools, and even making salt using the local seawater. Eventually, an order from GHQ to make yarn from cotton imported from America finally gave Suzuki the chance to sell textile machines in the kind of numbers that made the business viable again. By summer 1948, when the business was restructured under the Enterprise Reconstruction & Reorganisation Law, the capital of the company had increased to 18,000,000 yen (double the value quoted at the end of the war), and profits, although marginal, were being achieved once more.

The dream quickly came to an end, however, with cancelled orders and the growth of a strong union movement, and by 1950, although the company's capital now stood at a healthy 54,000,000 yen, losses incurred were huge and Michio Suzuki actually ended up approaching Toyoda Automatic Loom Works (the firm behind today's Toyota empire) for help.

Hope revived

With the company shored up by Toyoda's cash injection, Shunzo Suzuki (another son-in-law of Michio's who had played an important role in the company in prewar days, and now an executive board member) was able to concentrate on other things. Having been inspired by the early Honda machines, in the autumn of 1951, he set the ball in motion that would see his bicycle converted into a motorised vehicle to use on his beloved fishing trips.

Under Suzuki engineer, Yoshichika Maruyama, it was decided that for better balance, the engine should be placed low down and use the existing chain for drive. A 30cc prototype was built, but it was soon decided that more power was needed, calling for the adoption of a slightly bigger unit. Ultimately, all of the parts that made up the air-cooled 37cc two-stroke production engine were manufactured in their entirety at the factory to ensure a perfect installation. One of the most interesting features was a double sprocket gear that allowed the

The Power Free kept in the factory collection, along with a contemporary shot of Power Free engine production at the Takatsuka works.

The 30cc 'Atom' prototype that laid the foundation stone for the Power Free series.

SUZUKI MOTORCYCLES: THE CLASSIC TWO-STROKE ERA

rider to use the engine's power only, assist it using the pedals, or use the bike in a conventional manner.

Coming a month after the Type F/FM Cub, the Suzuki Power Free 36 was eventually launched in June 1952, selling for 22,000 yen (for the E-1 single-cylinder engine only) or 36,000 yen as a complete machine based on a sturdy bicycle. To put that into perspective, the average wage was 152,400 yen in 1952, while a fixed exchange rate of 360 yen to the US dollar was in place throughout the fifties and sixties.

Although there had been some resistance to the project in the boardroom, the Power Free engine evolved into E-2, NE and E-3 (all 37cc) variants, with sales of this original Suzuki bike finally ending in the autumn of 1954.

In the background, no sooner had Ridgway left than PM Shigeru Yoshida started reversing a lot of the GHQ-imposed policies, allowing power to be restored in the *zaibatsu* (industrial empires) of old, and soon Japan was back to its more familiar working practices. In reality, not that many cared as long as there was food on the table, and now, unlike a few years earlier, there was. Granted, the boom years were still a long way off, especially after an acute recession followed the end of the Korean War in 1953, but at least the country was recovering at a steady pace. This, and the unprecedented success of the Power Free line, helped by a relaxation in the rules regarding the ownership and use of motorcycles, as well as a strong dealer network established in the summer of 1952, allowed Suzuki to develop the power-assist idea further.

The SJK Diamond Free (the SJK initials standing for Suzuki Jidosha Kogyo, or Suzuki Automotive Industries in English, which perhaps pointed toward an ultimate goal) came about from user feedback and the exploitation of the latest rules, introduced in July 1952, which allowed a 60cc two-stroke or a 90cc four-stroke bike to be ridden without a licence. The 2bhp Diamond Free was expensive, with the 58cc DF-1 engine alone costing 38,500 yen at the time of its launch in March 1953, as it equated to about three months' worth of wages. Nonetheless, this speedy machine was a

Advertising for the 58cc Diamond Free engine (top centre) in amongst a selection of rival machines available in 1955.

The three-man team that did a proving run the whole length of Japan in late 1953 to show the reliability of the Diamond Free unit. The original DF-1 was sold from 1953 to 1956, with the 50cc and 70cc versions surviving a little longer, the latter until the end of 1957.

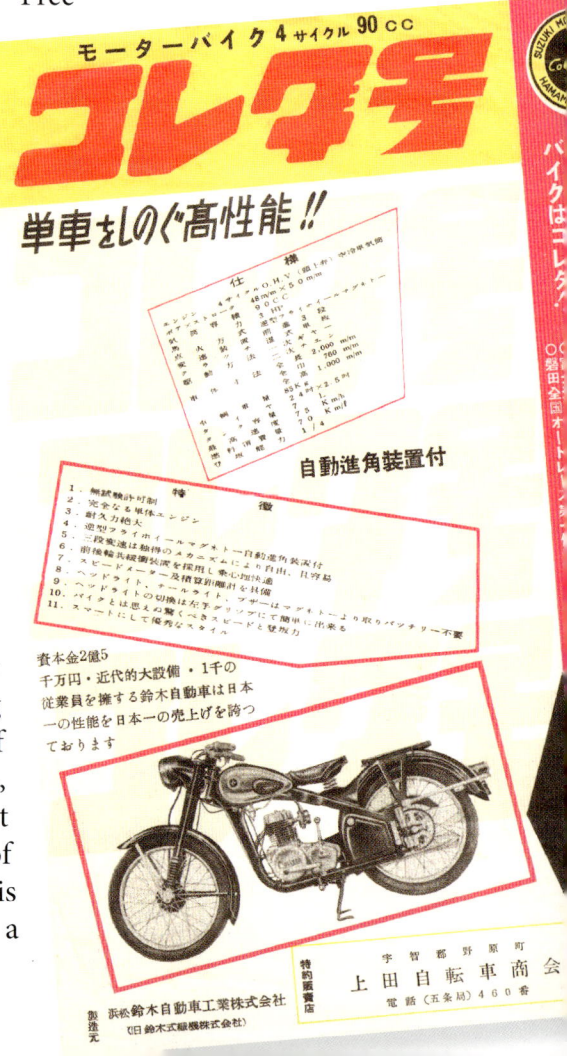

BIRTH OF THE MARQUE

huge success, even compared to the Power Free line, and the original production schedules of 4000 units a month had to be increased to 6000 by the autumn, such was demand, both at home and abroad. By the end of 1953, the Diamond Free had helped Suzuki clear all of its debts incurred after the war, and the company was a prominent member amongst the 28 firms originally registered in the important but sadly ephemeral Hamamatsu Motorcycle Manufacturers' Association (or HMMA).

From December 1954, there was a more compact 50cc Mini Free motor kit made available as well, the lightweight two-stroke MF-1, which made use of a belt drive, going through a series of modifications until the final MF-4 version was released, which, amazingly, sold until 1959. More exciting things were afoot at the SJK works, though …

The Suzuki Motor Co Ltd

The Suzuki Motor Company was registered as a limited company on June 1, 1954, with a share capital of 250,000,000 yen. While Suzuki looms were still being manufactured (this side of the business wasn't separated until April 1961), this move was made for several reasons – three with two wheels, and one with four.

Michio Suzuki was pleased with the way the sales of the Diamond Free motorcycle engines were going, and instructed his engineers to start research on a small car project in January 1954. However, Shunzo Suzuki said that it was too soon to enter the market, given regular income levels, and suggested concentrating on building complete motorbikes instead.

A single page flyer from the author's collection depicting the first Colleda, which was Suzuki's first proper motorbike. By the way, one will often see an 'S' followed by a few numbers on Japanese adverts and catalogues. This is the date in emperor years, with S for Showa era, and adding 25 gives you the year. While the S is missing (being taken as read at the time), the '29.8' in the lower right-hand corner tells us the piece was printed in August 1954.

The Colleda CO-K, Diamond Free, and Colleda CO-L outside the works, just before the company name on the building was changed to the Suzuki Motor Company. The Colleda moniker came from a translation of the Japanese for 'that's the one' – a play on words, although the straight conversion of the characters would be *koreda*, so obviously some thought was put into making the brand name look and sound more attractive.

As it happens, the motorbike idea was already well advanced, with the first Colleda CO completed just before Christmas 1953, allowing sales to begin in May the following year – a month ahead of the company name changing. This three-speed 90cc four-stroke machine was sold in two versions – the deluxe CO-K, with an engine guard and body fairings over the frame, and the naked CO-L, with its chrome fuel tank garnish. The latter was the most popular variant by far, selling for 103,000 yen, although even that was a rarity.

Despite doing well in competition, the CO hadn't been on the market long when the beautifully crafted single-cylinder engine was bored out by 8mm to give a 56mm x 50mm bore

Promotional paperwork for the CO-K and CO-L.

13

SUZUKI MOTORCYCLES: THE CLASSIC TWO-STROKE ERA

and stroke and take the cubic capacity up to 123cc, thus releasing a little more power (4bhp versus 3bhp for the CO), and bringing forth the Colleda COX model as a result.

Seeing as the CO had picked up a fin on the front mudguard not long after production started, the only distinguishing features of note are the badge on the fuel tank (a number '90' can be seen behind the Colleda script on the CO models, with '125' on the COX), along with a heavier kneepad, giving the COX tank a slimmer appearance.

Launched in March 1955 to coincide with a rule change on bike use (which basically bracketed bikes in two new categories of under 50cc and from 51cc to 125cc), although it lasted longer than its predecessor, the COX was still short-lived nonetheless, surviving only until the summer of 1957. In reality, Suzuki had found a better way to garner volume sales, and that was by concentrating on two-stroke models – the core subject of this book, and the thing we'll start covering in the next chapter.

Before moving on, though, we should mention the Suzulight – the four-wheeled machine we'd hinted at earlier. As we know, Michio Suzuki had been interested in making an automobile since before the war, and, at last, after a prototype was built in 1954 based on a combination of contemporary Lloyd, Volkswagen and Citroën technology, a thoroughly practical production model taking full advantage of the latest rules on Japan's domestic *Kei* (or light) cars was launched in October 1955.

It could be said that Michio Suzuki had often followed Soichiro Honda's lead up to this point, but on this front, Suzuki was a long way ahead of Honda, whose first car didn't appear until 1963. In fact, thanks to the sterling work of a five-man team led by Saburo Suzuki, the front-wheel drive model, powered by an air-cooled twin and

The Mount Fuji Ascent Race was the first serious form of two-wheeled competition in postwar Japan, held annually between 1953 and 1956, and sponsored by the *Mainichi Shimbun* newspaper. Rinsaku Yamashita won his class in 1953 on a Diamond Free, then won the second edition outright with the CO, similar to the one pictured here.

The original Colleda COX (or COX-I), which would be the last four-stroke Suzuki for quite some time. The COX-II, the final version, introduced in November 1955 and identified by the lack of rubber boots on the front forks, sold for 125,000 yen.

BIRTH OF THE MARQUE

Wonderful picture of a Suzuki dealer in Kagoshima in the mid-1950s, with a Colleda COX and Diamond Free engine stealing the limelight on the shop front.

Suzulight production with a few bikes in the background. The Suzulight *Kei* car was sold in sedan, van and pick-up form.

with independent suspension all-round, was a real trailblazer in the 360cc category, beating the Subaru 360 and Mazda R360 Coupé to the marketplace by quite some margin. With profits minimal, or even non-existent in the early days, Shunzo Suzuki was less than keen on the Suzulight, convincing his father-in-law to continue at a slow pace now the marque had become established as a car maker, but the majority of the company's effort should be directed towards two-wheeled machines for the foreseeable future.

By the way, Japanese bike production had risen to 170,000 units a year by this time, with over 200 makers at the peak of Japan's postwar motorisation boom. Indeed, thanks to another licence rule change, the number of registered bikes in the Land of the Rising Sun jumped from 94,500 in 1952, to 383,500 two years later, and would top the million mark in 1955! Suzuki's neighbours at Yamaha also decided to turn to motorcycles in 1954, with the DKW-based 125YA being successful enough to allow the company to establish a new business at Hamakita purely for two-wheelers. Sales began in February 1955, and while the musical instrument trade was as important as ever, the firm was able to build on this fresh foundation and simply never looked back. It was certainly an exciting time in the Hamamatsu area …

www.veloce.co.uk / www.velocebooks.com
All current books • New book news • Special offers • Gift vouchers

15

2 The Fabulous Fifties

While the Suzulight car was in production, Shunzo Suzuki recommended to his father-in-law that the company should concentrate on motorbikes, which were far more profitable, and, given the overall financial climate in Japan at the time, sales were much easier to come by, too. Indeed, with incomes increasing, allowing workers to spend on goods that had only a few years earlier been unthinkable, it's fair to say Japan was experiencing something of a motorcycle boom.

Having gained a good amount of experience with both two- and four-stroke motorcycle engines, following an unprecedented testing programme to prove overall reliability, along with advice from Tokyo University's Kiyoshi Tomizuka (the man that had led the famed *Koken-Ki* aircraft project), Suzuki fell for the charm of the two-stroke unit – it was easier and cheaper to make, and gave more power compared to a four-stroke engine of a similar size. From now on, for over two decades, the Suzuki name would be readily associated with these high-revving powerplants, the company ultimately becoming a world leader in this field of technology …

Variations on a theme

Before going on, given the core subject of this book, it's probably well worth outlining the differences between a traditional Otto-cycle petrol engine and its two-stroke counterpart. While we are at it, we may as well go into the advantages and negative aspects of both units, for they are quite different in terms of character and efficiency.

The Otto-cycle is a term for the four-stroke system applied to internal combustion engines. The word 'Otto' comes out of respect for Nikolaus August Otto (father of the four-stroke principle), while the four-stroke moniker itself describes the four piston movements necessary to complete one combustion cycle in conjunction with suitable inlet and exhaust valve operation, a method of igniting a measured fuel/air mixture, and a crankshaft with offset crankpins to keep pistons moving in the desired direction. The four 'strokes' can be summed up as follows:

<u>Intake</u> – As the piston moves down the cylinder, a suitable fuel/air mixture is drawn into the combustion chamber through the open inlet valve. The exhaust valve is closed at this stage.

<u>Compression</u> – Both valves are closed, allowing the fuel/air mixture to be compressed within the combustion chamber as the piston rises in the cylinder.

<u>Power</u> – With both valves closed, the fuel/air mixture is ignited either by a spark or an increase in heat through

The Suzuki factory pictured in the mid-1950s, with the name across the front now reading the Suzuki Motor Company, in kanji reading left to right rather than the old-fashioned right to left.

extreme pressure (via a higher compression ratio, as in the diesel engine), the resulting controlled explosion pushing the piston back down again.

Exhaust *– As the piston starts to rise again, the inlet valve remains shut, but the exhaust valve opens allowing burnt gases to exit the combustion chamber.*

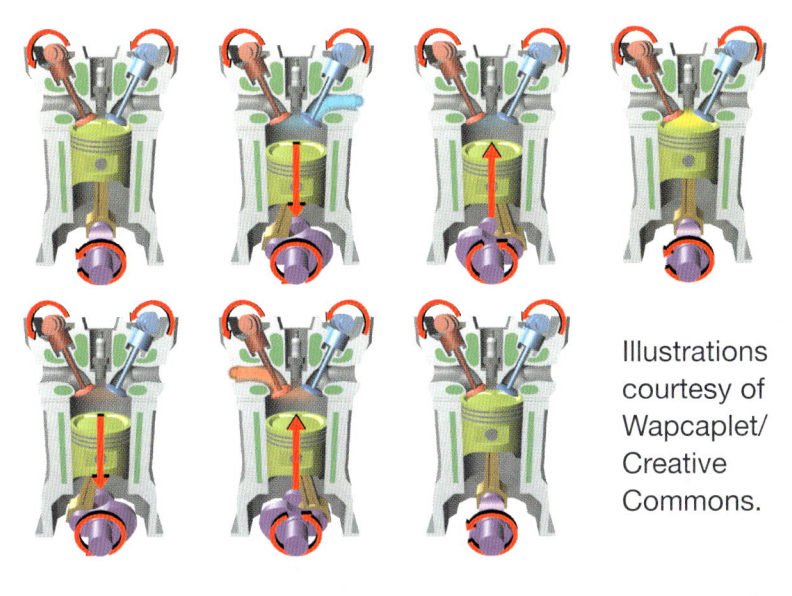

Illustrations courtesy of Wapcaplet/Creative Commons.

With hybrid vehicles now commonplace on today's roads, one may hear about Atkinson- or Miller-cycle engines, but the basic theory is the same as the Otto-cycle. With a two-stroke ICE, one follows the same sequence but in two piston strokes instead of four, by taking away the traditional valve system and using the piston's shape and travel combined with careful port positioning to complete the combustion cycle.

This allows these units to be lighter and more compact, as well as less complicated, meaning they are cheaper and easier to manufacture – these benefits are further increased with air cooling. They also deliver a power stroke on every rotation of the crankshaft (instead of every second rotation, as on a four-stroke engine), giving them a high power-to-weight ratio, faster acceleration and a free-revving character.

As it happens, the two-stroke idea has been around for a long time, since 1889 in fact, with the Englishman Joseph Day being responsible for the two-stroke as we know it. His designs were quickly refined, with the classic 'crankcase-scavenged' two-stroke unit coming about after a modification by Frederick Cock, who worked for Day's engineering company. This is how the engine works:

THE FABULOUS FIFTIES

Upstroke *– As the piston moves to the top of the cylinder, it compresses the air/fuel/oil mixture already delivered via the transfer port, and exposes the intake port beneath it as soon as it reaches TDC (top dead centre) in the case of a cylinder wall port (a reed valve or rotary disc valve could also be employed for intake purposes, as seen in the illustrations, with slightly quicker induction timing). This allows a fresh charge to be drawn into the crankcase. The exhaust port is blocked off by the piston skirt, as is the transfer port that connects the combustion chamber and the crankcase. Compression is followed by combustion, with a spark igniting the mixture to push the piston back down again.*

Downstroke *– As the piston moves downwards, this closes the intake and exposes the exhaust port, with the underside of the piston starting to pre-compress the fresh charge. On reaching BDC (bottom dead centre), the transfer port is now*

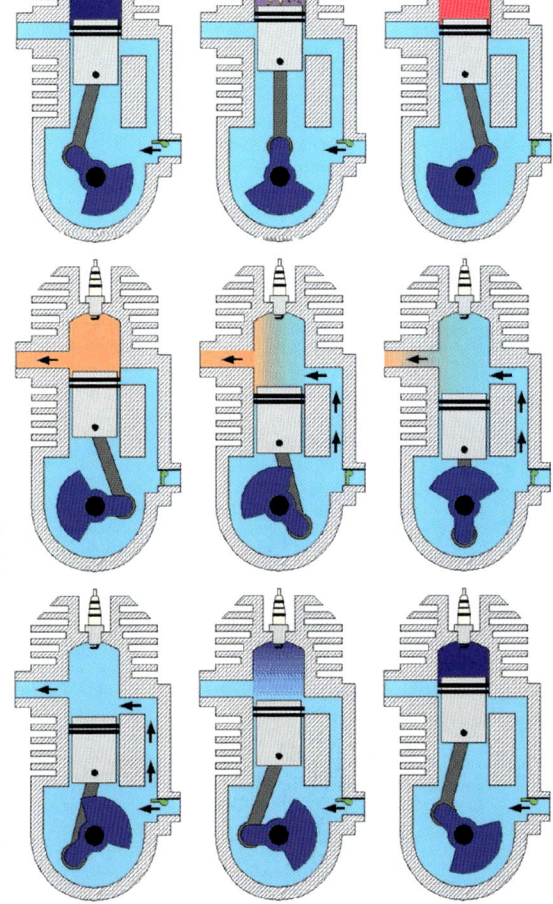

Illustrations courtesy of A Schierwagen using OpenOffice Draw/Creative Commons.

17

SUZUKI MOTORCYCLES: THE CLASSIC TWO-STROKE ERA

fully exposed, allowing the partially compressed charge to move from the crankcase into the combustion chamber and push out any remaining exhaust gases. The weight of the flywheel sees to it that the piston starts moving upwards again, first covering all ports and compressing the mixture before the intake port is exposed (or opened in the case of a reed valve or rotary disc valve) for the cycle to start again.

The two-stroke power-unit can boast a number of worthwhile advantages. However, while oil passages are not required (saving a fortune on machining), a small amount of engine lubricant has to be mixed with the fuel, meaning extremely high levels of particulate matter (PM) emissions from cross-contamination; due to the layout of the combustion chamber this more often than not leads to part of the air-fuel charge being wasted, leaking through the exhaust port before it is ignited. While thoughtful exhaust pipe designs can reduce this inevitable waste to a minimum, HC emissions are therefore very bad as a result, although CO and NOx emissions are actually lower than those of four-stroke engines, generally speaking.

There were a few automobile manufacturers that used two-stroke engines, with Saab being one of the last notables – ultimately, while they tend to release more power for a given displacement compared to an Otto-cycle unit, the lack of low-end torque and a fairly narrow power band makes the two-stroke option less attractive in a heavy application like a car. But as fuel consumption concerns increased and the environmental damage became more apparent, even motorcycle makers started moving almost exclusively toward four-stroke units at the end of the 1970s.

The early ST and DH lines

The four-stroke Colleda COX had been launched in March 1955, but it's the bike released in the following month that holds more interest for us given the subject of this book – the two-stroke 123cc Colleda ST. This attractive motorcycle exploited the new rules on user types to the maximum, being just under the critical 125cc upper bracket (allowing users to ride with no licence required, with the same limit set for both two- and four-stroke machines), and went on to be immensely popular.

Christened by Shunzo Suzuki (with the S standing for Suzuki, and the T for two-stroke), the ST followed the basic design of the Colleda CO and COX, which meant it followed the design trend established by many Japanese bikes of the period, such as the Honda Dream E, Miyata's Asahi FA, the Yamaha 125, and the contemporary Meguro, Tohatsu, Hosk, Lilac, Pointer and Cabton, to name but a few.

Shunzo Suzuki with an early Colleda ST.

The channel-type steel frame was, in fact, much like that of the prewar Harley-Davidson and a lot of British bikes from the time in profile, with the top tubes sloping steeply back from the neck stem to the rear wheel. There was a single downtube at the front, with telescopic forks ahead of it, and a plunger-type rear suspension – something that was considered the norm by a lot of companies in the early-1950s, including the likes of BSA, Ariel, Norton, BMW, Adler and Indian. Comfort was aided by a hefty coil spring under the seat, which was located to the frame at its leading edge.

The 5.5bhp engine was a single-cylinder two-stroke with traditional piston-port induction, and a hint of DKW RT125 about it. At 52mm x 58mm, the bore and stroke relationship was quite different to that of the COX, which, as we noted in the previous chapter, had a larger bore and a shorter stroke to arrive at the same 123cc displacement. It employed four caged roller main bearings (a type of bearing whose need for oil is minimal, thus suiting the two-stroke application perfectly) in the split alloy crankcase, a cast iron cylinder barrel, an Amal carburettor, and a magneto-type ignition system for the single sparkplug in the centre of the alloy head. Interestingly, the Colleda

THE FABULOUS FIFTIES

four-stroke models had a kickstart on the rider's left, while the two-stroke machine had it on the right, although the single exhaust pipe ran to the right-hand side on both, albeit with a less stylish end on the STs.

Like the CO and COX, the three-speed transmission was in unit with the engine, with the change on the left (as was the clutch lever), while a chain took drive to the rear wheel's sprocket on the left-hand side of the bike. The front drum brakes were operated by a lever on the right-hand side of the handlebars, with the rear drum using rod activation via a right foot pedal – an arrangement that was quite popular on prewar motorcycles, and would hang on for decades to come.

With a Suzulight sedan costing 420,000 yen, or over twice the national average wage of 185,000 yen a year, the ST was a much more realistic proposition at just over 100,000 yen. Even more realistic was the 83,000 yen DH-1 Porter Free model, released in October 1955. Or at least it would seem that way …

The Porter Free was a 102cc two-stroke model, using much the same engine as the original ST (retrospectively known as the ST-I), but with a shorter 48mm stroke to give the smaller displacement. Even so, the catalogue quoted not far off the same kind of power available as the COX, and with less weight thanks to a lighter, tubular frame and its rigid back axle, it gave a more than acceptable level of performance. Identifying features included a chain drive on the same side as the exhaust pipe, and a painted (albeit very elegant) fuel tank. The 102cc model was augmented by the 90,000 yen DH-2 spec model during the spring of 1957, sporting a fraction more power and a different rear luggage rack, before being allowed to quietly disappear from the line-up.

On the other hand, the ST was selling well, gaining some extra poke thanks to a new exhaust and air cleaner arrangement at the end of 1955 (to take the total first up to 6.5bhp and then ultimately 7bhp if catalogues are to be believed). This updated ST-II model also gained new shocks front and rear (the loss of the rubber dust boots on the front fork in favour of an attractive steel cover, giving a useful identifying feature) and a new rear light, before eventually becoming the ST-III at the same time as the DH-2 was launched.

Priced 5000 yen cheaper than the contemporary 125,000 yen COX-II, the COX and ST models had actually looked very similar until a fashionable new cowled headlight design aping that of the contemporary twin (which we'll come to in a moment) was adopted on the two-stroke machine at the end of the second generation model run (and duly continued for the third). However, as we noted in the first chapter, time was rapidly running out for the four-stroke series, especially now the 123cc 7bhp ST-III (listed at 130,000 yen) had moved the styling forward with a new fuel tank, a more comfortable saddle beyond it, fresh mudguards, and a redesigned bi-colour rear light.

There was also an oddity we need to mention – the ultra-rare 150ST of February 1956 vintage, which was a racier version of the 125ST. Listed 5000 yen

> Catalogue for the ST-II, already rated at 7bhp according to the data block. Later ST-II models gained a cowl over a new horseshoe-shaped headlight.

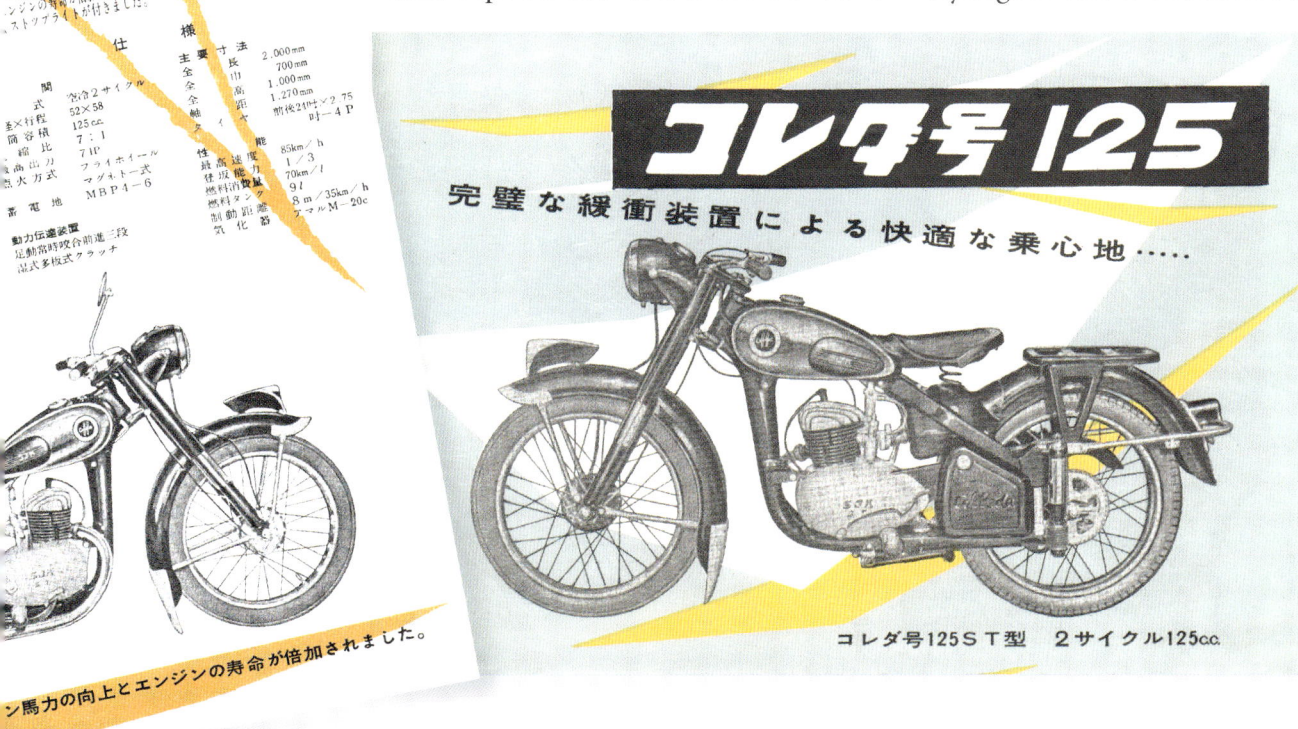

SUZUKI MOTORCYCLES: THE CLASSIC TWO-STROKE ERA

Inside pages from the 150ST brochure, dated February 1956.

A useful flyer from April 1956, showing the 150ST (the quality of the print can be misleading here, as it almost looks like it has a painted black tank, which simply wasn't the case), an early ST-II and COX-II on the top row, the Colleda 250TT in the middle (soon to reach dealerships), and the Mini Free and Diamond Free engines, next to the DH-1 Porter Free, with its two-tone painted fuel tank, along the bottom. For the record, all two-stroke bikes with the exception of the Porter Free came with a rearview mirror as standard at this time.

above the contemporary ST-II (and therefore having the same price-tag as the four-stroke COX-II model), the Colleda 150TT had a bored-out 150cc (56mm x 58mm) version of the ST's two-stroke engine, developing 8bhp off a 7.0:1 compression ratio. It had a different, more luxurious seat and a revised rear light compared to the ST, but had already disappeared from the line-up by the summer of 1957. However, the 150 concept would be revived in Hamamatsu in due course, albeit as a twin-cylinder model.

Progress

Up until this point in the story, Suzuki had concentrated on single-cylinder power-units, gradually turning its back on the four-stroke engine along the way. However, wanting to show the outside world what it was capable of, having announced it during the spring, the company officially launched the exciting Colleda 250TT in July 1956, with the TT name standing for touring two-stroke.

Based on the Adler MB250, this had a parallel twin (also referred to as a vertical twin) sporting a 54mm x 54mm bore and stroke to give 247cc. Whilst not as well balanced as a V-twin, the inline configuration – made popular by bikes like the Triumph Speed Twin – certainly offered more refinement

THE FABULOUS FIFTIES

Fuel tank badge used on the contemporary Colleda machines.

The short-lived ST-III. The fuel tank is the correct shape, although contemporary adverts show it should be in partial chrome and fitted with grey kneepads, as per the bike in Suzuki's museum. The same advert confirms that side boxes were fitted as standard.

than a single-cylinder engine, and its compact nature (allowing more freedom in positioning), good cooling characteristics and ease of manufacture held great appeal for the motorcycle makers.

The cast iron cylinders featured piston ports, fed by a Mikuni-Amal MC22 carburettor setup, while the pair of exhausts ran one along each side of the bike. A fairly high 7.0:1 compression ratio was specified, endowing the Type J air-cooled unit with a healthy 18bhp at 6000rpm – a figure that allowed Suzuki to tout it as Japan's most powerful bike in its class. A four-speed transmission was employed, as per the Adler, with the gearshift being on the left (below the kickstart lever) and the fully enclosed chain drive being on the right-hand side of the machine.

The pressed-steel backbone frame represented another big step forward, incorporating the latest Earles-type fork, made popular by BMW (although few others adopted it in reality), and a modern swing-arm suspension at the rear, with a spring and damper unit on both sides of the bike. The braking system was similar to the ST-series in principle, with a pedal still being used for rear brake activation, although the tyres were completely different to those of the earlier Colledas, with beefy 3.25-16 rubber being used on the newcomer, as opposed to the skinny tyres with narrow sidewalls used on the ST and COX range.

Indicators were added for the first time, cased in bullet-shaped housings either side of the streamlined headlight fairing at the front (which also played host to the speedometer and a gear indicator, as well as the horseshoe-shaped headlight and separate foglight), and on a special chrome pannier rack that extended beyond the passenger seat at the back and also carried the red rear lamp and reflector.

At 235,000 yen, the 81mph (130kph) Colleda 250TT cost more than a Honda 350 and was even seriously close to the asking price of a contemporary Meguro model, but it still attracted over 200 orders a

The Colleda 250TT making a splash at a launch event.

SUZUKI MOTORCYCLES: THE CLASSIC TWO-STROKE ERA

The 250TT in the Suzuki collection, this angle readily showing why the bike picked up the 'Cadillac of motorcycles' moniker.

Compared to the 250TT it was based on, the 250TT-P was toned down to a huge extent.

month nonetheless, becoming known as 'the Cadillac of motorcycles' amongst enthusiasts in Japan.

During the spring of 1957, with the TT still commanding 235,000 yen, Suzuki introduced the TT-P variant (the 'P' suffix standing for 'Popular') to sell alongside it. Priced at 198,000 yen, the Earles fork was dropped in favour of a regular telescopic one. In reality, a telescopic fork, with a coil and damper inside the fork tubes, has been the most popular type of front suspension for as long as anyone can remember. Although it tends to allow a bike to 'dive' under braking, the fact that it's so simple (and cheap to produce) outweighs any of the disadvantages that only really make themselves known at the extremes of the performance envelope, hence its longevity.

THE FABULOUS FIFTIES

A new frame (with a pair of downtubes added ahead of the engine) was made to fit in with this new front suspension arrangement, and the specifications were toned down a little to make the bike more affordable, including things like deleting the front foglight and dropping the back seat in favour of a luggage rack. Weighing in at 158kg (348lb), it was 12kg (26lb) lighter than the TT, despite having a slightly longer wheelbase. With 18bhp on tap, the new TP (the shorter TP moniker, which was actually an internal code, seemed to be in more common use than the TT-P one) was no slouch, but with increased competition in the domestic 250cc arena, it was still priced too steeply to attract high-volume sales.

A new broom

With Michio Suzuki becoming 70 years old, a few days after opening a new wing at the works that brought true mass-production to Suzuki via an automated conveyor line for the company's motorcycles, the man that had given the Suzuki marque life decided it was time to retire and hand over the reins to his son-in-law, Shunzo Suzuki.

Born in Okazaki in May 1903 as Shunzo Kimura, he studied as an engineer at Kanebo, and entered Suzuki after his marriage in 1931. He was the one that had done the research for exporting Suzuki looms in prewar days, visiting numerous countries across Asia, and had more recently surveyed the motorcycle markets in America and Europe in person. He had a very good eye for business, leaving little to chance and even less to whims. He was a shrewd character to say the least, and given the fact that Japan's motorcycle makers had dwindled from over 200 in 1953 to half that amount in 1957 (with the number of survivors set to fall off rapidly thereafter), this was no bad thing …

Shunzo Suzuki was named President on February 28, 1957, by which time the company's share capital stood at a hefty 500,000,000 yen. Michio stayed on in an advisory capacity, but it was Shunzo that now dealt with the day-to-day running of the business. Having experienced union troubles, he was quick to modernise as many systems as possible, making each worker's role and responsibilities far clearer than before, but was also keen to encourage team spirit and raise morale within the company. This 'new broom sweeps clean' approach would pay dividends in productivity and the management's relationship with the workforce.

To take advantage of the new state-of-the-art production

Shunzo Suzuki, who proved to be an excellent ambassador for the company.

Superb photograph from mid-1957 showing a trade stand with the 250TT-P (left), 250TT (up high) and ST-III sharing space with a Suzuki loom.

23

SUZUKI MOTORCYCLES: THE CLASSIC TWO-STROKE ERA

An early 250TM with one of the workers trying to get in on the act.

One of the later 250TMs sporting the new 'S' tank badge. The 'Colleda' name was still found on the side boxes and engine cover, though, along with an 'SJK' plaque on the transmission cover. Note also the different saddle and kneepads compared with the original.

facilities he'd inherited only days before stepping into the President's office, it was obvious to Shunzo Suzuki that the two-wheeled range needed streamlining if reasonable profits were to be secured. After all, if the various products in the catalogue called for a large number of different items to be made, the line workers would ultimately spend more time setting up than the automated production methods could save.

In January 1958, it was decided to concentrate on the 250cc TP, 125cc ST and Mini Free (MF) lines, although the latter, whilst selling reasonably well at the time, would disappear in 1959, giving way to a new range of more modern mopeds that would have to face up to the mighty Honda C100 Super Cub and Tosho Echo, as well as slightly bigger machines like the Tohatsu Birdie and the restyled Rabbit.

The 250cc line-up was still complicated, though, with the TT and TP still listed as partners until the end of 1959 (albeit with the pair being built in increasingly small numbers), and then there was the short-lived TM, combining the twin-cylinder engine and what was basically the old ST-III frame with its plunger-type rear suspension. Listed at 159,000 yen when it was introduced in the spring of 1958, with basic flashing indicators included in the price, it limped into the 1959 season carrying the new stylised Suzuki 'S' on its fuel tank – a new company logo that had officially been adopted on the first day of October 1958. However, the TM failed to fire people's enthusiasm, being built down to a price and too function-orientated in its specification, as opposed to sporting or fashionable, and duly failed to make it into the 1960 line-up.

Things were much easier to follow on the ST front, with the 150ST already gone and the ST-III giving way to the ST-5 at the tail-end of 1957 (note that there was no fourth generation in terms of numbering, and Roman numerals had been superseded by Arabic ones in the model designation) in time for the 1958 season. Priced at 125,000 yen, which was actually a fraction cheaper than the outgoing ST-III, the ST-5 came with a pressed-steel frame incorporating a swing-arm rear suspension, and a slight increase in power – now up to 7.5bhp at 5500rpm, giving the bike 53mph (85kph) performance. The front brake drums were duly enlarged to keep things in check.

The ST-5 inherited the horseshoe headlight shape from

THE FABULOUS FIFTIES

The ST-5 was not the prettiest Suzuki ever made, but it did represent a huge leap forward from a technical point of view. The ST-IV (or ST-4) was almost certainly missing in the run because four is considered an unlucky number. The same thing happened with the Hustler 250 over a decade later, with the internal numbering system skipping the four again. The ST name is still in use to this day, as it happens, reserved for a retro-style 250 sold in Japan.

its predecessor, along with heavier mudguards aping those of the early Suzuki 250s (the fin on the leading edge of the front guard was dropped at the same time). The fuel tank carried 'Colleda' badging, along with 'SJK' markings on the engine crankcase, although 'Suzuki' branding would soon become the norm with the launch of the ST-6. At the time, the stylists were very proud of the chain cover design on the left-hand side, but combined with the other body details (including plenty of chrome flashes and a selection of cubbies, the latter added with practicality in mind), the new machine looked a lot less racy than its low-slung predecessor, despite having a fractionally longer 1300mm (51.2in) wheelbase. This was especially so if the optional rear seat was added to the luggage rack. The ST-6, however, would represent a huge leap forward on the styling front.

More progress

As far back as 1956, the country had announced it was officially free of the postwar blues as far as the economy was concerned. There would still be better years and worse years to come, but Japan had at least turned a corner. As wages increased, while not everyone was in a position to buy a full-sized motorbike, this brought about a healthy market for things like mopeds. Indeed, it's fair to say that, like Europe, Japan was gripped by something of a moped boom during the second half of the 1950s.

At this time, a moped was basically a small motorcycle (under 50cc) with auxiliary pedals, which was much the same in concept as the Diamond Free in reality. In later life, the moped would lose its pedals, but the name survived nonetheless. The word 'moped' originally came from a combination of 'motor' and 'pedal', but as is often the case, the Japanese had their variation on a theme, with 'mopet' often being seen, implying this little two-wheeler was more like a motorised pet than merely a vehicle with no attachment to the owner. To add to the confusion, while catalogues and advertising copy often used the 'mopet' spelling, the badge on the vehicle could just as easily use the proper spelling, as was the case with the little Suzuki!

The first true Suzuki moped was the 50cc Suzumopet SM, released in May 1958 at 39,000 yen in its cheapest guise. This was basically a more civilised version of the Diamond Free bike using an SM-type Mini Free (38mm x 44mm) engine in a dedicated pressed-steel backbone frame. Keeping things simple, including rigid front forks (although a swing-arm rear suspension was employed) and a belt drive allowed Suzuki to hit the moped market just behind Tanaka

25

SUZUKI MOTORCYCLES: THE CLASSIC TWO-STROKE ERA

Advertising for the Suzumopet SM, inviting people to guess how long it would take the 50cc machine to do a complete circuit of Japan in order to win a bike.

University of the Arts being called in to look after the styling, which incorporated five-sided shapes on the fuel tank and the boxes underneath the modern-looking saddle, and a streamlined appearance – the 'Jet Line' name being used to describe the steep angle of the components mounted on the steel frame, running back from the headlight to the tail. This more integrated look would be nurtured as the years passed, but in the meantime, the ST-6 attracted a huge amount of attention in the 50-125cc *Gentsuki* class.

The Suzumopet SM-2 with a modified drivetrain and styling upgrades.

Kogyo, but ahead of its rivals. As a result, with younger riders able to use one from just 14 years old, 40,000 units were built in the first year of sales, until others started taking healthy chunks out of the pie for themselves.

For 45,000 yen, one could buy the Selpet SM – the 'Sel' element of the name implying that an electric starter was fitted in this instance – and in face-lifted guise (the SM-2 of 1959 vintage), with chain drive and a more attractive fuel tank, rear mudguard and chain cover design, the Suzumopet had matured enough to keep Suzuki ticking over against some tough competition until the Selpet MA could take over the crown. The last of the SM models were sold in the summer of 1960.

The single-cylinder ST line was also evolving, with the ST-5 giving way to the 125,000 yen ST-6 in October 1958. This shift in generations represented another monumental change for the bread-and-butter model, with Toru Sasaki of Tokyo

Incidentally, the ST-6 featured the familiar Suzuki 'S' badge from the start, although the Colleda brand name was still being used on catalogues and suchlike at this stage. Indeed, it could still be seen in the early sixties, and may have continued beyond that had those in influential export markets not asked to keep things simple by using the Suzuki moniker only. After all, the racers that had flown the flag at the Isle of Man in 1961 and 1962 were part of the Suzuki team, and promoted as such, with the vast majority of foreigners hardly recognising the link between Suzuki and Colleda, despite the latter name having been used for the TT race in 1960.

Anyway, tweaking the engine (which also carried the ST-6 designation, incidentally) released 8bhp at 6000rpm. In addition, the exhaust was now on the left-hand side with the chain drive on the right, opposite to the ST-5. Otherwise, the specifications were much the same, with the three gears

THE FABULOUS FIFTIES

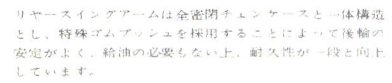

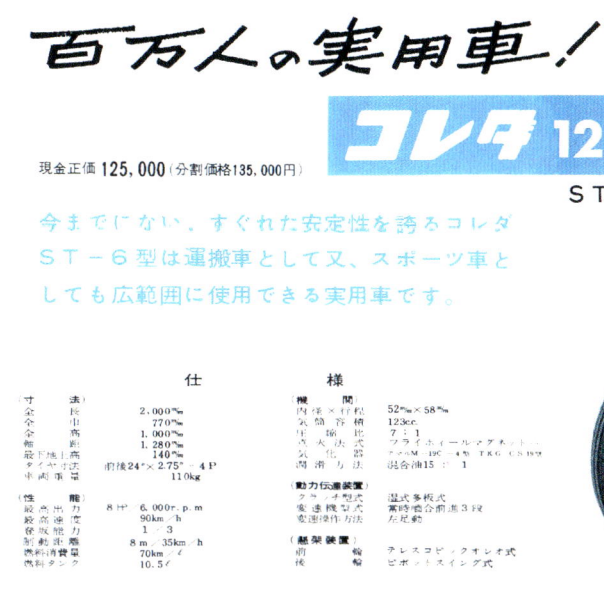

Domestic catalogue for the ST-6 model.

selected on the left, the clutch operated by the left hand, and the drum brakes (still no hydraulics as yet, only cables and rods) via the right hand and right foot; the kickstart was also on the right-hand side of the bike. Suspension was via a telescopic fork at the front, and swing-arms at the rear. The horseshoe-shaped headlight was carried over, by the way, with TM-type indicators on the headlight cowl and rear mudguard.

The ST-6A was launched at 128,000 yen in the middle of 1959, although one would be hard pushed to spot the difference beyond the all-black paintwork underneath the saddle, and a

SUZUKI MOTORCYCLES: THE CLASSIC TWO-STROKE ERA

An advertising board pictured in Hamamatsu in 1959. The lettering underneath the 'S' badge spells out 'Colleda' in *katakana*, incidentally.

1950s production

These early figures include the powered cycles and four-stroke machines built at the start of Suzuki's motorcycle odyssey. For ease of reference, the numbers are broken down into bikes with an engine capacity of up to 50cc, 51 to 125cc, and 126cc and over.

	Up to 50cc	51cc to 125cc	126cc +	Total
1952	9993	–	–	9993
1953	37,251	5	–	37,256
1954	25,699	6336	–	32,035
1955	11,279	11,267	–	22,546
1956	14,129	15,783	2525	32,437
1957	18,150	19,754	3933	41,837
1958	41,261	34,085	5907	81,253
1959	45,264	45,118	7050	97,432

subtle redesign of the fuel tank and the kneepads attached to it. The ST-series was a massive hit, with around 100,000 units being sold before the line was replaced by the SH in 1961. This success was part of the reason Suzuki was able to increase its share capital to 750,000,000 yen in February 1959, before doubling it in 1960, and then doubling it again, up to 3,000,000,000 yen, in August 1961.

Not surprisingly, by the end of the fifties, dealers were queuing at Suzuki's doorstep. The old system of three main distributors had broken in 1956 with the collapse of Shoji Kogyo, who'd looked after the eastern side of Japan, with Suzuki supplying bike dealers directly from Hamamatsu from that date on. Those handling cars at this time were often dismayed, but the bike side of the business just kept growing and growing, with more than enough customers to keep things ticking over, no matter how many shops popped up. However, by 1961, a more organised dealer network had been put in place on the home front.

The new twin

Before moving on to the 1960s and the next chapter, we need to discuss one more bike introduced in August 1959 – the Colleda Seltwin SB. First announced as a prototype almost a year earlier at the 1958 Tokyo Show, the SB was famous for becoming the world's first two-stroke twin with a self-starter.

The SB took the Jet Line styling of the ST-6 models a stage further, with the chromed fuel tank and box covers aft of it taking on a straight line approach that was, to be perfectly honest, quite unlike anything else on the market. While European makers were still pushing very traditionally-styled machines, the SB was incredibly modern, with beauty very much in the eyes of the beholder – one was either attracted to the bold design or put off by it. One thing's for sure, it was hard to ignore a bike like this one!

The front fork was disguised to look like a lower link (Kawasaki also adopted this design trick for its 125-60 from the

The first catalogue for the Colleda Seltwin SB.

same era), with the handlebars styled to appear more integrated. The fuel tank had straight lines flowing back from the headlight; the sides were decorated with chrome pieces broken up by the Suzuki badge and the black chequered insert that was becoming a common sight on the Colleda range. The sharp saddle was purpose-made to fill the gaps and match the tank insert lines, while the black painted frame and chain cover (on the left-hand side, aft of the four-speed gearchange) provided contrast for the chrome and alloy surfaces.

Hooked up to a four-speed rotary transmission, the Type SB engine was basically a scaled-down version of the 250cc unit, introduced to offer users more refinement in the up to 125cc class, with the 42mm x 45mm bore and stroke giving a cubic capacity of 124cc. With a single Mikuni VM19H carburettor (the Mikuni concern was a Moto Guzzi dealer in prewar Japan, by the way) and a 7.0:1 compression ratio, it delivered 10bhp at 7000rpm, its twin exhausts (one pipe on each side) giving it a healthy bark. Although an electric starter was part of the spec,

SUZUKI MOTORCYCLES: THE CLASSIC TWO-STROKE ERA

The Seltwin SB with optional leg guards, which were quite popular at the time.

there was a location provided for a kickstart on the right, added as a back-up.

Lighting was revised, with a new headlight surround brought into use (its cowling playing host to the speedometer and ignition switch), while the front indicators were now positioned on the handlebars. The indicators at the back were in a familiar place, but styled to match the housing used for those up front, and on the tail, the simple reflector of the ST-series was replaced by a proper red light unit.

> Range catalogue dating from August 1959, with the new Seltwin SB taking pride of place on the cover. The inside spread shows the contemporary line-up with, from left to right, the 360cc Suzulight TL (the 21bhp *Kei* car had only been launched in the previous month), the 250TM, the Suzumopet SM-2, the ST-6A (note the new fuel tank and side covers compared to those used on the strict ST-6), and the SB. The lack of the 250TT and 250TP in the brochure shows they were no longer being pushed.

THE FABULOUS FIFTIES

The wheels were fractionally bigger than those of the contemporary 125cc Honda, giving better ride quality on the still rough roads of Suzuki's homeland, with whitewall tyres listed as an option. For those more interested in beating the weather than looking trendy, a two-piece bolt-on front fairing was available, and can be seen in several catalogues; the bike in the factory museum also has a fairing fitted. As usual, a rear seat squab was also listed, ready to be attached to the luggage rack over the back wheel, or there was a full-length saddle for two. One could also specify a brown frame, which came with a two-tone red and grey saddle.

With 3,040,000 bikes now in use in Japan (against 2,175,000 cars), the next chapter looks at the early sixties – an era in which the Suzuki marque would make its international competition debut, and mature in a way that would have been difficult to imagine only a few years earlier …

By the end of the 1950s, Suzuki was using the more specialised RB for racing, but it was still a long way from perfect, and usually sported knobby tyres more suited to off-road work than paved surfaces. The next decade would see some remarkable progress on the competition bike front.

Road bike evolution

The Suzuki motorcycle range is complex, and very often frustratingly confusing. This simplified table, following the evolution of each two-stroke model covered in this chapter, should hopefully allow things to become a lot clearer.

Model	1955	1956	1957	1958	1959	1960
Porter Free (102cc single)		DH-1	DH-2			
Colleda 125ST (123cc single)		ST-I / ST-II	ST-III	ST-5	ST-6	ST-6A
Colleda Seltwin SB (124cc twin)						SB
Colleda 150ST (150cc single)			ST			
Colleda 250TT (247cc twin)			TT			
Colleda 250TT-P (247cc twin)				TP		
Colleda 250TM (247cc twin)				TM		

Note: Four-stroke models, pure mopeds and cyclemotors are not included in this table, although they are all covered within the text.

3 The Early Sixties

The SM-series Suzumopet and Selpet models ran until the summer of 1960, although their more modern replacement – the Selpet MA – had already made its debut by then, having been introduced at the 1959 Tokyo Show for sales to start a couple of months later in January 1960. In reality, the MA arrived just in time, as Suzuki was rapidly losing ground to the Honda Super Cub and Yamaguchi Autopet, as well as the proliferation of scooters being fielded by other domestic makers.

While I have no intention of going in-depth on these machines, they should at least be mentioned in passing as they allowed Suzuki to thrive in an era when many fell by the wayside.

The Selpet MA. The ME had a different fuel tank and side box arrangement in order to make it easier to mount and dismount the machine, although the general impression was similar.

Selpet MA mopeds on the production line.

When the moped line evolved into the more modern-looking M30 line, the 52cc version (seen here) was known as the M31.

THE EARLY SIXTIES

Cover of the domestic range catalogue printed in March 1960.

They also spawned some interesting offshoots that we'll look at properly in due course, despite their minute 50cc engines. For now, though, we need to clear up a huge jumble of model numbers on the Super Cub fighters, just in case the designation leaves folks scratching their heads years on from now.

The single-cylinder MA (or MA-1 in retrospect) became the MA-2 (or MA-C with a kickstart only) in 1961 before being renamed the Selpet ME in the following year. This bike, which had no clutch, then evolved into the restyled 50cc Selpet M30 of 1963 vintage, which looked uncomfortably similar to its Honda rival, despite clearly taking its styling cues from the 50MD/MC.

Politics were playing a part in model development in the meantime. Until January 1961, a proper licence had not been required for the use of mopeds of under 50cc capacity in Japan, although from this date, a test (and the related pennies) became necessary to enable a person to ride one. There was also a 19mph (30kph) speed limit put in place on these tiddlers, along with other road rules imposed, and a ban on pillion passengers. To get around these rules, which would have doubtless hurt sales, makers introduced a line of mopeds with engine capacities just over the 50cc bracket, thus enabling users to continue much as before, two-up and

Cover and a couple of images from the 12-page Colleda 125SH brochure.

SUZUKI MOTORCYCLES: THE CLASSIC TWO-STROKE ERA

without speed restrictions. It was cheeky, but there's no doubt that the cunning ploy worked for a while. For reference, the 52cc version of the MA-2 was the Selpet MA-B of March 1961, which duly became the M31 in 1963.

Bigger brothers

The Colleda 125ST (type ST-6A) continued into the 1960 line-up, having only been introduced in mid-1959. Interestingly, for Suzuki, modern 12-volt electrics were already the norm by this time, even on the smaller 125s. With a top speed of 53mph (85kph), the ST-6A sold until 1961, when it evolved into the 125SH, which basically looked like a Seltwin with a different engine.

Introduced in September 1961, the SH had the familiar 123cc single-cylinder unit, with an Amal VM20 carburettor and the compression ratio lowered a fraction to 6.5:1. With the exhaust now exiting on the right-hand side instead of the left (due to a gearbox change), power was maintained at 8bhp at 6000rpm, while maximum torque was stated as being 7lb/ft at 4000rpm; fuel economy was said to be exceptional, with the catalogue quoting close to 200mpg imperial, with 140 being the average return one could expect. The SH didn't just inherit the Seltwin frame (the additional standardisation at least helped keep the price in check), it also gained the four-speed transmission used on the twins at this time. Sporting the Seltwin's 2.75-17 tyres (quite different to the ST-6A's 2.75-24 rubber), and the Seltwin's proven mechanical braking system, the 113kg (249lb dry) SH was capable of hitting 56mph (90kph).

Advertising sheet for the Colleda Seltwin 125SB from March 1960.

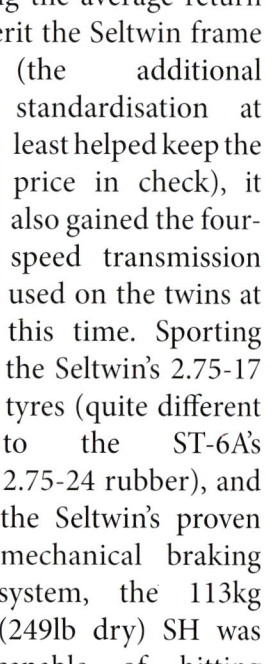

The early SB pictured with the 150SB-S model.

Like the ST-6A, the Colleda Seltwin SB was also continued into 1960, having been released only a few months earlier, in August 1959. This vertical-twin had a top speed of 69mph (110kph), which wasn't far off the performance level of a 250. After being proved at the 1960 Isle of Man sortie (the meeting being held in June that year), twin VM19SC carbs were adopted for the SB-2, taking power up from 10bhp to 11.5bhp, developed at 8000rpm with the standard 7.0:1 compression ratio.

The SB-2 gained a front fairing as standard, but otherwise looked the same as its predecessor at first glance – even more so if the original model had the pieces added as an option, or if they were removed on the SB-2 (something that can easily be done, as they've been taken off the author's 1960 example, and no one would know). Careful inspection, though, revealed thinner exhaust pipes, elongated shields surrounding the carb setup, and a switch on the left-hand side, aft of the new carburettor arrangement (the old levers on the opposite side of the lump disappeared at the same time). Moving this switch activated a choke, allowing the owner to start the bike on the electric starter at freezing temperatures with ease. The catalogue says this is the first

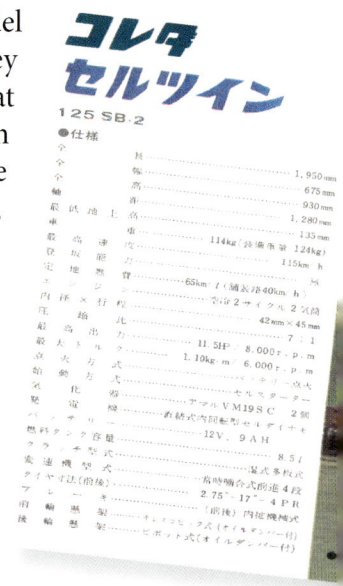

THE EARLY SIXTIES

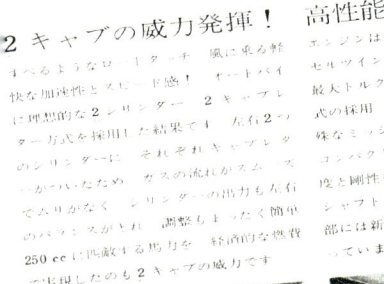

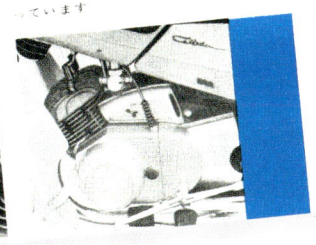

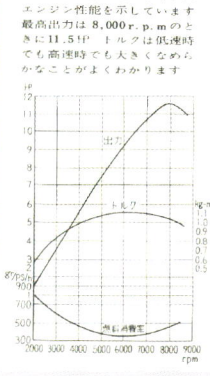

The pages that really matter from the SB-2 catalogue, showing the uprated engine.

time such a device was made available on a motorcycle.

It should be noted that a good while before the SB-2 was launched, as early as the first days of spring, in fact (publicity material goes back even further), a sportier Colleda Seltwin SB-S – aka the Sport 150 model – was also put on the market. This had a bored out (46mm x 45mm) 150cc version of the twin-cylinder engine giving 12.5bhp at 8000rpm, and a fraction more torque, along with a repositioned exhaust, mounted higher up and covered like a scrambler pipe.

Both Seltwin models were available in the regular black finish with a black saddle, as well as a brown frame with an all-red saddle combination. The front fairing (used on the SB-2 only) was always painted in a cream shade; the saddle was usually the short type for one, although a full-length two-person version could be bought as an option. For the record, as it gets confusing, the 125SG and 150SGB designations were often assigned to the equivalent export models.

Moving on to the biggest of the bigger stuff, with the 250TT dropped, the TP duly evolved into the Twin-Ace (or TA) in January 1960. This used a new pressed-steel frame, with its distinctive Jet Line styling still in evidence but toned down somewhat. The restyled nine-litre (two imperial gallons) fuel

Front and side views of the Twin-Ace, or 250TA.

The SB-2 page from the 1960 Tokyo Show brochure. No less than 812,000 people attended the Harumi event, which ran from October 25 to November 7 that year.

SUZUKI MOTORCYCLES: THE CLASSIC TWO-STROKE ERA

tank was combined with new covers under a beefier saddle and augmented by front fairings, but otherwise things fell into line with the Seltwin, including the mudguard designs and lighting arrangements. However, it also featured a revised version of the 250cc twin and a new braking system.

The latest vertical-twin had a bore and stroke of 52mm x 58mm, giving a 246cc displacement. With a pair of VM20 carbs for the traditional piston-port induction, petroil lubrication and a 6.3:1 compression ratio, maximum power was listed at 18bhp at 7000rpm, while the peak torque of 14lb/ft came in 1000rpm lower. Making full use of the four-speed transmission (it should be noted that the chain drive was on the left – the opposite side to the earlier 250s – along with the rotary-type gearchange), this enabled the 148kg (326lb) bike to be propelled up to a heady 81mph (130kph).

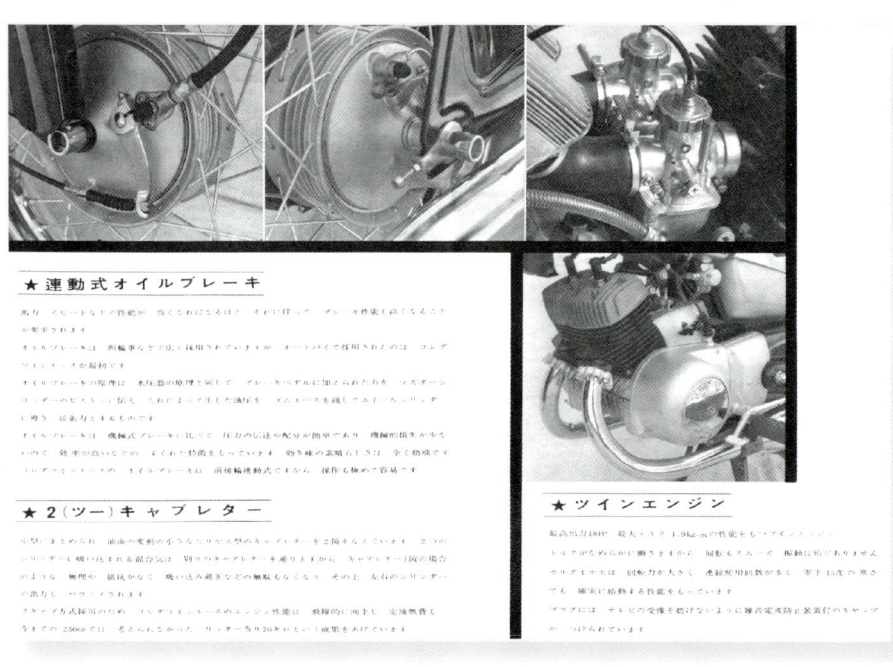

To keep this performance in check, the TA used 3.25-16 tyres and was given hydraulic braking, on both the front and rear drums. This novel, trailblazing system used a common master cylinder brought into play by what was the rear brake pedal on the earlier 250s. To add to the complexity and weight, though, the traditional front lever and cable was left in place as a back-up. With difficulty experienced in getting the brake balance right for the wide range of road speeds (and weather conditions, of course), Suzuki duly dropped the idea at the end of the TA run.

The TA (available in black, red or blue) was ultimately a short-lived two-stroke variant, as in November 1960 it was replaced by the 175,000 yen Colleda Super Touring TB – a sporting model that had made its debut at the Tokyo Show and looked every bit as modern as the Seltwins did quaint. In reality,

Technical details regarding the 250TA.

The 250TA in the catalogue issued to visitors to the 1960 Tokyo Show. Both TA and TB models were featured in the handout.

THE EARLY SIXTIES

it came about as an acknowledgement that something practical and having a certain 'wow' factor was necessary now that Suzuki had entered the world scene via its Isle of Man race campaign.

The styling was quite different to that of the TA. The lashings of chrome were replaced by a two-, sometimes three-tone paint scheme, based around red, white and stone grey, although the front mudguard was now plated, with its profile hugging that of the tyre rather than sitting high above it. Either side of the mudguard was a new telescopic fork design, losing the covers to give the bike a more lithe appearance – a move further enhanced by the use of traditional chrome handlebars and revised indicators, along with a new gauge pack, although the shape of the headlight the latter was contained in still looked familiar enough.

Moving back, there was a larger capacity (10.5-litre/2.3-imperial gallon) fuel tank that looked a lot less harsh on the eyes, but there's no doubt that the loss of the chrome item with its chequered-pattern insert and giant badge made the bike less distinctive as its maker sought more universal appeal. At least the fairing was gone (although the author has actually seen a Japanese catalogue picture of a Twin-Ace without one), with the styling update completed by revised boxes under an upswept saddle made for two, a lighter-looking rear mudguard, and new rear lighting units.

The 250TA finished in its alternative red and blue paintwork schemes.

Although all the leading specifications for the "silky smooth" air-cooled engine were the same as those of the TA on paper (including the Mikuni carburettor setup and c/r), parts were lightened wherever possible, and the compression ratio was raised in reality, even though the method of measurement meant the 6.3:1 value stayed the same; maximum power went up to 20bhp at 8000rpm, while peak torque output increased by ten per cent, developed at 7000rpm. The four-speed gearbox was carried over, but the hydraulic brake system was now used on the rear wheel only, and the tyre sizes were changed as well, now being 3.00-17s (black tyres were the norm, with whitewalls as an option). Being a touch lighter and coming with the extra pair of horses, top speed was now quoted at 87mph (140kph).

In its test of the TB, the UK's *Motor Cycling* magazine

said: "Without doubt, the Suzuki 250TB is an excellent example of Japanese know-how and engineering. There's nothing quite like it in Britain."

The 1960 and 1961 racing seasons

The racing world is full of premier events – those timeless classics that are held up above all others for whatever reason, even if it's only the romance attached to it. In car racing, there's the Le Mans 24-hour Race, or maybe one of the two main Monte Carlo bashes; in horse racing, it's without doubt the Epsom Derby; in bicycle racing, the Tour de France, and in motorcycle racing, it's the Isle of Man TT …

Based on the tiny island situated between the north-west coast of England and the east coast of Northern Ireland, the TT started life as a car race (the Tourist Trophy) at the turn of the 20th century, with motorcycles joining the fray in 1907. As it happens, the car races quickly fell by the wayside, but the bike races took on a legendary status, offering riders and manufacturers the greatest challenge in the racing calendar.

The Honda team had been the first to try its luck, with modest results in the Ultra Lightweight (125cc) Class in its 1959 debut year. But Honda would be back, and they would soon start winning, too, with some of the biggest names in racing duly riding their machines. In the meantime, however, not long after returning to Japan following his Manx debut, Soichiro Honda encouraged Shunzo Suzuki to join him next time and take a team to the Isle of Man. Sure enough, the good-natured advice was heeded, and after a meeting between some racing figures and Suzuki's

Cover and selected images from the 16-page 250TB brochure. Note the blue TA in the background on one shot.

38

Michio Ichino and his RT60 in front of the pits during the 1960 Manx challenge. (Courtesy Yaesu Publishing)

Suzuki making the most of its Isle of Man sortie in the brochure handed out at the 1960 Tokyo Motor Show.

Jimmy Matsumiya and Yoshichika Maruyama, a Colleda team was duly entered alongside a Honda one for the 1960 event.

The Suzuki contingent (including race manager Takeharu Okano, who came from an aeronautical engineering background, plus seven Suzuki members to look after the bikes) left Japan for the Isle of Man on May 9, giving the team plenty of time to recce the Snaefell Mountain Course and prepare for the race, for the Tourist Trophy meeting wasn't due to begin until June 13. By that time, Shunzo Suzuki had turned up to show support, even though he knew deep down there was little hope of a win first time out.

Riders for the Suzuki team were Mitsuo Itoh, Michio Ichino and Toshio Matsumoto, although Britain's Ray Fay replaced Itoh at the time of the race, as the Japanese lad had a tumble in practice. The works used a 125cc (44mm x 41mm, giving 124.7cc) twin-carb version of the Seltwin piston-port engine (the latter carburettor setup later being adopted on production models) in a modified frame, giving birth to a six-speed 13bhp machine known as the RT60.

39

SUZUKI MOTORCYCLES: THE CLASSIC TWO-STROKE ERA

While 33 bikes started the 1960 edition of the Ultra Lightweight (125cc) race, Italy's MV Agusta was able to claim the first three places, the winning machine being a full 14mph (22kph) faster on overall speed compared to the best of the Okano-designed Suzukis, or Colledas if we're to be technically correct. Okay, the highly-experienced MV Agusta team won everything in sight at that year's TT meeting, but it was obvious there was still a lot of work to do, with Matsumoto 15th, Ichino 16th and Fay 18th; Honda had five bikes in the top ten, with only Moto Kitano falling behind on the sixth Honda, one place behind Fay.

All finished the course, however, proving reliability in the toughest of conditions, and a Bronze Replica was duly secured by Matsumoto, so all was not lost. The key thing to come from the aftermath of the 1960 TT is that Shunzo Suzuki got the racing bug, and a proper competition campaign – one with the necessary finance and resources in place – would follow as a result.

With the Suzuki name now proudly being used for the works racing team, 1961 marked the first time that the Japanese maker contested the full Grand Prix World Championship season. Like the races in Spain, West Germany and France, though, the 1961 Isle of Man experience was a painful one – Honda filling the top five spots in the 125cc class, while all three Suzukis (124.7cc 15bhp RT61 rotary disc-valve twins ridden by Michio Ichino, Mitsuo Itoh and Sadao Masuda) failed to finish. The 250cc race didn't bring much better results, with Honda again dominating, and Yamaha coming sixth on its TT debut. Hugh Anderson was the top Suzuki finisher, the Kiwi rider claiming tenth and a Bronze Replica, with Ichino two places further back on his 248.6cc 28bhp RV61; there was a DNF mark against Itoh and Masuda, as well as Paddy Driver and Alistair King. Just for the record, with MV Agusta toning down its racing activities that year, it was Norton that took the spoils in the Junior TT and Senior TT event.

There was, however, one good thing to come out of the Manx sortie, for a meeting between Jimmy Matsumiya (who ran the newly-opened Suzuki office in London by that time) and Ernst Degner ultimately saw the latter defect from both East Germany and the MZ team, and take up a position with Suzuki from November 1961. Stories of intrigue abound, but the bottom line is the engineer and ace rider would bring experience to the Suzuki camp, as well as a great deal of know-how built up after years of working alongside MZ's Walter Kaaden, who was probably the leading authority on two-stroke race engines at the time. For a very handsome fee, not to mention more than a fair bit of personal risk, Degner joined the Japanese team with his family and his old friend from West Germany, Paul Petry, a renowned two-stroke tuner. While the 1961 season was best forgotten, with the rotary-valve engines proving unreliable throughout the year, regulation changes in the wind and a top class rider and mechanical engineer in the fold, there would be no looking back for either Degner or Suzuki after this ...

The RV61 at the time of its announcement.

Poster for the 1961 Isle of Man TT race.

THE EARLY SIXTIES

The original Selpet 50MD model, known as the 50MC when fitted with a self-starter arrangement.

The complete catalogue for the M10-series MD and MC models, with mention of the 52cc M16 on the back panel, as well as the M12 and 80cc line-up in the tiny illustrations. It should be noted that the *katakana* used on early publicity material says 'Sports,' although the English used in the majority of export markets, and Japan as well later on, uses 'Sport' as the correct designation.

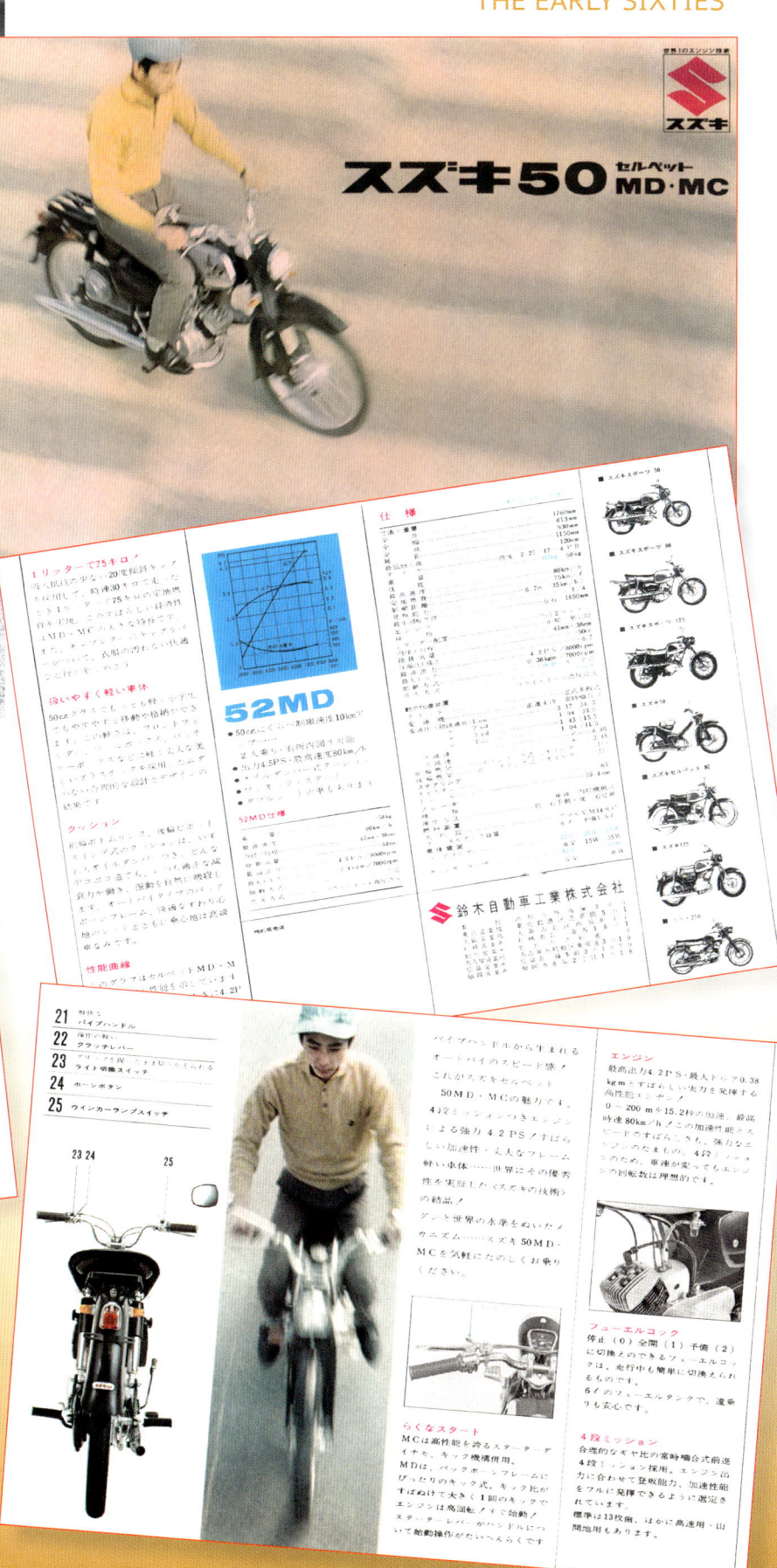

SUZUKI MOTORCYCLES: THE CLASSIC TWO-STROKE ERA

The early Sport 50, or M12 model. Note the lack of a badge on the side box (the 80cc model was given 'Selpet 80' ones).

Super tiddlers

By 1961, the moped boom had pretty much peaked, but there were still 15 makers in Japan producing these small machines as 1962 dawned. Serious competition followed, though, combined with a lull in the market, leaving only seven in the game in 1963, with Suzuki thankfully doing very well out of the Selpet moped line. Indeed, with this valuable contribution to overall production figures, Suzuki now found itself in the enviable position of being the world's second largest motorcycle manufacturer.

In the meantime, scooters – small motorcycles with a step-through frame, generally coming with a platform for the rider's feet, with the Lambretta and Vespa being perfect examples of the breed – were the new thing on the block. This fad was to be a short-lived one in Japan, though, with only the Rabbit (built by Fuji, or Subaru as we know it today) and Mitsubishi Silver Pigeon left by 1963. This was somewhat ironic, given the loss of the more attractive Yamaha SC1, Honda Juno, and others like it.

While Suzuki avoided scooters, motorcycle racing's governing body, the FIM, announced a Coupe d'Europe series for 50cc machines in 1961, leading to a World Championship class status for the following year, after which interest in smaller-engined bikes picked up; Japanese makers quickly saw this as a golden opportunity to shine and claim a market niche, with only the West German Kreidler and (then Yugoslavian) Tomos concerns offering any sort of real rivalry in this arena.

The works decided it was time to launch a sporty 50cc line-up, introducing the Selpet MD in 1961. This pretty little bike looked a lot like a scaled-down version of the ST-5 in reality, although close inspection reveals that many of the parts were sourced from the MA moped. Indeed, the shared front end (with traditional Suzuki handlebars and the speedometer recessed into the centre of the shallow vee formed by them), engine and transmission, 2.25-17 tyres and the familiar tail were easy to spot, but the classic fuel tank (painted on the early machines), the exposed single-cylinder air-cooled lump, and a short saddle (no pillion passengers allowed on smaller bikes, remember) harking back to the days of the first STs, provided the machine with a very different impression compared to its significantly more mundane donor vehicle.

The MA engine was a high-revving 49.9cc (41mm x 38mm) unit, benefiting from an intensive weight reduction programme to offset the heft of the cast iron barrel, which simply couldn't be avoided. With a VM14SC Amal carburettor, it developed 4.2bhp at 8000rpm off a 6.7:1 c/r, and was hooked up to a four-speed rotary transmission (a world first in this class when it was launched on the MA). It still seems incredible that the MD provided Suzuki with the foundation for its 50cc racer, although a selection of factory racing parts was made available for enthusiasts.

While the 58kg (128lb) 50MD had a kickstart and 6-volt electrics (unusual for Suzuki), the 50MC model sold alongside it added a 12-volt battery and self-starter into the equation, with the kickstart facility still there as a back-up. This added 2kg (4lb) to the base weight, which was next to nothing, so the top speed remained at 50mph (80kph).

With the arrival of the new M30 in 1963, the little 'boy racer' model inherited the revised handlebar arrangement of the moped (meaning chrome bars, available in three heights, and a fresh speedo, which now sat atop the headlight), fresh front indicators, a chrome finish on the original fuel tank, and redesigned boxes under the saddle. Engine changes included larger cooling fins to improve air-cooling efficiency, and the adoption of a VM15 carb to supersede the existing VM14 one, although power output remained the same nonetheless.

While the 50MD name was still used in catalogues and the like, the M10 code was applied internally to differentiate between the old and new models. Likewise, the 50MC became known as the M10D, although the start lever mounted by the rider's left hand (a change brought about by the newly-adopted handlebars) looked a little out of place on such a sporting machine, it has to be said. From January 1963, there was also a 5bhp Sport 50 variant, which had the scrambler-type exhaust, the Sport 80 front-end (which we'll come to in a moment), a different rear light unit, and a slightly bigger saddle (albeit still too short for two). Although available in Japan, the Sport 50, costing 60,000 yen and carrying the M12 moniker, was aimed mainly at export markets.

As with the mopeds, there was a 52cc (42mm x 38mm) version marketed to overcome the rules on bikes with engines smaller than 50cc, and for 1962, the 50MD duly spawned the 4.5bhp 52MD (type M11) with a longer saddle made for two. When the M10 line was introduced, this model was given a fresh M16 code, which can often be seen expressed as 52M16 in official paperwork. There was also a short-lived M13 version, which was an M16 with the high-mounted sports exhaust.

Any other business?

With bike sales falling off and the country slowly but surely becoming more suited to automobiles, Suzuki once again took a serious look at the car market. Research indicated that while the situation was improving for car makers, it was still business and working vehicles that dominated the figures of four-wheeled machines registered during the mid-1960s, with *Kei* trucks accounting for a huge

The elegant lines of the 125SL of 1962 vintage.

percentage. With a cool, calculating man like Shunzo Suzuki at the helm, it's not surprising that Suzuki had launched the FB Carry in 1961 – the foundation stone for a line that survives to this day, and popular enough to justify building a new factory at Toyokawa (a new foundry had also been built, reducing Suzuki's reliance on outside suppliers). This evolved into the L20 series, but at least the private car market was not ignored, with the Suzulight TL giving birth to the first of the Fronte models in March 1962. This name was later used on the Fronte 800, which made its debut at the 1963 Tokyo Show, powered by a water-cooled 785cc two-stroke three-cylinder engine rated at 41bhp. The two-stroke triple was a significant piece of technology, and brought the company (with its share capital now up to 4,500,000,000 yen) a lot of good publicity.

Another revamp

If you've followed the story thus far, you'll have spotted that Suzuki rarely left things alone in the fifties and early sixties – no sooner was one model range introduced than another would spring up to run alongside it, with lines superseded on such a regular basis it's enough to make your head spin!

Sure enough, in the spring of 1962, all hell broke loose, with the 125SH becoming the SL, and the 125SB-2 becoming the SK; only the SB-S kept its old

The modern Fronte 800 made its debut at the end of 1963, although it didn't go on sale until 1965.

43

SUZUKI MOTORCYCLES: THE CLASSIC TWO-STROKE ERA

An A4 flyer produced to announce the arrival of the 125SL model.

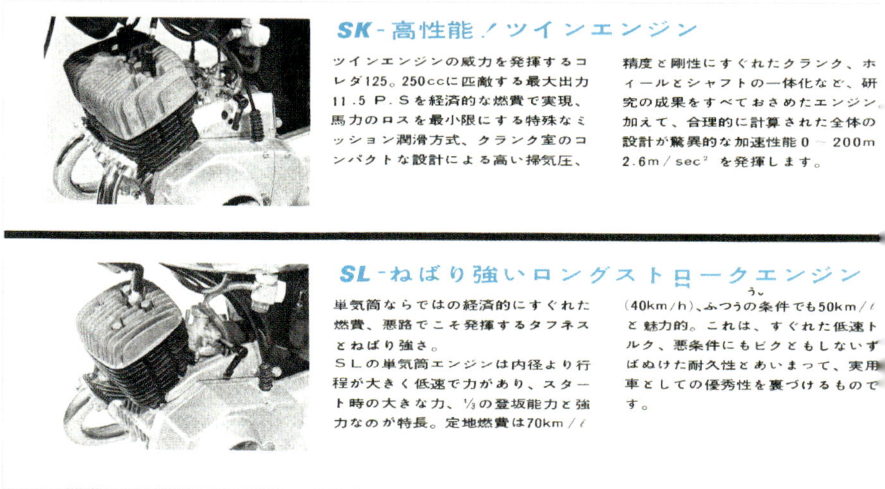

Cover and a couple of inside pages from the combined 125SK and 125SL catalogue.

designation (at least at home, for it was now listed as the 150SKB abroad), although time was running out for the latter, as the model ultimately failed to make it into the 1964 season line-up. In addition, 250TB evolved into the TC. As if that wasn't enough, by the middle of 1962, there were new 80K10 and 80K11 models to add into the equation as well.

The 128,000 yen 125SL had more traditional styling than its predecessor, signalling an end to the highly-distinctive Jet Line design, as well as a return to traditional chrome handlebars, with the indicators now mounted at the top of the fork tubes. A tighter front mudguard, squatter fuel tank, redesigned boxes under the saddle and a new rear light cluster finished up the main changes to the 8bhp 125cc single-cylinder model.

As before the face-lift, the 125SK was basically the same as the SL sister model, but fitted with the twin-cylinder engine rather than a single, so twin exhausts were fitted, providing a useful distinguishing feature along the way. As with the SL, the leading mechanical specs were carried over, so the SK was still endowed with 11.5bhp, and came with a four-speed rotary-type gearbox. In fact, all Suzukis, even the little mopeds, had a rotary transmission at this time.

The TC looked much like the TB at first glance, although there was a return to the older-style front mudguard (albeit tighter to the wheel), a more sporting angle on the handlebars,

44

THE EARLY SIXTIES

a chrome fuel tank with a slightly different profile, a shorter saddle (and redesigned boxes underneath), and a longer rear mudguard. Mechanically, there were no real changes, so the 20bhp engine and four-speed transmission was carried over, as well as the hydraulic rear braking system.

Production of the new Selpet 80 (80K10), which looked a lot like the 50MD in reality, began in May 1962, with the same seat on the original models (later changed to a fatter, more comfortable one, like that found on the SL and SK), but with lighter mudguards up front, proper handlebars from the start (it will be remembered that the contemporary MD was landed with the heavier, moped-inspired ones), and revised rear lighting that would duly find service on both the Sport range and the M15 versions of the MD/MC line-up. The 80 also had a downtube added ahead of the 6.5bhp single-cylinder engine, which itself had a different appearance compared with the 50cc unit.

The engine was comprised of a cast iron barrel, playing host to a piston-port induction system, and an alloy head and crankcase. With a 45mm x 50mm bore and stroke measurement, the unit's displacement was put at 79cc. In regular guise, the air-cooled single developed 6.5bhp, although the Sport 80 (80K11) version, introduced around eight months later on the first day of February 1963, was rated at 7.3bhp thanks to its high-mounted exhaust; both models were equipped with a four-speed transmission. The 77,000 yen Sport 80, with its chrome forks (duly revised to lose the exposed springs for the 1965 season) and lightweight pearl silver front mudguard, had a seat change early on, by the way, with the model gaining a full two-person saddle during 1963, in plenty of time for the 1964 season.

At its peak, the 80K10 model was pulling in 18,000 orders a month due to a combination of its reasonable price point (close to the cost of a true moped) and low overall running expense, its peppy performance, and the way it managed to gel with people's needs, especially after gaining a

Publicity shot of the early 80K10, with the 'Selpet 80' badging used for the home market.

The rather short-lived Colleda 250TC. A longer saddle was available as an option, but this shorter version was standard fare for Japan.

Single-page flyer using much of the full-size 80K10 brochure's artwork.

45

SUZUKI MOTORCYCLES: THE CLASSIC TWO-STROKE ERA

self-starter option for 1964. All told, over half a million were sold over a five-year run.

Incidentally, the 1962 Tokyo Show witnessed no less than 14 manufacturers exhibiting motorbikes and scooters, with the emphasis on 50cc machines (a proposed rule change may have had a bearing on 30cc models, but this was not really Suzuki territory – indeed, only Tohatsu fielded one at the event), followed by 125s and 250s. Only two motorcycles with engines of over 350cc capacity were shown, meaning the bigger stuff was still the realm of the Europeans and Americans.

The 80K11 (or Sport 80) as it appeared soon after the time of its announcement.

British advertising making the most of the company's success during the 1962 Isle of Man TT event.

The 1962 and 1963 racing seasons

This season marked Suzuki's arrival as a team to be reckoned with. Having been the laughing stock of the pit lane in 1961, the ridicule was taken as a useful lesson, and the ease with which Honda had started winning was no longer taken for granted. At the end of the day, Honda's racing budget was huge by this time (even putting aside enough money to build Suzuka racetrack), while Suzuki was coming from behind in an era when technology played an ever-greater role. Those in the game with a head-start and/or the wherewithal to fund a racing programme properly were always going to have an advantage …

While the bigger-engine classes were always going to give Suzuki's engineers a headache, the newly-introduced 50cc category looked almost custom made for the Japanese manufacturer, and with Degner onboard, the gap between the newcomer and the established teams could quickly be reduced. Shunzo Suzuki was sure his men were in a position where they could at last compete on an equal footing, and the management ultimately gave the project its rubber stamp.

To win, though, even the littlest Suzukis needed to sport at least 87mph (140kph) performance at the top end, which proved difficult to achieve given the engine power available. Numerous design changes were made, with trouble never being far away as the power target was slowly but surely

A small but interesting piece of contemporary promotional material, punched for binding and perforations to separate each band. Ernst Degner (then 31) and a slightly younger Hugh Anderson (aged 26) are profiled.

THE EARLY SIXTIES

brought into sight. Finally, in March 1962, just before setting off for Spain (the team left Tokyo's Haneda Airport on April 24), the 9bhp output engineers had sought – even though it looked unthinkable given the power-per-litre ratio in a 50cc unit – was duly achieved, giving the bike the speed it needed on the straights if the calculations were right.

The Suzuki team was led by Takeharu Okano, with the six works riders being Mitsuo Itoh, Michio Ichino and Seiichi Suzuki from Japan, Ernst Degner (described in Cycle World as "the brilliant East German rider technician"), Hugh Anderson from New Zealand, and Canadian-born Frank Perris, who'd resided in the UK from an early age. Bikes included the 42bhp RV62 in the 250cc class, the 24bhp RT62 in the 125cc category, and the eight-speed RM62 with a rotary induction valve in the 50cc class.

The season kicked off with the Spanish GP on May 6, but it was Kreidler's race in the 50cc category, with home makers Derbi and Honda filling the podium. A week later, Kreidler and Honda once again dominated amongst the tiddlers, but at least Suzuki and Itoh got some points on the board in the 50cc class, and work began on improving the bikes almost as soon as the flag fell at Clermont-Ferrand, as the TT was next.

While MV Agusta took the 500cc and 350cc classes in the jewel-in-the-crown Isle of Man TT, with Honda picking up the 250cc and 125cc silverware, Suzuki was able to claim 50cc honours on its first attempt. As well as recording the best lap, Degner averaged 75.1mph (120.2kph) to win with ease, with Itoh fifth, Ichino sixth, and Suzuki eighth, just outside the points. All got a Silver Replica Award, though, plus a Team Award for the Japanese maker.

The victory formed the basis for a ten-second TV advert aired in Japan on the next day, and in a message in the works journal, Shunzo Suzuki was ecstatic at the fact that his company was able to claim a world level win within just three years of Grand Prix racing. One has to tip a hat in his direction, too, for congratulating Honda on their achievements, and paving the way. This modesty could do nothing to dampen spirits or hide the solid foundation stone created by Suzuki alone that June, though – the Isle of Man race had been an excellent advert for two-cycle technology, and an excellent advert for the Suzuki brand.

Degner duly won the next three races (in Holland,

The RT63 and RM63 featured in a contemporary Suzuki catalogue. Spot the 'deliberate' mistakes in the numbering!

End of season celebrations for the 1962 works Suzuki team. From left to right: Anderson, Perris, Degner, Suzuki, Itoh and Ichino.

SUZUKI MOTORCYCLES: THE CLASSIC TWO-STROKE ERA

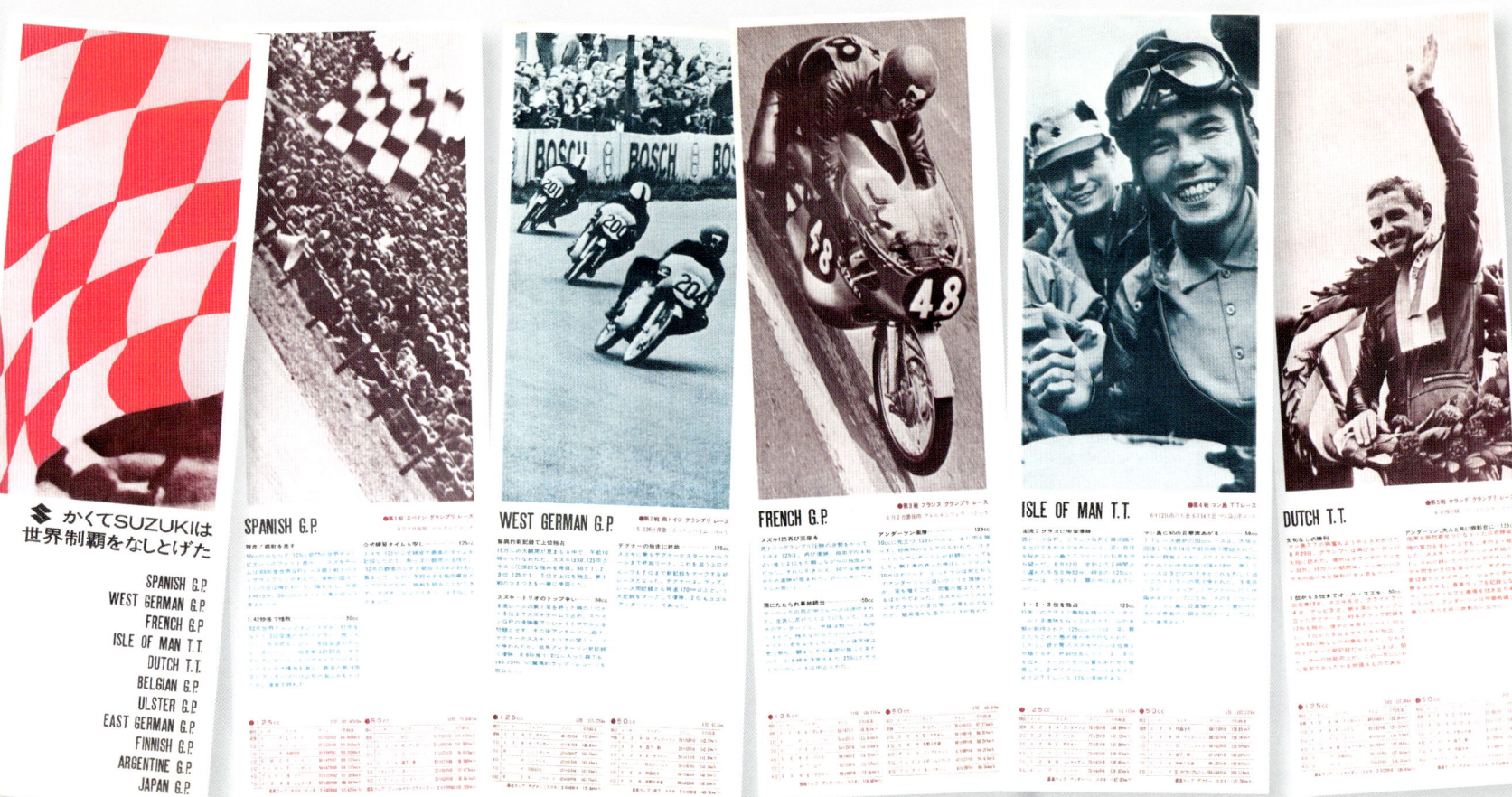

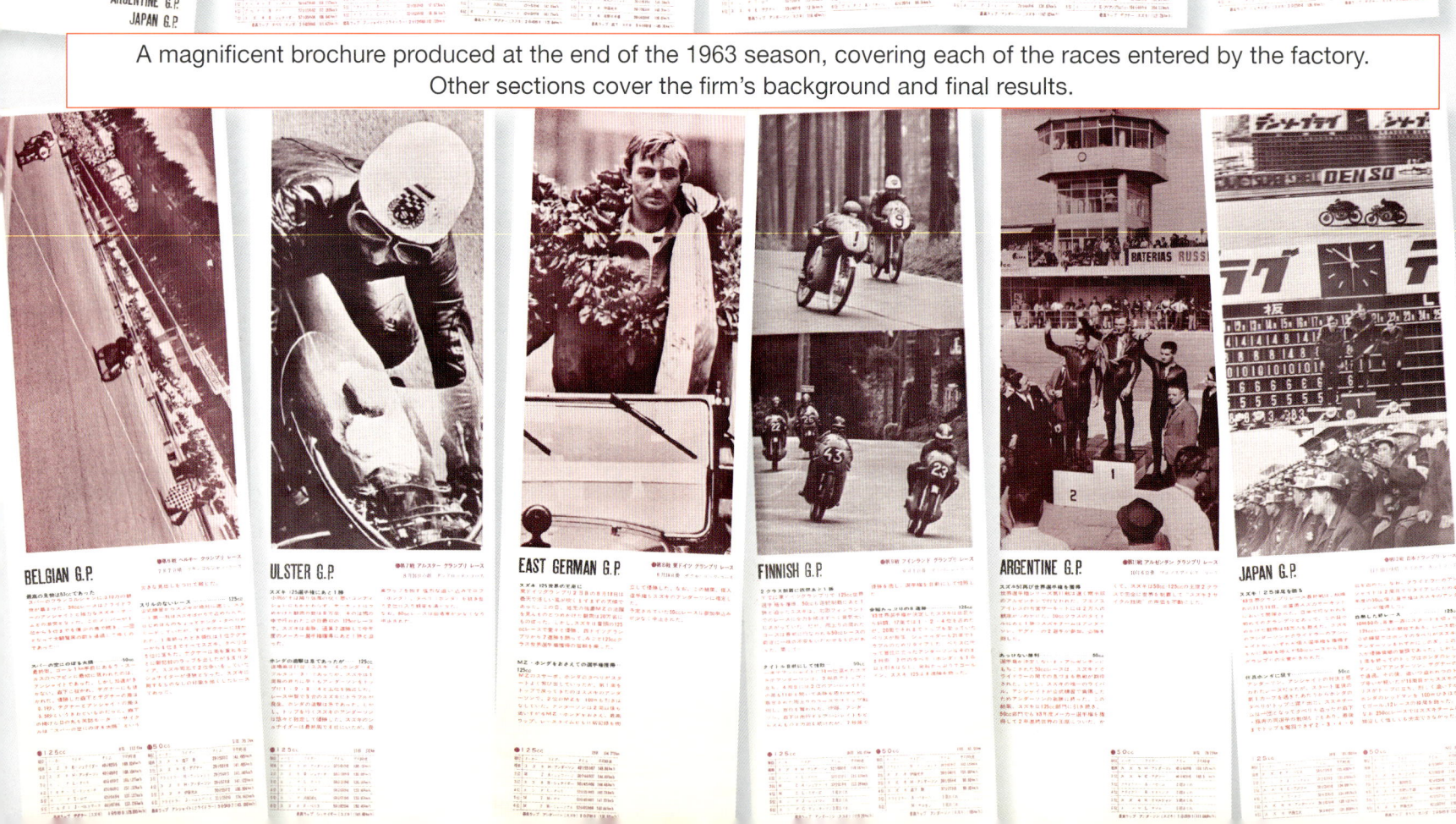

A magnificent brochure produced at the end of the 1963 season, covering each of the races entered by the factory. Other sections cover the firm's background and final results.

THE EARLY SIXTIES

Hugh Anderson (with his Kiwi helmet) on the cover of the 1964 Model Year road bike brochure. Suzuki was able to use the race programme as both a mobile R&D laboratory and an excellent form of publicity.

The 50M40, illustrated in road and race trim.

For the 1963 Grand Prix season, there was the 10bhp nine-speed RM63 fighting for 50cc class honours, the all-new 24bhp eight-speed RT63 twin in the 125cc category (there was also an RT63X with a different exhaust arrangement), and the four-cylinder RZ63 in the 250cc class. This latter six-speed machine was an amazing contraption with an engine consisting of what amounted to two RT units, one in front of the other, with a common crankcase, and liquid-cooling to help keep the rear pair of pots at working temperature. While this level of complexity added a fair bit of weight, the 52bhp output was impressive nonetheless, and had the reliability been there, it could have been a serious challenger no doubt. It certainly turned heads, almost as much as the return of the Gilera team. Riders were Degner, Itoh, Ichino, Anderson and Perris from the previous season, while newcomers included Isao Morishita and Bert Schneider.

Before the world championship season kicked off, Suzuki took a team to the USMC Grand Prix at Daytona, and filled the first five places in the 22-lap 50cc race, as well as claiming a one-two in the 125cc event, with Degner leading home Haruo Koshino. Hardly anything was made of this, yet Yamaha took out double-page adverts to celebrate its 250cc and GP victories.

Anyway, there was a second and fourth in the 50cc class in the 1963 opener in Spain in May, followed by a one-two-three victory at Hockenheim; the RT63 came good in West Germany, too, delivering Ernst Degner a nice win, and then gave Hugh Anderson one in the next meeting in France, with the 50cc models second and third in their race.

Suzuki had a superb Isle of Man meeting in June, with the RT63s totally outclassing the Hondas – Anderson won, with Perris second, and Degner third; only Luigi Taveri could hold off Schneider from taking fourth. The 50cc class also belonged to Suzuki, with Mitsuo Itoh becoming the first Japanese rider to win a Manx TT race, followed in by Anderson, Morishita in fourth, and Ichino in fifth.

As the circus moved to Holland, Degner led home the first of five Suzukis in the 50cc race, while Anderson took the flag in the 125cc race. Morishita and Schneider won in Belgium, with Anderson winning the 125cc class in both the Ulster GP and East German GP events (there were no 50cc races in Ireland or East Germany that year); Anderson won again in Finland, sealing the 125cc title.

Belgium and West Germany), which was enough to secure the world championship title for himself, and a win in Argentina for Anderson sealed things once and for all for Suzuki in the 50cc class. While the 125 and 250 racers had been also-rans, with Hugh Anderson giving the RT62 its only GP win of the season in the 1962 finale at Buenos Aires (the RV62 couldn't pick up a win at all), Suzuki was able to display its 50cc single-cylinder RM62 racer at the 1962 Tokyo Show with a true sense of pride.

Suzuki's know-how had now been proven on the track over a gruelling season, and lessons learnt could duly be passed onto the customer in old school fashion. This victory enabled Suzuki to lead the tiddler class at home, adding enthusiasts that would have previously scoffed at such small engines to its client list. Indeed, the same thing happened all over the world judging by the reactions in contemporary issues of Cycle World magazine and the like. A new era had begun.

49

SUZUKI MOTORCYCLES: THE CLASSIC TWO-STROKE ERA

With no 50cc race at the Nations GP held at Monza, Suzuki decided to stay away from the meeting, but Anderson secured the 50cc world championship in Buenos Aires in October, adding it to his 125cc title. In the season finale, the second Japanese GP, Perris won the 125cc race on Honda's Suzuka track, as if to rub salt into the wound, as he was the first non-Honda man to lift the winner's trophy there.

As it happens, the Suzuka meeting marked the debut of the fascinating RZ63 four, although it was a dramatic one for all the wrong reasons. Degner suffered a bad accident that put him in hospital for a month with serious burns, Perris stopped to help his team-mate, and Anderson finished ninth after trouble struck – he had been as high as fourth, which would have given Suzuki something to build on if nothing else.

At least Suzuki was able to celebrate a fantastic season in the smaller classes, establishing the maker as the brand to beat in the 50cc and 125cc categories. To celebrate, amateur racers that followed the marque could even buy an off-the-shelf racing bike – the 50M40, which came with a 6.5bhp 49cc piston-port engine and six-speed transmission, a unique lightweight frame (keeping weight down to just 70kg, or 154lb), a choice of exhaust systems, sporting saddles, and suitable body fairings. There was also the six-speed MR41 version, further lightened and coming with a highly-tuned 8.5bhp 49cc single for serious enthusiasts.

Export drive

The value of export sales had always been clear at Suzuki – its very survival was thanks to opening up new markets in its prewar days, back when looms were the firm's staple product. Official 'authorised distributors' were few and far between according to documents from 1961, with outlets in Belgium and France, one on each side of the African continent, and three in the Middle East.

Naturally, this doesn't mean these were the only places Suzukis were sold, as the SE Asian market once more came to the rescue, and there was even a

A couple of UK adverts from 1962. Note the adjustable steering damper on the 250TB, as well as a list of the various foreign distributors at the time.

An advert that appeared in *Motorcycle Mechanics* in February 1963.

THE EARLY SIXTIES

CKD operation established in Taiwan in 1961. There was a sales outlet set up in London, too, at this time, although no distributor as yet, and this story was repeated in numerous countries across Europe, as well as America, for an advert from early 1964 placed by Ken Kay proudly states it was his fourth year handling the brand in the States. Mathematically, this would be before distribution rights were granted, while the UK office even had press machines on hand a couple of years ahead of Associated Motor Cycles becoming official distributors. AMC was actually the umbrella company behind such great English marques as Norton, AJS and Matchless, and would start handling the Suzuki brand from its Birmingham premises from the summer of 1963.

Despite a heavy 15 per cent import tariff being imposed during the year, around 18,000 Suzukis were sold before 1964 came to an end, mostly 50cc tiddlers, although there were also the 80cc and 250cc bikes in the mix. During 1964, the Sportsman (M15) was listed at £96 in the UK, with the Sovereign (M15D) at £114; the £109 Super Sport (M12), with its high-mounted exhaust and extra chrome, made up the 50cc range. At the same time, the 80K10 commanded £123, the 80K11 £128, and the T10, which had silver-painted front mudguards rather than chrome ones by now, £249.

Motor Cycle tried a K11 in early 1964, and concluded: "The Suzuki K11 Sports is a

Cover of a 20-page supplement that appeared in a March 1964 edition of the UK's *Motor Cycle* magazine. It was duly reprinted for dealers to hand out.

Selection of adverts from 1964, after the formation of Suzuki GB and Associated Motor Cycles taking on the distribution rights for the United Kingdom.

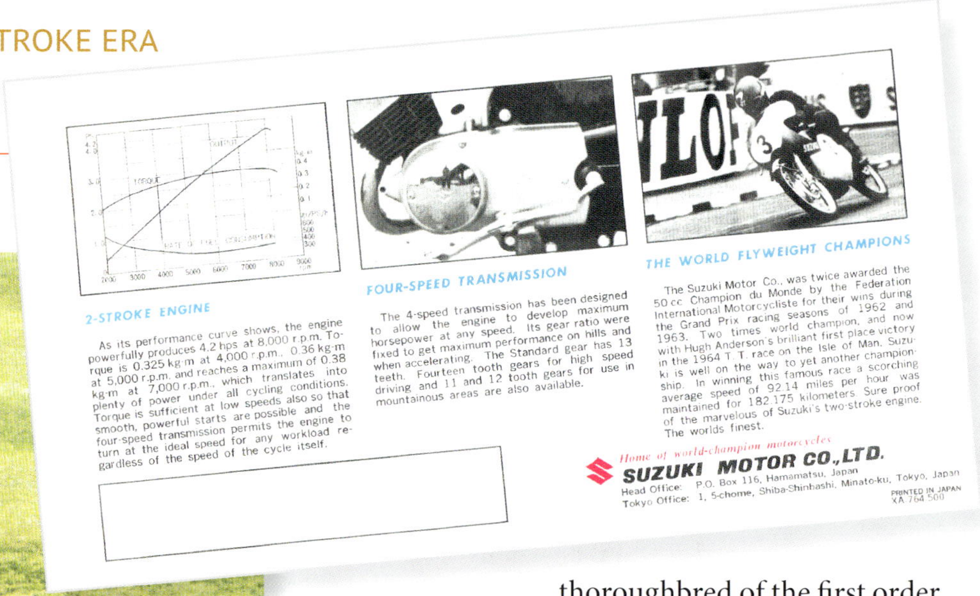

SUZUKI MOTORCYCLES: THE CLASSIC TWO-STROKE ERA

An English language brochure for the M15 models, printed in the summer of 1964.

Part of the English language catalogue for the M12 and 80K11 from the same era.

thoroughbred of the first order. Full marks to the manufacturers for an excellent product – and for 600 of the happiest miles for some time." It was the T10 luxury tourer that impressed the most, though, moving the testing team to compare the Japanese bike with a Rolls-Royce!

At about the same time as the AMC deal was going through, Suzuki decided to create a European base in Brussels. The timing was right. While 1962 to 1965 was a difficult era for all motorcycle makers, becoming something of a fight for survival, the company's success in the Isle of Man TT races had brought a lot of attention to the marque, helping to increase awareness of the brand in export markets.

This expansion outside the Land of the Rising Sun proved crucial, for in the bloodbath of the early sixties, hardly any Japanese makers were able to pull through. Tohatsu (Tokyo Hatsudoki) fell by the wayside in 1964, and the respected Meguro marque was swallowed up by the Kawasaki empire.

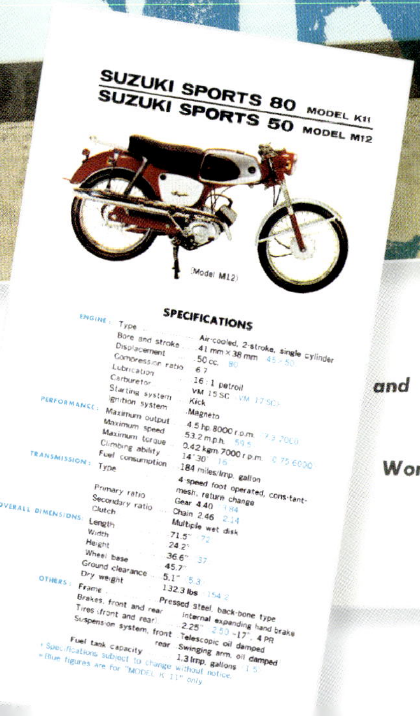

52

It all seemed rather at odds with the buoyant atmosphere at home, with the Tokyo Olympics and the first bullet train service starting. Ironically, this may have been part of the problem. Wages kept increasing rapidly, with the national average going up from 260,000 yen a year in 1960, to 450,000 yen in 1965, at a time when a bowl of noodle soup was around 150 yen, and the average magazine just 50 yen. All of a sudden, cars became an affordable object of desire, and motorbike sales fell as a result, leaving only the fittest in the game.

Indeed, by 1966, between them, Suzuki, Honda, Yamaha and Kawasaki now accounted for 95 per cent of domestic market sales (Bridgestone made up the rest). This situation would have seemed unthinkable only a decade earlier, but at least with Suzuki specialising in two-stroke engines, Honda in four-stroke technology, and Kawasaki and Yamaha having their own appeal, this avoided a direct clash in the showrooms. More than ever before, the American market would hold the answer to Suzuki's prayers.

California Dreamin'

The American market was truly huge, with machines being shipped over from various parts of postwar Europe at a pace that some makers could only just keep up with. Then, of course, Honda arrived on the scene, and the complexion of the playing field simply changed overnight.

When Suzuki made its first tentative steps into the US sales arena, with Ken Kay Distributing Co of Sherman Way, North Hollywood, CA, handling the imports and distribution at this time, Honda was already taking double-page adverts in the leading Stateside magazines, listing 11 models for the 1962 season, and boasting of their excellent track record in European racing. Equally, Yamaha was buying a full page to push its 250s and the 125 YA-5 with its high-efficiency rotary valve technology, with the snappy catchphrase: "The name that says 'quality' in any language."

What was interesting was that both Honda and Yamaha had their own corporate offices in Los Angeles to punt their wares, which was a luxury afforded to few of the import brands. For instance, Norton was handled by Joseph Berliner of the Berliner Motor Corporation of New Jersey, who also looked after the Ducati, Steyr, Zundapp and Sachs marques, as well as Matchless as 1962 came to an end. NSU and Motobi models were imported by West Valley Cycle Sales of California, MV Agusta, Bianchi and Parilla lines by Cosmopolitan Motors of Philadelphia, Gilera by C&N Enterprises, German Maico bikes by White Motors, and Triumph by Johnson Motors Inc. for the west coast. Only BSA could really rival the Japanese when it came to brand representation. In other words, there was nothing unusual in having an outside party handle things, but, as the author's old friend Yutaka Katayama quickly concluded on a recce trip for Nissan, if one was to succeed in the States, one needed a base there, offering all the back-up a customer would expect in a product's native land.

For now, though, the Ken Kay outfit was the face of Suzuki in America, listing the single-cylinder 50cc Suzuki 50MC (with a four-speed transmission, turn signals and a longer saddle, as the restrictions on pillion passengers in Japan had no bearing in the States) at $295, and the twin-cylinder 250TB (with 12-volt electrics and an electric starter) at $595 in early 1962. This compared with a Pointer 125cc Senior at $390, or a 250cc Honda CB-72 Hawk at $640.

There was no mention of the Colleda name, and things went decidedly quiet until the start of summer, when the first adverts starting appearing – and they were tiny, too! But the 50cc model was now called the 'Classic' and the 250cc 'El Camino' (now carrying a TC designation rather than a TB one in line with domestic production) came in three guises, suitable for street and touring use, town and trail work, and full-blooded scrambling. Not until the tail-end of summer did Ken Kay have the nerve to go for a big advertising splash, taking a double-page to show the new dealer network (49 shops) and larger pictures of the $625 El Camino and $295 Classic, alongside a new $350 Trojan 80, and a couple of other imports that had nothing to do with Suzuki.

In the meantime, looking through old magazines, it's clear that while a traditional market still existed in the States, interest was rising in off-roaders (giving a welcome financial boost for the likes of Jawa, Greeves and Cotton), and scooter sales were really taking off, too, with 33,000 units sold in 1961 and figures set to rise further. Adverts for the likes of the Lambretta, Rabbit and Steyr Venus may have been unthinkable only a few years earlier, but even Harley-Davidson was downsizing, badge-engineering the Aermacchi 250 for its diehard customers. This move towards smaller engines also opened up the way for 50cc bikes, which were no longer a laughing stock in American eyes due to their well-documented success in the racing arena. The

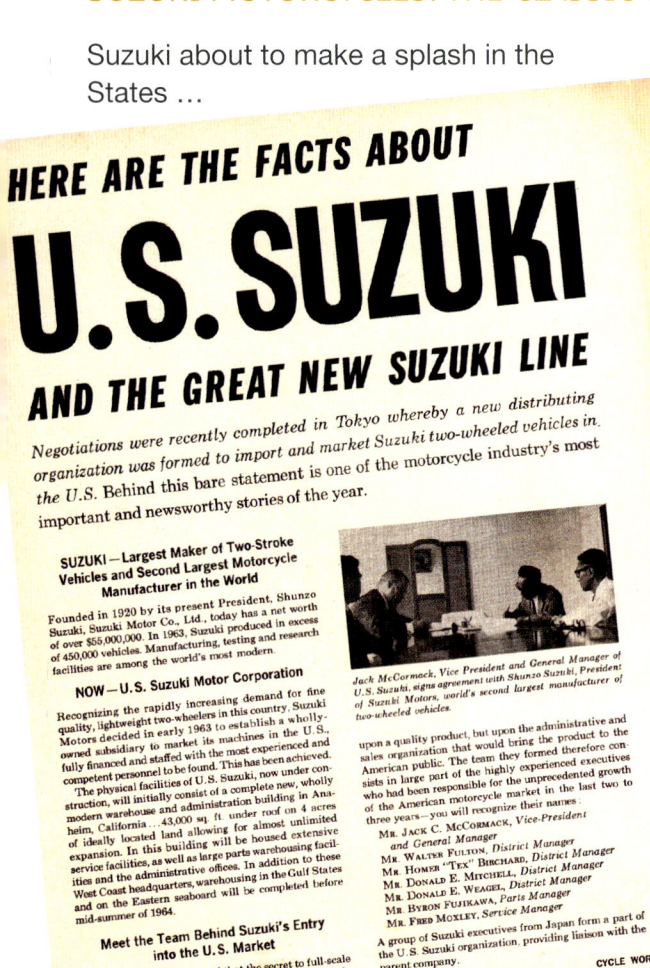

SUZUKI MOTORCYCLES: THE CLASSIC TWO-STROKE ERA

Suzuki about to make a splash in the States ...

[Vintage advertisement reproduction: "HERE ARE THE FACTS ABOUT U.S. SUZUKI MOTOR CORP. AND THE GREAT NEW SUZUKI LINE" — Cycle World, January 1964]

timing was definitely right for Suzuki to establish itself across the Pacific.

As it happens, there was one more double-page spread from the Ken Kay concern (along with a test of the 250TC, which the highly-respected *Cycle World* described as "a very interesting piece of machinery"), and then, by the time winter was setting in, it was back to a quarter of a page for a whole season, while rival Honda (proclaiming itself as "the world's largest motorcycle manufacturer") was hogging three pages plus the odd dealer piece. With Walt Davis doing his best in a PR capacity, it was obvious the funding wasn't there, and by early 1963, Suzuki ads were a similar size to those for the Mustang tiddler, loitering in the back pages.

There was one last hurrah at trying to promote the Trojan 80 Super Sport as the summer of 1963 gave way to autumn (red and blue versions of the little bike were listed to augment the regular black one), followed by a large ad for the $295 50cc Classic, the $350 80cc model and $589 El Camino, but basically time had ran out for the Ken Kay operation – from now on, Suzuki would be going it alone, joining the ranks of Honda and Yamaha with their own US offices.

Interestingly, the Ken Kay Distributing Company was still an important part of the Japanese bike scene, taking on the Kawasaki brand in the States in 1964, badged as Omegas while under his watch. He also continued to use the Trojan brand name, and offered his services as a Suzuki spares supplier.

The US Suzuki Motor Corporation started business on the first day of October 1963, with a capital of $100,000 and a large new $750,000 headquarters planned in Santa Ana, California, allowing sales to begin in January. The VP/GM was Jack McCormack, who'd previously headed Honda's American arm, while Shozo Hashimoto was another VP and the factory contact, and Yoshito Itoh looked after the service department and race activities; Walt Fulton joined the team soon after as the sales manager.

Aiming to sell a modest 8000 units in 1964, while there had been a giant splash announcing the new organisation, the full-blooded advertising campaign only really started in the summer of that year, after Suzuki had taken out full-page adverts in a number of leading publications to try and secure US dealers, following it up with radio interviews and other

An advert that could only be placed in an American magazine!

THE EARLY SIXTIES

Inner pages of the US Suzuki T10 catalogue.

forms of publicity. There was also a $500,000 east coast office opened in Jacksonville, Florida. Suzuki still had a long way to catch up with Honda and Yamaha operations Stateside, which were already extensive, but progress was definitely being made; Suzuki's position as Japan's number two maker (a long way behind the 564,000 production figures posted by Honda but ahead of Yamaha) would become easier to hold on to from now on.

For 1964, Americans had a choice of the M30 moped at $245, the M15 and M15D at $267 and $297 respectively, the M12 'Cavalier' at $292, the K10 'Sport' at $334, the K11 'Super Sport' or 'SS' at $353, and the T10 at $603. This compares with $285 for a Honda four-stroke Sports 50, or $665 for the 305cc Honda Super Hawk. Colours available included black, red, blue and white for both the 50cc and 80cc models, as well as the T10. There were also thoughts of importing the S31, along with a 150cc version in regular guise (S32) and with the sports exhaust (S33), although it's difficult to say whether any made it across the Pacific in volume.

However, production of the K15 trails bike started in May 1964 – an incredible success story for Suzuki, as its launch coincided perfectly with a US boom for this sort of machine. Originally named the 'Bearcat', the $350 'Hill-Billy' was designed specifically for the US market by McCormack, and tested extensively in Mexico to ensure authentic scrambling capabilities, backed up by knobby tyres and a dual drive sprocket arrangement to make the bike suitable for on- and off-road work.

After its first test of the new 80cc 8bhp bike, *Cycle World* noted: "In short, the Hill-Billy has everything necessary to make it a success on today's extremely competitive trail bike market. We can throw into the bargain the fact that it is nicely finished and a very good-looking piece of equipment as well."

Much like the first Japanese cars to find their way to foreign shores, there were certain areas that were lagging behind (such as tyre technology and suspension setups that were fine in their place of origin, but hardly in tune with their new surroundings), but the value-for-money element soon had people forgiving certain things when the bike was looked at as a whole package. These early offerings also had a 'character' that was nothing if not distinctive – styling being a case in point, and something you either loved or hated. Interesting times lay ahead …

The 1964 racing season

After the success of 1963, expectations were high for a good result in 1964. Suzuki fielded the RM64 in the 50cc class, its new 49.8cc engine having a 41.5mm bore and 36.8mm stroke (as opposed to the 40mm x 39.5mm relationship found on the RM62 and RM63 to give 49.6cc). With an 8.8:1 c/r, power was now quoted at a heady 12.5bhp at 14,000rpm, enabling the 60kg (132lb) machine to do the ton (160mph) with those brave enough.

The 125cc fighter was the RT64, with the same 123.7cc (43mm x 42.6mm) air-cooled twin as 1963, albeit tuned to give 30bhp at 13,000rpm in its latest guise. The RT64 tipped the scales at just 90kg (198lb), so its performance was quite sprightly to say the least. In addition, work was going on behind the scenes on the so-called RK64 four, although this 125cc contender never saw the light of day. Meanwhile, the big RZ64 was rolled out for 250cc honours.

Anderson, Perris, Schneider, Morishita and Itoh kept their seat in the works team, but Degner was out for the start of 1964 due to the injuries he'd sustained at the end of the last year, so Australian Jack Ahearn was called up for service, along with Japan's Yoshimi Katayama and Teisuke Tanaka.

The US GP was brought into the world championship fold for 1964. Anderson won both the 50cc and 125cc races (Suzuki claimed a one-two-three finish in both events), although Austria's Bert Schneider had impressed everyone at Daytona with his remarkably fast lap on the RZ before it expired.

Sadly, the 54bhp RZ64 was no better than the RZ63 it was based on, and despite numerous extensive changes, the engineers just couldn't get it right. As such, the works 250cc campaign was nothing to write home about, with only three finishes in the points during the whole season – Schneider's

SUZUKI MOTORCYCLES: THE CLASSIC TWO-STROKE ERA

Shell advertising – the petrol giant was proud of its links with the Japanese bike manufacturer.

The opening of the Ryuyo test track, with racing bikes in attendance. A new site is being built after the massive 2011 earthquake raised fears of tsunami damage.

Suzuki making the most of its racing success on the cover of the 1965 Model Year road bike brochure.

Advertising telling the world about Suzuki's success at Daytona in 1964.

third at the French GP being the best result of 1964 for the big bike.

Anyway, while there was no glory in Spain, Anderson managed to win the 50cc race in the French GP, and then sealed Suzuki's hat-trick in the 50cc category at the Isle of Man TT classic. Anderson won at a remarkable 80.6mph (129kph) average, with Honda's Ralph Bryans close behind – in fact, these two battled hard all season. For the record, Morishita was third, with Itoh fifth, making up for the disappointment in the other Manx categories, even the 125cc race, in which none of the works bikes managed to complete the six laps.

Honda dominated at the Dutch TT in front of an almost 200,000-strong crowd, and then took the flag in the 50cc race at Spa, too. The two German races saw Anderson win the 125cc category in the East German GP, and he repeated the feat in Ulster. Reliability problems plagued the RT in Finland, but at least Anderson was able to win the 50cc race, sealing the championship for both himself and Suzuki in the process, as

THE EARLY SIXTIES

Bert Schneider in action with the RZ64 in the French Grand Prix. (Courtesy Yaesu Publishing)

there was no 50cc class at the Nations GP at Monza, and the one held at the Japan GP didn't count towards the title chase.

Being Suzuki's third 50cc title, not surprisingly there was something of a media frenzy back home – the Hamamatsu maker had won the class in all three years of the championship's existence after all! Although the 50cc Suzukis were not campaigned at Suzuka in the season finale, it was nice to see Ernst Degner back in winning ways, taking the silverware home from the 125cc race, in which Honda's Luigi Taveri was second, and Suzuki's Yoshimi Katayama third.

Incidentally, Suzuki's first dedicated test course was completed at Ryuyo (to the west of the head office, on the Hamamatsu coastline) in December 1964. Measuring four miles (6.5km) in length, it was designed specifically for bikes, with a long straight, a hairpin turn and a series of different curves to help simulate race conditions. Having been shown where earlier testing was carried out, it would have called for some very understanding local law enforcement officers! Ah, the good ol' days …

Advertising sheet and a front three-quarter view of the M15 model that superseded the M10 series.

Cover for the Japanese S30 catalogue.

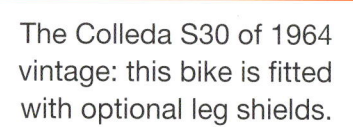

The Colleda S30 of 1964 vintage: this bike is fitted with optional leg shields.

The S31 model, introduced in June 1963. Note the 'Colleda' badge used on the side boxes.

58

THE EARLY SIXTIES

More catalogue updates

While most of the tiddlers were continued unchanged, the M10 became the 55,000 yen M15 very early in 1964, having a different rear light unit, which was actually similar to the one originally used in America (as well as Britain, but to clear the UK number plate, the mounting post had to extend both upwards and back), and relocated rear indicators. It seems odd, though, seeing as the US market required a larger rear light in 1964, that Suzuki should adopt the version used before the change in Federal lighting rules made the newer lens necessary. Not to worry, at least the difference has been noted. Not surprisingly, with a pattern established, the M10D was now called the M15D, which continued to sport a self-starter, with a kickstart facility still there as a back-up.

As for the 125s, the SK became the S30 just in time for the 1964 Model Year, with the S31 (or Sport 125) named as an indirect replacement for the SB-S (aka the 150SKB) alongside it, albeit launched a few weeks earlier in June 1963 at 143,000 yen.

The S30 could be bought with or without front fairings (or leg shields if you want to call them that), and had a number of detail changes compared to its predecessor, including a redesigned fuel tank to suit the tubular steel downtube added up front, new front forks with more chrome showing in the lower section, and a Sport-type rear lighting arrangement, with the indicators now separated from the enlarged taillight. With a 7.0:1 compression ratio and Amal VM18SC carburetion, power was now quoted at 12bhp at 7500rpm, delivered via a four-speed rotary transmission.

The sister model, the S31, had 12.5bhp thanks to its high-mount sports exhaust, and came with a lighter TB-type front mudguard (as used on the Sport 50 and Sport 80), exposed springs on the front forks and rear damper units (also adopted on the

The S31 as illustrated in the 1964 MY catalogue, complete with the machine's basic specifications.

SUZUKI MOTORCYCLES: THE CLASSIC TWO-STROKE ERA

other Sport models for the 1964 season), and a longer saddle than the S30, again fitting in with the other Sport machines, which had also gained new seats. Striking blue paintwork was available on the Sport range, making the bikes even more eye-catching.

The 250TC became the Colleda T10 at the start of 1964 proper, with a lighter front mudguard (back to TB era again!), a longer seat, and a couple of more horses to play with, taking the model's maximum power output to 22bhp at 8000rpm, while torque increased to 15lb/ft at 7000rpm. Incidentally, the early T10s had the TC's rear braking system, but this was soon changed to a mechanical version.

The next move was the introduction of the single-cylinder S10 to replace the 125SL in the autumn of 1964, in time for the 1965 season, although in reality both models ran alongside each other until the spring of 1965. This 130,000 yen machine had a brand new 123cc (54mm x 54mm) rotary valve engine, developing a healthy 10.5bhp and 9lb/ft of torque, and was unusual in that it had double ports and twin exhausts, despite being a single (the solitary sparkplug sticking out of the aluminium head gave the game away). This hike in power justified the downtube added for this model, which meant using the S30 tank. Other than these things, S30-type front forks and the latest rear lights, the S10 looked very much like the bike it superseded. By the way, a 250cc rotary-disc valve prototype known as the R250 was displayed at the 1964 Tokyo Show, but unfortunately this 32bhp machine failed to achieve production status.

Production version of the T10, introduced at a price of 170,000 yen. The badges on the side boxes read 'Colleda' by the way.

Cover of the Colleda 250 (T10) brochure.

The S10 panel from the Suzuki range catalogue produced in readiness for the 1965 season. The 125SL was still listed at this time, as there were doubtless stocks to clear in dealerships.

60

THE EARLY SIXTIES

Road bike evolution

The Suzuki motorcycle range is complex, and often confusing. This simplified table, following the evolution of each two-stroke model covered in this chapter, should hopefully allow things to become a lot clearer.

Model	1960	1961	1962	1963	1964	1965
Selpet 50MC (50cc single)		MC		M10D	M15D	
Selpet 50MD (50cc single)		MD		M10	M15	
Sport 50 (50cc single)				M12		
Selpet 52MD (52cc single)			M11	M16		
Sport 52 (52cc single)				M13		
Selpet 80 (79cc single)				K10		
Sport 80 (79cc single)				K11		
Colleda 125ST (123cc single)	ST-6A		SH	SL		
Suzuki S10 (123cc single)						S10
Colleda Seltwin SB (124cc twin)	SB	SB-2		SK	S30	
Sport 125 (124cc twin)					S31	
Colleda Seltwin SB-S (150cc twin)	SB-S					
Colleda 250TA (247cc single)	TA	TB		TC	T10	

Note: Pure mopeds and models made specifically for export are not included in this table, although they're all covered within the main text.

www.veloce.co.uk / www.velocebooks.com
All current books • New book news • Special offers • Gift vouchers

4 The Late Sixties

A bruised and battered, but nonetheless valuable, document – a magazine supplement printed in the first days of 1965.

By the time 1965 rolled along, the Colleda name (and the Selpet one for that matter) had all but disappeared, quietly allowed to slip into the history books in favour of the Suzuki moniker. This made sense, for the export markets had never adopted anything other than the Suzuki nameplate for their machines, and the works racing team also went under the Suzuki banner. There doesn't appear to be a formal changeover of any sort, it just happened as model introductions occurred or new catalogues were printed, with the Colleda S30 becoming the Suzuki 125 S30 for instance, the Suzuki Selpet 80K10 becoming the Suzuki 80K10, and the Colleda 250 T10 the Suzuki 250 T10 in later brochures and advertising. We can see this shift in naming policy on the bikes themselves, too, with new badges introduced along the way.

Notwithstanding, the line-up for the 1965 season looked

The M80 moped as per the time of its introduction.

THE LATE SIXTIES

much the same as it had for 1964, as the 125SL limped on into the spring, sold alongside its ultimate replacement, the Suzuki S10. For a change, there were no new machines either, at least until May 1965, when the M80 moped and the sporty B100 were introduced. There was also a domestic version of the 250 T20 launched – a bike that had been introduced at the 1964 Tokyo Show, but was initially destined for export markets.

Starting with a brief résumé of the mopeds, the 70,000 yen M80 was much like the M30 and M31, but fitted with a 79cc engine borrowed from the 80K10, albeit in de-tuned form. This was to be a short-lived model, however, for the autumn of 1966 saw a complete revamp of the moped line, with the M30 being replaced by the 47cc U50 and U50D, the M31 falling by the wayside, and the M80 being superseded by the 69cc U70 (coded K40 internally). The new U-series was somehow more stylish than the M30-based machines, with rotary valve induction and CCI technology coming as part of the package. More on the latter in a moment …

The 108,000 yen B100, available in black, red or blue, looked similar to the 80K11, but minus the

Part of a range catalogue showing the new T20 model, with the original fork and spring arrangement.

front downtube, and with toned-down front forks (with rubber boots) and rear shocks, a traditional low-mounted exhaust on the right-hand side, and a less racy but nonetheless stylish seat for two sat atop the pressed-steel frame. It also had a much larger rear light unit, similar to that found on the new T20, run off the same magneto as the ignition. As for the single-cylinder engine, this was an all-alloy air-cooled 118cc (52mm x 56mm) piston-port lump developing 8bhp (adjusted to 9bhp in later publicity material) and plenty of torque, put down to the road via a four-speed transmission with a primary kickstart feature that allowed the bike to be started in gear as long as the user had pulled in the clutch lever. Traditional petroil (self-mix) lubrication was used on the first models, although, as we shall see, this was changed to a far more convenient system during 1966.

The other newcomer was the 250 T20, with the kickstart 247cc twin now pumping out 25bhp at 8000rpm – enough to endow the machine with a 94mph (150kph) top speed and a 15.5 second standing-quarter time. Many reports from the time, and later catalogues, too, said it would do the ton, but whichever way one looks at it, figures like these put the bike firmly in the 500cc class on the performance front.

Following two-and-a-half years of development (an amazingly long period, with testing on the new road course at home, plus extensive mileage in America, through deserts and the Rocky Mountains), the production T20 sported a strong but light tubular double-cradle 'valve' frame with twin downtubes at the front. The styling was traditional enough for followers of Suzuki lore to instantly recognise the design cues associated with the brand, such as the horseshoe-shaped headlight (containing a beautiful combined speedometer and tachometer within) and signature fuel tank, with B100-type minor lights and fork trim, three-step adjustable chrome rear shocks (quickly changed to a version

Brochure for the original B100, this example finished in red. It was also available with black or blue paintwork, and came with 'Suzuki' badges from the off.

SUZUKI MOTORCYCLES: THE CLASSIC TWO-STROKE ERA

1966 T20 with the later forks and rear springs.

A Sport 50 with the forks introduced on the M12 and K11 for 1965.

The 80K11 as it looked at the start of the 1965 season, with the new front fork design that was also adopted on the Sport 50 model at the same time. This bike still has 'Selpet' badges, but they were a real rarity on the updated machines.

with exposed coil springs), chrome handlebars with an adjuster for the steering damping rate, a colour-coded flash down the mudguards on machines that weren't painted in silver, a single chrome exhaust pipe on each side, a seat for two kicked up slightly at the trailing edge and a chrome luggage carrier beyond, and revised boxes underneath, with the offside one housing an oil supply to lubricate the engine – it was basically the first sight of the CCI system, although it wasn't called this at the time.

New technology for the big twin (54mm x 54mm) included aluminium cylinders with sleeves to reduce wear, the automatic lubrication system we've just touched on (a development of the Selmix system introduced for the Suzulight automobiles in 1963), and the first six-speed gearbox for a production road bike in Japan. With a pair of Mikuni VM24SH carbs, the engine developed 25bhp (or 29bhp SAE), and to keep these horses (and the 17.5lb/ft of torque) in check, the T20 was given powerful brakes – uprated, with twin leading shoes at the front, and a cable-operated SLS setup at the rear, which was something new for Suzuki, even though a right-hand foot pedal was still used for initial activation – and the latest high-speed tyres, 2.75-18s up front and 3.00-18s at the back.

Weighing in at 145kg (319lb), the 187,000 yen Suzuki 250 T20 – also known as the X-6 Hustler and Super Six in export markets – would prove to be a huge success amongst sporting enthusiasts both at home and abroad, with 5000 units a month being produced at one point. With quantities like this involved, it's not surprising that we can spot differences within the same model run, with the exposed springs being one obvious change

THE LATE SIXTIES

new 6.5bhp K10D once the 1965 season got under way. While all this was happening, in the early spring, it appears that the S31 was dropped from the domestic line-up (the latter sporting exposed springs right up until the end of its run, incidentally.) The S30 was also modified at the same time, becoming the S30-2, losing the leg guards for good, and inheriting painted side boxes along the way.

For the record, helmets became compulsory on faster roads in Japan at this time, and pillion passengers were being frowned on as well.

The 1965 racing season

The 50cc challenger for 1965 was the ten-speed RK65 (a 12-speed gearbox was also available), with an all-new water-cooled 49.7cc (32.5mm x 30mm) parallel twin for motive power. With an 8.6:1 c/r, plus the familiar Kokusan magnetos for the ignition, and Mikuni carburetion allied to rotary disc induction, it developed 14.5bhp at a heady 16,500rpm. Drum brakes were still the norm, of course, but then the bike weighed just 60kg (132lb), so even at racing speeds of over the ton, they hardly had a great deal of work to do.

The RT65 was more familiar, with its water-cooled 123.7cc twin being a straight development of the power-unit found in the previous year's 125cc racer. There was a slightly lower compression ratio, bigger carbs, and a new nine-speed gearbox, but power and speed increases were minimal – Suzuki was really pushing the performance envelope with its two-strokes.

The eight-speed RZ65 was also a carry-over as such, though a weight reduction programme thanks to an engine redesign that allowed a shorter frame and an increase in power up to 56bhp gave the 250cc machine a top speed of 148mph (237kph), which was quite enough given the skinny tyres and drum brakes.

As it happens, both three- (type RJ) and four-cylinder (RS) engine configurations were tried for the 125cc class at this time, but both of these water-cooled designs were duly dismissed in favour of keeping the tried-and-trusted twin-cylinder layout. The 48.9cc triple (type RP) was also given a miss, but if nothing else, this experimental work allowed Suzuki's engineers to perfect a two-stroke triple for road use, thus creating a legend along the way.

Hopes to secure Mike Hailwood's services were dashed at the last minute, so the rider line-up was much the same

Brochure for the deluxe 80K10D (announced in mid-December 1964), which came with more chrome and a self-starter system. Note also the 'Suzuki 80' badging, previously reserved for export models.

The S30-2, which usually came without leg guards. However, as this illustration shows, they were still available as an option.

(the rears first, followed by the fronts not too long after), and larger indicator lenses another.

As for the Sport series, the M12 and K11 gained new front forks with a chrome upper finish – something also fitted to the

Frank Perris taking the RZ65 to third place in the 1965 Isle of Man TT race. (Courtesy Yaesu Publishing)

THE LATE SIXTIES

Publicity material issued following the 1965 Czechoslovakian Grand Prix, and used as part of a contemporary catalogue.

as before, with Mitsuo Itoh, Michio Ichino, Yoshimi Katayama, Haruo Koshino, Hugh Anderson, Frank Perris, Jack Ahearn, and Ernst Degner. Toshio Fujii joined the stable in the summer, making his debut at Spa.

The season opener promised much, with Degner winning the 50cc race at Daytona, followed home by Anderson, Ichino and Koshino, and Anderson claiming the spoils in the 125cc class, with Degner and Perris in second and third. Perris got the big 250cc machine up to fourth, but Yamaha had this class sewn up on the day. Notwithstanding, Suzuki was able to take out full-page adverts in all the leading US publications boasting of their fine performance.

In the West German GP, Suzuki had to settle for third in the 50cc event, but was first and second in the 125cc race – enough to offset the disappointment resulting from a poor showing in the 250cc category. It was actually quite a similar story in Spain and France, although Anderson managed to take the flag in both the 50cc and 125cc races at the Montjuic circuit.

Next up was the big one – the Isle of Man TT. Ahearn had a bad spill with the RZ in practice for the Manx race, and although Perris got a fighting third place with the machine in the 250cc class, its days were numbered. Indeed, the square-four had been dropped from the Grand Prix scene by the summer (despite reasonable results at Spa), with only Katayama taking one out after that for the season finale in Japan. Meanwhile, a number of problems saw the smaller Suzukis struggling, too, with Anderson a distant fifth in the 125cc category, and the 50cc race falling to Honda's Luigi Taveri in difficult conditions. At least Anderson was second and Degner third, so the team had a few bits of silverware to show for their efforts. But no winners on the TT, that was unusual …

With nothing to celebrate in the Dutch TT either, at least Degner came out ahead in the 50cc race at Spa (there was no 125cc race), and Frank Perris made the most of Anderson being sidelined with an ankle injury in the East German GP at the Sachsenring, winning the 125cc race. There was no 50cc category in Germany, the Czechoslovakian GP, Ulster GP or the Finnish GP, but 125cc wins for Perris, Degner and Anderson at the last three Grands Prix sealed the title for Suzuki with remarkable ease. With competition being the ultimate proving ground, no one could question Suzuki's leading-edge technology in the two-stroke field.

Sadly, Degner crashed in the wet at Monza, effectively ending his career as a top competitor in the Nations GP. Some consolation came via a 125cc win for Anderson, with Perris following his team-mate home. In the last race of the Grand Prix season, the Japanese GP, Anderson fended off the challenge of the new five-cylinder Hondas in the 125cc race, although Katayama crashed heavily with the RZ in its last outing, and Honda's Taveri reigned supreme in the 50cc event.

Ultimately, Honda picked up the 1965 50cc title (and the 350cc one, too, as it happens), but Hugh Anderson and Suzuki won the 125cc category with ease. At the end of the season, Anderson finished on 56, with Perris on 44, and MZ rider Derek Woodman a long way adrift on 28 to claim third in the 125cc title chase.

67

SUZUKI MOTORCYCLES: THE CLASSIC TWO-STROKE ERA

Export market update

Wages kept increasing rapidly in Japan, with the national average standing at 450,000 yen a year by 1965. Unfortunately, this new-found wealth led to a fall in personal motorcycle sales, as the automobile was now king – the latest list of desirables being a car, a colour television, and air-conditioning.

With Japanese bike makers dropping like flies, it was becoming increasingly obvious that in order to survive, Suzuki would have to further nurture its presence in export markets. Surprisingly, it wasn't until 1965 that an export department was formally established at Hamamatsu, despite the large number of global distributors established in the years prior to this. In reality, this was not so much a promotional office, for Suzuki's success in racing had heightened the marque's profile to the point that there was no shortage of interested parties abroad, but more a centre to co-ordinate what had suddenly become a big part of the business – only 3251 bikes were exported in 1960, but the number was well over ten times that figure by 1963, and robust sales saw further increases, up to no less than 106,591 units in 1965.

The growth of the American market was important here (despite a huge choice of bikes available from Britain, Italy, Germany, Czechoslovakia and Spain, as well as Japanese rivals, the company was able to boast about attracting a new dealer almost every day during 1964 – some, like Suzuki City in Venice, CA and Suzuki Fun Center in Burbank, also in California, being truly massive and luxurious, offering rental services to entice potential buyers to try the bikes properly), allowing Suzuki to build on its traditional strongholds in SE Asia and the African continent, along with increased penetration across Europe.

Thanks to the success of bikes like the $350 Hill-Billy, the capital of Suzuki's US arm was increased to $300,000 in 1965, and no less than 70 American dealers were invited to Japan at the end of the year, their visit timed to coincide with the 12th Tokyo Show.

Meanwhile, for the 1965 season, the Stateside dealerships were able to offer the $245 M31 'Suzy,' which took the place of the M30 on the latest price lists, the $260 M15 'Collegian,'

American dealers visiting Japan in the autumn of 1965.

The X-6 Hustler gave Suzuki the bike it needed to make serious inroads into the American market. The 29bhp is an SAE measurement, by the way.

THE LATE SIXTIES

the $285 M12 'Cavalier,' the K10 'Sport' (also available as the K10D 'Deluxe'), the $345 K11 'Challenger,' the K15 'Hill-Billy,' the new B100 and S10 models, the US-only 150cc (46mm x 45mm) 16bhp S32 'Olympian' twin at $450, and the $589 T20 'Crusader,' which replaced the T10 at the start of the season, although it would be several months before deliveries began. By that time, the X-6 Hustler moniker had been adopted for the new twin in the States, and a new 12-month/12,000 mile warranty had been introduced – a remarkable show of faith for this era.

It was particularly ironic that even Harley-Davidson was moving towards smaller machines with a vengeance, punting the $225 M-50 alongside its more traditional wares. With tiddlers and step-through models from Honda, Suzuki and Yamaha selling in huge numbers, as well as the Fuji Rabbit (at least for a little while longer) and the more stylish Vespas and Lambrettas from Italy, I guess one cannot blame the American giant for wanting a piece of the action.

But the big news at Suzuki this season was its big bike – the X-6 Hustler, which was available in Candy Red (a different shade to the traditional Permanent Red), Candy Blue (likewise, a different hue to the norm), or Metallic Black. *Cycle World* enthused: "Handling is exceptionally good. The X-6 has a frame and suspension that show a strong family resemblance to Suzuki's road racing motorcycles ... A lot of attention has been given to making the X-6 stop as well as go. The machine is fitted with brakes of no more than moderate size, but they do the job very well indeed."

All change

In amongst the racers and an extensive range of domestic models, Suzuki displayed its S32 model and K15 trials bike at the 1965 Tokyo Show, although both were only ever destined for US shores. Interestingly, Kawasaki showed something similar to the K15 in the F1TR, confirming the off-road boom was still in place, at least in the States.

The CCI automatic lubrication system was formally introduced to the Suzuki range in February 1966, the technology (generally known as Posi-Force in export markets) having already been proved on the T20 for the best part of a year. The main merit of CCI (an abbreviation of Crankcase Cylinder Injection, sometimes teamed up with the Selmix moniker) was it took away the need for users to mix oil in with the petrol every time they filled up, for this pre-mix method was a rather hit-and-miss and messy process, even if it was devised in order to keep the engine bearings in good condition. Anyway, there was now a separate tank for oil to augment the traditional fuel one, with a pump metering the amount of oil injected into the crankcase according to the position of the throttle. It wasn't the first such system, as Yamaha had announced 'Autolube' at the 1963 Tokyo Show (and indeed Velocette had something similar decades earlier, followed by Puch some time after), but it was refreshingly reliable and a significant step forward in reducing oil consumption and emissions, as well as eliminating a lot of stress for users along the way.

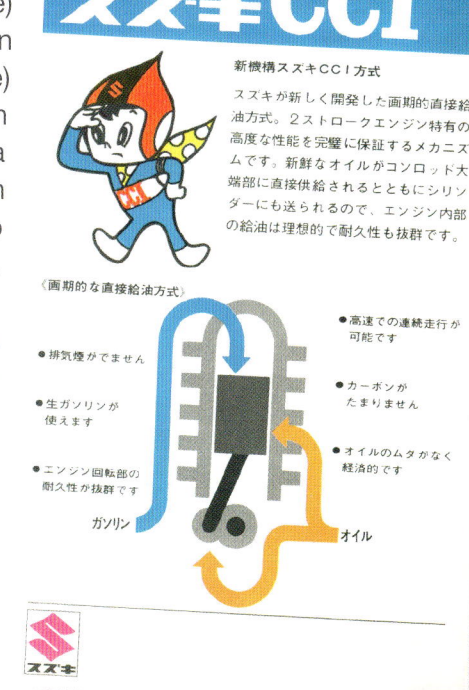

It seems odd, therefore, that CCI was not employed for the M15 or M12 models, presumably because costs needed to be kept in check and replacements were waiting in the wings.

CCI explained, in typical Japanese style. Petrol (blue) is fed into the combustion chamber, while oil (orange) is directed towards parts in need of lubrication. It was a far more efficient system than using an oil-petrol mix to do everything ...

The M15-2 of early 1966 vintage, bringing the tiddler into the modern era.

The M12-2, which probably looked less sporty than the original, but an attractive package nonetheless.

An 80K10-2 with CCI lubrication.

The B120 and T21 featured in a contemporary domestic range catalogue.

SUZUKI

The K10-2 on the cover of a Japanese brochure. Foreign models were used in quite a lot of Japanese advertising during this time, with Nissan's Ken and Mary series for the Skyline being a particularly memorable campaign.

The S10 as it appeared in the 1966 catalogue, seen here fitted with optional leg guards.

スズキ B120
総排気量 118cc 最高速度 100km/h 最高出力 8PS/7,000r.p.m 前進4段ロータリー式
125c.c.級の高性能で扱いやすさは80c.c.級

スズキスーパー 250 T21
総排気量 247cc 最高速度 160km/h 最高出力 30.5PS/8,000r.p.m 前進6段リターン式
マニアがうなった爆発的ダッシュ！

A super photo used for a 1966 brochure cover, showing the sporting T21, the latest U50 moped, and the A90 model in the background.

THE LATE SIXTIES

Notwithstanding, the Suzuki 50 M15 duly became the M15-2 (likewise the M15D became the M15D-2 after the upgrade) in February 1966, thanks to a slimmer fuel tank, modern-looking forks, a tighter front mudguard, redesigned side boxes and a fresh saddle, as well as new indicators and a slight increase in power, up from 4.2 to 4.5bhp.

As for the M12-2, treatment was similar to that of the Mark 2 M15s, with the fuel tank, front forks (which gained rubber gaiters at this time), rear springs (now plain) and side boxes receiving the most attention. There was actually a 52cc M16-2, too, but this was not actively marketed in Japan.

In addition, the 125 S10 and 125 S30-2 models were carried over exactly as before, adding to the confusion. The K10 did get the CCI system, though, as well as the latest M15-style front-end, a new fuel tank, an M15 saddle with an extra seat added beyond it, and a bigger rear light unit. Naturally, new side boxes and badges came thanks to CCI, along with a new Suzuki 80 K10-2 or K10D-2 moniker depending on whether or not a self-starter was fitted. The K11 Sport 80 was allowed to continue in updated K11-2 guise, but only until mid-1967 in Japan, when it simply faded away without ceremony.

The Suzuki B100 received CCI in the spring of 1966, after which time it was known as the B120 on the home market, although the only real change was the automatic lubrication system (which brought with it a smaller main jet in the Mikuni VM20 carburettor), and the badging that came with it on the side covers. Careful inspection, however, did reveal a subtle difference in fuel tank shape and seat design, compared to the original B100s. Available in black, red, blue or white, like the K11-2, the B120 would soon disappear from Japanese catalogues, albeit not until the end of 1967 in this particular case.

At about the same time as the B120 was launched, the 250 T20 evolved into the T21, with exposed springs on the shocks at both ends from the off. Apart from CCI badges being added (the system was already there on the T20, of course), there wasn't much else to distinguish the latest model from its predecessor. Those used to riding the old model, though, would have noticed the extra horsepower – with a raised compression ratio (upped from 7.3:1 to 7.8:1), this was now quoted at a healthy 30.5bhp at 8000rpm.

Another newcomer was announced in April 1966 – the 73,000 yen A70, with the 'A' supposedly signifying 'Ace,' a word the Hamamatsu concern seemed to like, having used it on numerous occasions. As usual during this era, nothing is straightforward when it comes to Suzuki, and the A70 was shown as the 70K30 in early catalogues, although a look in the parts book clarifies the situation, with the A70 frame and engine numbers starting on K30-10001.

With a 7.1:1 compression ratio, the 69cc (46mm x 42mm) engine developed 7.3bhp at 7500rpm, and came with CCI and rotary disc valve induction. More powerful than the equivalent single used in the U70 moped that was announced at the same time, this modern, all-alloy unit looked quite different to earlier singles, as the alloy lump was angled over to the point that it almost laid horizontal, exposing the induction system above and allowing the exhaust system to remain compact.

Styling was also fresh, exuding a feeling of quality. While the front looked similar to the M12-2, there were new indicators and a beautiful teardrop fuel tank beyond, plus a touch of chrome on the M12-style rear shocks underneath the full-length seat. The

SUZUKI MOTORCYCLES: THE CLASSIC TWO-STROKE ERA

Flyer for the 70K30 model, aka the A70.

The early version of the A90, complete with a '90' badge on the side box, and a different air cleaner to that of the A70.

A70 also had a chrome filter and crankcase cover, a new lightweight rear mudguard, separated from the frame and painted to match the front one, and large rear lights borrowed from the K10-2. With a four-speed transmission, the 78kg (172lb) machine had a top speed of 59mph (95kph), with an elegant new oval-shaped gauge pack informing the rider of how close they were – or weren't – to the bike's limit.

However, the A70 didn't last long in the Japanese line-up – only for one year in fact, but it did at least spawn the larger-engined A90, which was released at the start of 1967, and ran alongside the A70 for a little while.

The 75,000 yen A90 looked very similar to the A70, but the visible part of the induction system wasn't as attractive, and a '90' badge was added underneath a modified 'CCI' plate on the very early models (it was later deleted after the 70cc model was dropped). The 86cc (47mm x 50mm) single gave 8.4bhp at 7500rpm, but, strangely, had a cast iron cylinder barrel, whereas the A70 (and the A100 that followed) sported an alloy one. Teamed up with a four-speed rotary transmission, it allowed the A90 a fraction more speed, but it really was only a fraction. This was probably a crucial factor in the loss of the A70, as the performance of the two A-series models was far too close for comfort.

The 1966 racing season

With Ernst Degner no longer able to give his best, at least Suzuki managed to secure an able replacement in Hans-Georg Anscheidt – the man who had been Degner's team-mate at Kreidler and a fierce rival after the East German rider swapped camps and moved to Suzuki. It was a signing that was good for both parties, filling a void for the Japanese company, and giving the talented Anscheidt a decent shot at the title now that Kreidler was playing second fiddle to the might of Suzuki and Honda in the tiddler category.

Joining Anscheidt was the familiar line-up of Anderson, Perris, Itoh and Katayama, with Degner named for a couple of big races. As for the bikes, the 50cc RK66 had much the same engine as the 1965 warrior, but it now delivered 2bhp more, and

THE LATE SIXTIES

a 12-speed gearbox was the norm for the whole season. Indeed, the frame and engine numbers were still marked with a 'K5' serial number, so one can tell the changes were minimal. Likewise, the 125cc RT66 was basically an RT65 with an extra horse released.

The opening round in Spain fell to Honda's Taveri in the 50cc race (Anscheidt was second), and Yamaha's Bill Ivy in the 125cc event, with the Suzukis out of the points in that one. Next up, the circus moved to the West German GP at Hockenheim, with Anscheidt leading from start to finish, and making up for further disappointment in the 125cc category.

There was no Suzuki interest at the French GP, as there were no 50cc or 125cc races. In fact, the same was true of the Belgian GP at Spa. In the meantime, Degner made a cautious comeback at the Dutch TT, but was suffering with a 50cc engine that was distinctly off song. Honda won again, but at least Anderson was in touch with Taveri, while the 125cc race was a shoot-out between Honda and Yamaha.

There were no 50cc races at either the East German GP, Czechoslovakian GP, Finnish GP, or the Ulster GP. In Germany, Katayama was second with Perris fifth in the 125cc race, but fourth and fifth was the best Suzuki could do in the other Iron Curtain meeting, and it was the same story in Finland, falling to fifth and sixth in Ireland.

The Isle of Man TT had been delayed in 1966 due to a seaman's dispute, but at least it got under way eventually. It was Yamaha's year, though, in the 125cc class (claiming first, second and fourth), with Anderson third and Perris fifth. Honda was first and second in the 50cc race, adding to Suzuki's misery, with Anderson third and Degner a distant fourth in his last run for the Japanese manufacturer. Indeed, the German rider retired after this race, bringing a sparkling career to a rather sad end.

The Italian Grand Prix (or Nations GP) at Monza saw Suzuki enter only the 50cc race, but at least Anscheidt came back from a bad start in the searing heat to claim the silverware and tie the championship going into the finale in Japan.

For Suzuki fans, the Japanese GP at Fuji Speedway at least made up for what had been something of a disappointing season. Katayama won the 50cc race, followed home by Anscheidt, Anderson and Itoh, sealing things beyond doubt. Yamaha won the 125cc event, but Katayama was second with the RT66, showing his mastery of the course.

Ultimately, though, it was Honda that took the 125cc crown in 1966 after a tight battle with Yamaha. Sadly, the top Suzuki rider was fifth in this class (Anderson), with Katayama and Perris filling the next two slots, while Itoh was joint-ninth with just four points to his name at the end of the season. Thankfully, Hans-Georg Anscheidt won the 50cc title, finishing two points ahead of his Honda rivals, Ralph Bryans and Luigi Taveri, while Anderson was fourth, Katayama fifth, and Degner and Itoh joint-sixth.

While the 125cc class was disappointing for the works team, at least the 50cc title was secured, and Suzuki was also flying high in smaller events, as this UK advert from the summer of 1966 shows – Chris Vincent and Tommy Robb took the T20 to an excellent second in class in the 500-mile Grand Prix D'Endurance race at Brands Hatch, beaten only by a lap by a pair using something close to a pure racer. The T20 would be modified by a number of people over the coming years, with a good deal of success in non-world championship races.

SIX-SPEED LAUNCH WAS A-OK

Suzuki style success rewarded co-riders Chris Vincent and Tommy Robb who piloted the Suzuki Super Six 250 in its maiden flight at Brands.
179 gruelling laps during the 500 mile Grand Prix D'Endurance proved beyond doubt that the stamina characteristic of all Suzuki machines is there in plenty in the brand-new Super-Six. The price of power? Just £276-17-1d. Fly the Super-Six 250 at your dealers today!

SUZUKI Super SIX 250

SUZUKI MOTORCYCLES: THE CLASSIC TWO-STROKE ERA

As if making a deliberate attempt to try and annoy historians (or simply send them crazy) and add yet more confusion to things like the 70K30 actually being the A70, not long after the introduction of the A90 in the early part of 1967, Suzuki decided to rename a whole host of models after CCI and other revisions appeared on the spec sheets of bikes previously sold without the automatic lubrication system.

The M15-2 pairing became the K50 and K50D, with the familiar 4.5bhp engine, four-speed transmission and styling that at first glance looked exactly the same. Apart from the CCI-related parts and badges, one can also see that a larger rear light unit was fitted, along with bigger indicators at both ends, and a new gauge pack. The 59,000 yen machine (or 66,000 yen in K50D guise, with a self-starter) duly won a Good Design Award, which is highly-coveted in Japan.

Likewise, the M12-2 was transformed in a similar fashion to become the 62,000 yen KS50, while the K10 was given a new engine to give birth to the K90. As it happens, the styling was similar, though, with the seat extension taken away, larger indicators, K50-style forks and an A-series type fuel tank being the main changes, and the engine was the same as the one used in the A90, so the evolution made a lot of sense, with cleaner emissions and improved performance from the rotary valve powerplant. The sporty K90 also gained a MITI Good Design Award, offering excellent value at just 72,000 yen, with easy handling and low running costs.

Incidentally, for those that wanted one, while no longer in the mainstream catalogue, the K11 was still available to order, but was ultimately dropped at about the same time as the A70; the B120 lasted a little while longer. Meanwhile, having only just been released, the A90 was naturally carried over, being joined by the 9.3bhp A100 at this time – a 98cc model that was built mainly for export markets. Available at 83,000 yen, it looked just like the A90, as neither came with an engine size badge after the A70 fell by the wayside. However, those in the know would be able to tell which was which, as the A90 had a black finish on the cylinder barrel, while the A100 had a natural silver look due to the component being made in alloys rather than cast iron.

Continuing the changes, the S10 was transformed into the 135,000 yen K125, with a front fork design similar to the other K-series models (only the KS had rubber gaiters), new gauges,

Cover and inner pages of the Suzuki range catalogue from early 1967.

The new K50 grade captured in a delightful period shot.

The K90 model, which took the place of the 80K10 in the line-up.

Promotional paperwork for the KS50 – a bike and designation that would soon fall by the wayside.

The A100 model, which was short-lived in Japan, but successful abroad.

larger light units, and a new fuel tank and saddle. Although now boasting CCI lubrication, the 123cc single was still rated at 10.5bhp, however. At the same time, the T21 became the 187,000 yen T250, distinguished by having bigger indicators at both ends of the bike, although the trademark headlight shape remained pretty much intact across the entire Suzuki two-wheeled range.

By the middle of the year, the S30-2 had evolved into the T125, sporting a new lightweight frame based on that of the original X-6 line. The all-alloy 15bhp engine was also new, and while still a 124cc twin, the bore and stroke relationship was changed to 43mm x 43mm, much like the racing machines. With a five-speed transmission and modern tyres, the 145,000 yen T125 was capable of 81mph (130kph).

It was joined by the T200, TC200 and TC250 at the same time. Exhibited as a prototype at the 1966 Tokyo Show, the T200 was basically the same as the T125, but powered by a 196cc all-alloy parallel-twin (50mm x 50mm) coming with

75

SUZUKI MOTORCYCLES: THE CLASSIC TWO-STROKE ERA

The T125 in black. The one illustrated in the catalogue is finished in red.

The TC200 of 1967.

a pair of VM22SH carburettors and enhanced lubrication. Capable of delivering 21bhp at 7500rpm and coupled to a five-speed transmission, the 165,000 yen T200 was a fraction faster than its 125cc stablemate, but it was a marginal gain. The TC200 was a Sport variant, with an upswept exhaust system, while the TC250 followed the same pattern, being a Sport version of the T250.

The Sport variants were only a couple of thousand yen different to the versions with regular exhaust systems. Interestingly, while the T250 had exposed springs all-round, the front forks had gaiters on the T125, T200, TC200 and TC250, and all-chrome rear shocks for the T200, TC200 and TC250 (the T125 had partial-chrome rears.) All five T-series bikes had subtly different fuel tanks, although the Ts were kept similar, with the TCs having less chrome on them. Like the 200cc pairing, the TC250 was a short-lived model, though, lasting only until the tail-end of summer 1968 in Japan …

Before moving on, we should also mention that the 500bhp *Cyclone-Go* – the mount of Kamen Rider in the contemporary smash TV hit, was based on the 250cc Suzuki, adding to the popularity and myth surrounding the model after the television series was first aired in Japan in 1971. Indeed, Suzuki provided most of the bikes in the series during the Showa Era.

Foreign affairs

With so many changes taking place at home, and at very strange intervals as well, it must have been difficult for the various importers abroad to keep track at times. The confusion caused by using model year (MY) terminology within the car and motorcycle world in most European and North American countries is bad enough, as we could be talking about three or four months ahead of the actual calendar year (CY), and the lack of uniform release dates for upgrades and full model change (FMC, as opposed to MC, for minor change) is a real headache for anyone trying to follow the story on a chronological basis. Add in local names, nicknames and the use of partial designations, and to say that chaos reigns is something of an understatement.

Anyway, for 1966, the US dealers had the X-6 Hustler, which duly took on the look of the domestic T21 after it was launched, even though it retained the T20 code in America (and the UK, for that matter). This just about sums up the points made in the previous paragraph! Likewise, the B120 was sold in the States as the B100P 'Magnum' (with the 'P' suffix standing for pump, although the full name was the Suzuki 120 B100P. The B100P moniker was also applied in Britain, incidentally (where folks

The TC250, which looked very similar to the TC200, but careful inspection will reveal the different frame underneath the fuel tank, and a beefier exhaust pipe design.

76

The K15P 'Hill-Billy' for the US market.

The 'Bearcat' was a huge hit in America, perfectly in tune with the times.

Three pieces of rather glamorous American advertising from 1966.

The first X-5 advert appeared in April 1967. One magazine noted: "We rather believe that Suzuki have another winner in their line-up."

A selection of American advertising from 1967.

British advertising for the 250 and 125 models dating from early 1966. The advert also describes the Posi-Force (CCI) automatic lubrication system.

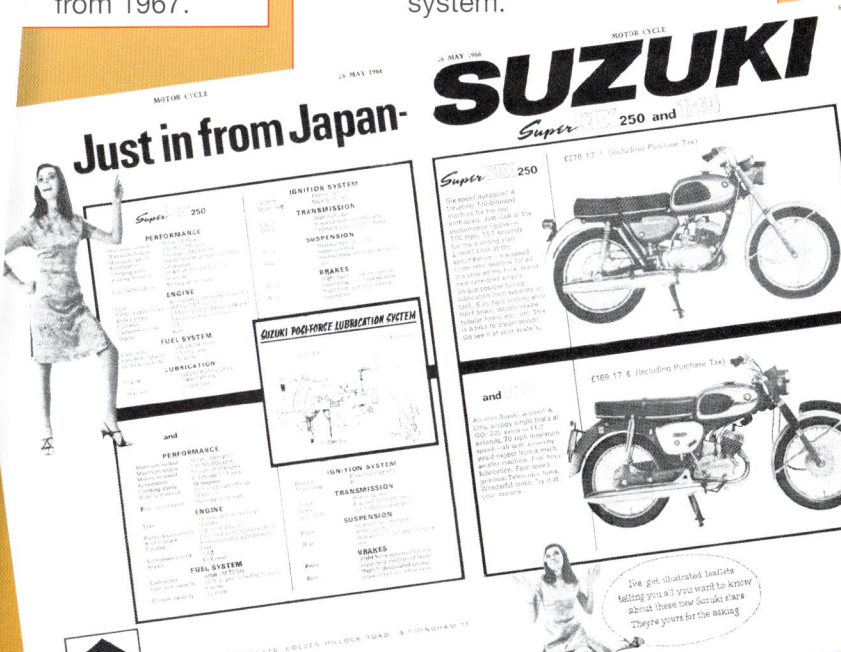

delighted in calling the model 'the bloop'), as well as the other export markets.

Cycle World had nothing but praise for the 11bhp 'Magnum': "Suzuki engineers seem to have arrived at a design balance that we are certain was conceived, to a large extent, on the race track. Braking and cornering are superior to most. We found little to fault the bike at all, as a matter of fact."

Other models included the S32, the K10, the M15, and the sporty M12, K11 and K15, each of which were modified as the production lines at Suzuki swapped over to the latest incarnations of the breed. As a result, a Mark 2 suffix was added to the M15 and M12 moniker (the S32 became the S32-2), while the K10 became known as the K10P 'Corsair', the K11 the K11P 'Challenger', and the K15 as the K15P in the process, or the Suzuki Trail 80 K15P 'Hill-Billy' to give the latter its full title.

From July 1966, there was also the US-only B105P 'Bearcat', which was the larger-engined equivalent of the 'Hill-Billy', with knobby tyres and a dual-range rear sprocket for a perfect on- and off-road performance compromise, plus the A100 with a larger 98cc (50mm x 50mm) version of the single used in Japan. Quoted as having 9.3bhp, this model was eventually called the 'Charger' to distinguish it from other A-series machines sold in the States.

Looking through American magazines from the time, it was interesting to note how there was – generally speaking – less advertising from Japan's 'Big Four' (Kawasaki was just starting to make an impact Stateside, so naturally made a bigger splash than before) and still a fair bit from the likes of Bridgestone, Hodaka and Marusho (aka Lilac); Bridgestone actually took six pages in the May 1966 edition of *Cycle World*, mainly in colour, which must be considered a last ditch stand in retrospect. Already, quite a lot of the familiar names from the early sixties had disappeared, and soon (with Bridgestone the last to finally admit defeat in 1971 after a long time spent on the ropes) only Honda, Yamaha, Suzuki and Kawasaki would be left to compete against Harley and the European imports, themselves dwindling in number as each year passed.

Meanwhile, during the 1967 season, the US dealerships stocked the M31 moped, along with the K10P, K11P and K15P. These K-series machines were replaced by the A100, B100P/B120 and TC120, along with the B105P as soon as stocks ran dry, while the T125 superseded the S32 line. Following its introduction at home, the T200 was marketed as the X-5 Invader, with the TC200 becoming known as the 'Stingray' in the USA – the X-5 duly made the cover of several magazines,

giving the model a flying start in the States. The X-6 Hustler was also sold in various guises, including a scrambler model introduced in the latter part of 1966.

The UK left the B100 out of its line-up until May 1966, when it started selling the £170 B100P – the updated model with CCI lubrication (or Posi-Force as it was called abroad). Although dropped in Japan quite soon, the B100P was sold for many years in the UK, picking up the B120 and 'Student' monikers along the way.

As in America, Britain adopted the K10P and K11P nomenclatures after the models received their respective upgrades, but the bikes being pushed during this period were the new '125' (aka the B100P) and the big '250' (or T20), the latter selling for £277 when it was introduced to the UK market in May 1966.

Motorcycle Mechanics tried the two newcomers side-by-side in its August 1966 issue, noting on the 250: "Unlike some five-speed bikes, the top gear was not a sluggish overdrive, and the bike would accelerate when sixth was notched just as easily as when you used any of the other gears.

"Handling was a bit of a shock – being used to the rather loose, easy feel of British machinery, the Suzuki shook me with its hairline handling. Not once on Brands Hatch's bumpy corners did the Suzy shake its head, and the rear went around without a wiggle."

As for the 125: "For everyday riding, the 125 is comfortable in the extreme, and silent and smooth into the bargain. Both bikes have virtually no vibration periods at all. Comparing prices with other bikes on the market, I think the 250 is the best

Publicity photo of the long-running B100P model.

THE LATE SIXTIES

British advertising promoting the benefits of Suzuki ownership.

value, the 125 being a trifle expensive, but worth it."

Motor Cycle was equally gracious in its comments about the T20: "The new Suzuki Super Six is one of the brightest stars to come flying over from Japan. With its 94mph/150kph best one-way speed, it is the fastest 250 roadster ever tested by [this magazine]. In appearance and in specification, the Suzuki is a winner [and] proved itself to be no less impressive on the road."

And *Motorcycle Sport*, who didn't hide the fact that they would have liked the bike to have been made in Britain, called it "the best-handling roadster of our experience." Perhaps more than any other bike, the T20 opened up the UK and European markets for Suzuki once and for all.

Generally speaking, exports continued to rise for a while, with foreign sales amounting to 187,717 units in 1966, but dropped off to half that figure in 1967 before recovering a little again as the sixties gave way to a new decade. However, even at this lowest point at the tail-end of the 1960s, it was still a significantly higher number than that posted in 1964, despite the Vietnam War slowing things down Stateside.

Suzuki was not only expanding its sales operations abroad, it was also slowly but surely building up a small empire of satellite factories, too – even in the sixties, labour and raw material was far cheaper in mainland Asia than the islands of Japan, and there was always the prospect that certain products could be shipped directly to large,

Exports were a crucial element of Suzuki's long-term success. This is a dealer in India from the time, with a line of T21-type 250s in the shop.

There's something very special about sixties adverts, and this is a typical piece from late 1967, announcing the arrival of the T200 on UK shores.

Dealer training in Thailand during the same period.

proven markets in the future. This latter train of thought saved on shipping costs as well, allowing the Hamamatsu concern to be even more competitive in a part of the world that was very price-sensitive – put simply, the cheaper the product, the more chance there was of it

79

selling. This statement isn't being unkind – it's just a reflection of the vast difference in wages being earned on opposite sides of the Japan Sea, a gap that has hardly closed in some Asian countries to this day.

Taiwan we've already mentioned in the previous chapter, with stronger links quickly being established, while March 1967 saw a CKD operation starting in Thailand, with a subsidiary formed to look after the assembly site. A couple of years later, a new plant was erected to produce A50, A70 and A100 machines, and this factory would play an important role in Suzuki's growth in the future. During the seventies, Suzuki would duly tie-in with firms in Indonesia, Pakistan, Malaysia, the Philippines and Ecuador to become a truly global concern.

The 1967 racing season

With Anderson, Perris and Degner all hanging up their racing leathers at the end of the 1966 season, Hans-Georg Anscheidt and Yoshimi Katayama carried the hopes of the Suzuki works team, with Stuart Graham (who'd raced Honda, Matchless and AJS bikes during 1966) taken on as a newcomer. Apart from Tommy Robb's run in the Manx classic, only the Japanese Grand Prix had more riders assigned to factory machines, namely Mitsuo Itoh and Hiroyuki Kawasaki, plus another local lad, who promptly fell off his 50cc mount – the less said about that, the better …

Suzuki employed the 14-speed RK67 in the 50cc class, with 17.5bhp now on tap thanks to a slight increase in the compression ratio (the leading engine specs were otherwise similar to the 50cc RK65 and RK66). A new batch of frames and engines were built, which must have been incredibly annoying for the FIM announced a number of rule changes in 1967, with 50cc bikes being limited to single-cylinder engines and six-speed transmissions for the 1969 Grand Prix season. Whilst aimed at reducing costs, thus encouraging entries from privateers, this move naturally consigned several prototypes to the scrapyard, and spawned the wrath of some big names in the sport. Indeed, Honda withdrew its works team from racing at end of the 1967 season in response, going out on a high with the 250cc and 350cc titles in the bag, and a close thing in the 500cc category. Others would follow Honda's lead, for in 1968, the FIM went further in stating that 125cc and 250cc bikes should be limited to two cylinders from 1970 onwards. As we shall see, this went against the grain at Suzuki and Yamaha, too, both of whom were moving towards V4s.

Meanwhile, the RT67 was again a gentle evolution of the previous season's 125cc twin, with power up to 35bhp by this time, and a new ten-speed transmission to help the rider make the most of the horses available. The other 125cc contender was the water-cooled V4 RS67. Making its debut at the Japanese GP, this two-stroke machine had a 124.7cc capacity (35.5mm x 31.5mm), and with an 8.4:1 compression ratio and a carburettor for each pot, it developed an incredible 42bhp at 16,500rpm. Weighing in at just 95kg (209lb), the 12-speed RS was capable of 137mph (219kph), but unfortunately it came too late for Suzuki to benefit from its potential.

The Spanish GP witnessed an easy win for Anscheidt in the 50cc class, with both the German and Katayama lapping the entire field. It almost justified the FIM's decision seeing such a dominant performance, galling as it was for enthusiasts who'd seen a new era of tiddler racing brought in thanks to the Japanese makers. Katayama was third in the 125cc race, trailing a pair of Yamahas.

With Honda leaving the 50cc class, Suzuki should have had an easy run in the West German GP at Hockenheim, but while Anscheidt took the flag, both Katayama and Graham failed to finish. At least Katayama was able to win the 125cc race after both Yamahas were involved in an accident, with Anscheidt second. Katayama was in winning mood again in the next round, claiming victory in the 50cc race in the French Grand Prix.

All eyes then turned to the Isle of Man TT, where Stuart Graham won the 50cc race at an average speed of 82.9mph (132.6kph). He was followed home by Anscheidt and Tommy Robb to make it a Suzuki one-two-three, with a gaggle of Hondas behind. Narrowly beaten by Phil Read (Yamaha), Graham was second in the 125cc race as well, so it was a good meeting for him.

In wet conditions, Katayama came

Yoshimi Katayama leading the pack on his RS67 in the 1967 Czechoslovakian Grand Prix. (Courtesy Yaesu Publishing)

SUZUKI MOTORCYCLES: THE CLASSIC TWO-STROKE ERA

through to win the 50cc race in the Dutch TT, with two Derbis coming next. The two-stroke Yamaha fours proved too fast in the 125cc category, but at least Graham got onto the podium with a third place. There was no 125cc race in the Belgian GP, but Anscheidt won the 50cc event ahead of his two team-mates for another Suzuki one-two-three.

The East German GP, Czechoslovakian GP, Finnish GP, Ulster GP, Nations GP, and the new Canadian GP at Mosport, all shied away from 50cc races. Bill Ivy proved too strong in the 125cc races, with his Yamaha claiming all but the Finnish GP in this batch of events; Graham was able to shine at the Imatra Circuit.

And so to the final round – the Japanese Grand Prix. Itoh was winning the 125cc race at his home event with four laps gone, when suddenly the red flags went out and a fresh start was called for by officials. Suzuki promptly walked away from the grid in protest, but Itoh and Graham were eventually persuaded to rejoin on their RS models. The restart saw Bill Ivy (Yamaha) run away with it, with the Suzukis about a second a lap down (Stuart Graham was second in the end), and the new Kawasakis another second a lap adrift. At least Mitsuo Itoh was able to claim the silverware in the 50cc race at Fuji Speedway (Anscheidt had engine trouble), with Stuart Graham second and Hiroyuki Kawasaki third.

Anyway, at the end of the season, with all the maths done, Hans-Georg Anscheidt was declared winner of the 50cc world championship, followed home by Katayama and Graham. Derbi riders filled the next two spots, with Itoh sixth. The RS67 had, sadly, come too late to prevent Yamaha winning the 125cc title, with Bill Ivy a worthy champion, and team-mate Phil Read second. Graham was able to claim third place for Suzuki, with Katayama a distant fourth, but still a fair way ahead of the MZ competition.

Another reshuffle

With Suzuki's capital now standing at 7,500,000,000 yen, the company chose the 1967 Tokyo Show to unveil something very special – the T500, which had gone on sale in the States a couple of months earlier, in August. Like the T20, this bike was largely the work of Masanao Shimizu, and made excellent use of his experience gained in the field of competition (Shimizu was one of the first members of the factory racing team, doing a lot of the design work on the early racers).

In most respects, the T500 looked very similar to the T250,

The LC10-type Fronte was launched in April 1967. A new factory at Iwata was built for the pretty little 356cc *Kei* model, while Stirling Moss was called in to partner bike racer Mitsuo Itoh on a European publicity run for the higher-powered SS in the summer of 1968.

The magnificent T500, making its presence felt in typical sixties manner.

although the bigger two-stroke engine naturally filled out the area below the fuel tank and aft of the downtubes to a far greater extent. There were plenty of other detail differences, too, such as the latest A-series front forks and indicators, and a pair of instruments in separate round meters (one housed the speedometer; the other a tachometer) above a headlight that was closer than usual to round. The fuel tank and saddle were slightly different, as were the mudguards at both ends, and the rear luggage rack and light unit: the rear shocks also followed the T125 pattern rather than having the exposed springs found on the T250.

After paying special attention to getting the air-cooling right (justifiable concerns over cooling meant that very few

82

THE LATE SIXTIES

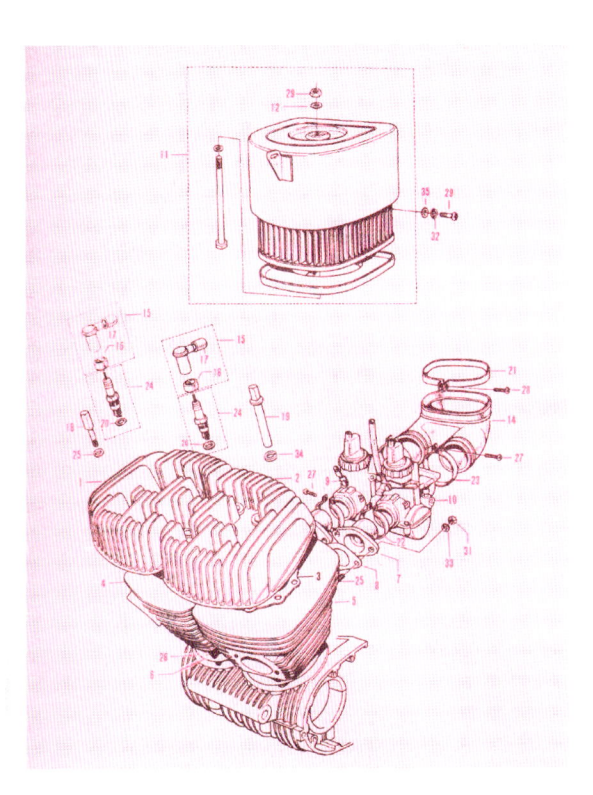

manufacturers had attempted such a large two-stroke unit since Zundapp in the early 1950s), the all-alloy twin had a 492cc displacement (70mm x 64mm), and with traditional piston-port induction, a pair of Mikuni VM34SC carbs and a 6.6:1 compression, it delivered 47bhp at 6500rpm, along with 40lb/ft of torque 500rpm lower down the rev-range. With this kind of power and a weight of only 176kg (387lb), the five-speed machine (with a left-foot change) was capable of dismissing the standing-quarter in 13.2 seconds before going on to a top speed of 113mph (181kph).

Priced at 268,000 yen, the T500 went on sale in Japan in March 1968, securing Suzuki's position at the top of the two-stroke league with its effortless performance, put down to the road via 4.00-18 rubber (a 3.25-19 tyre was chosen for the front-end) and kept in check via large cable-operated drum brakes (right foot-actuation was retained for the rear brake, incidentally). Despite the hefty sticker price, thankfully for the Hamamatsu concern, there was no shortage of takers.

Followers of Suzuki lore would have come to realise by now that numbering systems were wild and often meaningless in the early years. With the 1968 line-up, at least the new designations started to bring sense into the equation. Basically, the U-series models were mopeds, full-stop, then there were the traditional-looking Ks, the modern and sporting As, and the flagship T-series bikes; extra letters and numbers gave a fairly clear indication of the styling and engine type, with the T-series having helped establish the latest format. Naturally, there were oddities, but, at last, things became far easier to follow …

The U50 and U70 continued as the moped lines, and while the A100 went in the reshuffle, the K50 and K50D continued unchanged, as did the K90, K125, T125, T250 and TC250. The TC250s days were numbered, though, with production officially coming to an end in the autumn of 1968. Even so, it did appear in a few catalogues after that date, outlasting the

The early T500 engine as illustrated in the parts book.

The T500-I was a giant leap of faith for Suzuki, but it was a well-judged introduction, as the maker was now well known across the globe and no longer had to peddle tiddlers to survive. The company had matured, and here was a bike to make that statement in no uncertain terms. Suzuki had arrived, and was here to stay …

Japanese advertising from the summer of 1968.

SUZUKI MOTORCYCLES: THE CLASSIC TWO-STROKE ERA

T200 and TC200 pair in that respect, which proved to be very short-lived indeed from a Japanese point of view.

Moving onto the renumbered grades, the KS50 duly became the AS50, still priced at 62,000 yen, but with a separate rear mudguard (which justified the change in camps), a new fuel tank and saddle, a semi-exposed chain giving the bike a more purposeful look, and a revised gauge pack, indicators and back light. The most significant modification, though, was the adoption of rotary-disc induction on the A-series 50s (the cast iron barrel still sporting a 41mm x 38mm bore and stroke measurement), allowing power to increase by over 30 per cent. Maximum output was now quoted at 6bhp at 9000rpm. Incidentally, there was an official road racing kit listed for the 50cc model, enabling owners to convert their machine into a track bike.

Meanwhile, the A90 became the 75,000 yen AS90 in mid-February, which

Another Japanese advert, this one from the tail-end of spring 1968, and showing the latest AS and AC grades, as well as the T500.

The AS50-I, which took the place of the KS50 in 1968.

Promotional paperwork for the AC50-I, and the same model viewed from a different angle.

The AS90 of 1968 vintage. The chassis plate states 'A90-2,' by the way, perhaps helping to explain why a low-mount exhaust was retained on this grade?

THE LATE SIXTIES

for some reason retained the normal exhaust system rather than the high-mounted one of the 50cc bike, despite having an AS designation. Well, as we said, there were oddities! But otherwise the general upgrade checklist was followed. There was also an AS90G – a deluxe version boasting Candy Red paintwork (the normal grade came finished in the regular Suzuki red or blue shades), chrome-plated components (such as the mudguards, chain cover, et cetera), a different seat with a racing-type tail, and a sidestand, all for only 4000 yen more; this upgraded version was released in May.

As for the newcomers, these were the 63,000 yen AC50, 75,000 yen AC90 (launched alongside the AS90) and 79,000 yen AC90G, which came along a couple of months later (but a touch sooner than the AS90G). These all had a high-mount sports exhaust, and a revised saddle, fuel tank and handlebars compared to the AS grades. These were aimed at off-road types, having greater ground clearance than the AS models, as well as different tyres, with a scrambler conversion kit available for the 6bhp 50cc model. Both the AS and AC lines were given a Good Design Award in the summer of 1968.

The 1968 racing season

The factory team had planned to compete with the V3 RP68 in the 50cc class, and the V4 RS68 in the 125cc category, and indeed, signed up Anscheidt and Graham as part of the rider line-up as soon as the Japanese Grand Prix meeting ended. However, on February 21, 1968, two months to the day before the world championship season was due to begin, Suzuki joined Honda and pulled the plug on its racing programme.

The FIM ruling that sparked off this show of defiance sadly brought an end to the development of the 48.9cc V3 racing engine, for with 19.8bhp on tap and a 14-speed gearbox, it must surely have been an able competitor had it seen the light of day. As it happens, Hans-Georg Anscheidt asked Suzuki for a bike and factory mechanics for his own use, and competed with last year's RK67 – the last year in which the twin-cylinder model was eligible.

Anscheidt duly won the West German GP, Spanish GP and Belgian GP on the semi-works RK67-II, and with only five rounds counting towards the world championship in the 50cc class, this meant Hans-Georg Anscheidt won the title for the third time in a row, despite being the only Suzuki rider. He also had a few 125cc rides that year, but the best he could do was a second at the Nürburgring and a third in the Italian round at Monza. Yamaha won the 125cc title again, with remarkable ease, but Yamaha threw in the towel as well at the end of the 1968 season.

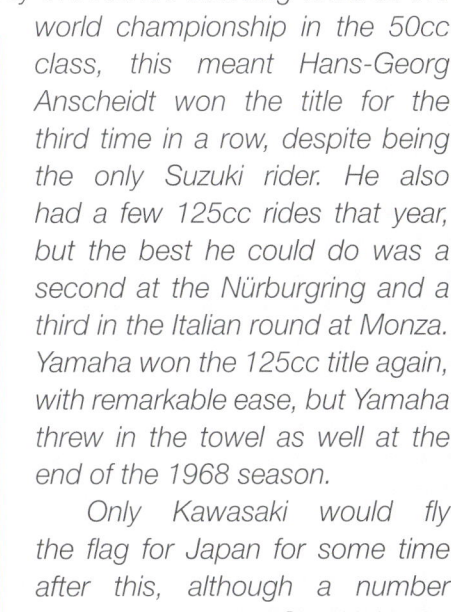

Only Kawasaki would fly the flag for Japan for some time after this, although a number of privateers kept Suzuki in the limelight, with Dieter Braun and

The AC90 in its original guise.

SUZUKI MOTORCYCLES: THE CLASSIC TWO-STROKE ERA

Cees van Dongen second and third in the 125cc world championship in 1969, and Braun ultimately going on to win the title in 1970 with an ex-Anscheidt machine. 1971 marked the arrival of Barry Sheene, with a second place in the championship using Graham's old RT bike. Thankfully, a return to factory interest was not far away …

Naturally, the biggest news from abroad at this time was the launch of the T500 (priced at $1039, it was given the 'Five' moniker originally, before gaining the more familiar 'Titan' nameplate) in readiness for the US 1968 season.

Featuring the model on its front cover, *Cycle World* noted: "Viewed as a package, a concept, a milestone, the Suzuki 500 Five qualifies as one of the most exciting and best-engineered bikes on today's market. It has exploded an absurd myth and may, itself, be destined to become a legend, or, at the very least, a bench mark at the beginning of a brand new game."

No less important, at least in terms of sales volume, was the KT120 'Trail' taking the place of the 'Bearcat' in the Stateside line-up. This came with a novel new Posi-Select feature, allowing the rider to change from the low- to high-range sprocket, and vice versa,

American advertising for the T500, or Suzuki Five.

Advertising for the US-spec T305 'Raider' of 1968 vintage.

Advert for the X-5 'Invader' from the May 1968 US edition of *Playboy*.

A selection of English language brochures produced in readiness for the 1968 season.

THE LATE SIXTIES

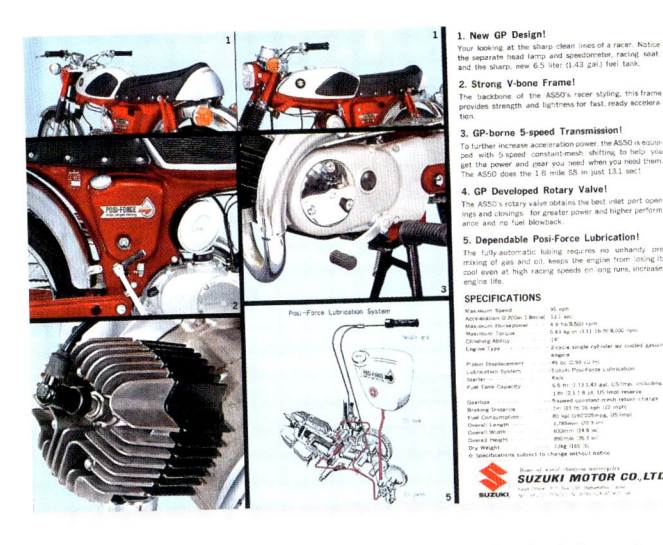

The AS50 brochure aimed at British and other English-speaking enthusiasts.

simply by pulling on a lever on the left-hand side of the engine casing – a far more satisfactory arrangement for the average user, who is generally not as mechanically inclined as a diehard off-roader or scrambler racer.

America also took on the AS50 and AC90 for the 1968 season, as well as two new 37bhp twin-cylinder models for export only – the $701 T305 'Raider', and the $722 TC305 'Laredo'. These were based on the 250s, with the engine bored out to give a 305cc displacement, and became available in the new year, taking pride of place on the Suzuki stand at the New York International Bike Show in April.

"Suzuki engineers have worked skilfully at producing the Raider," wrote *Cycle World*. "It's a bike with more charm and versatility than the Hustler, and proves equally acceptable as a ride-to-work machine or as a long distance tourer. The factory is fairly late in entering the 300-350cc displacement range, but the final product is going to win many friends."

Another interesting move was the launch of the $975 TM250, which was a pure scrambler sold for motocross enthusiasts. Suzuki was one of the first to see the opening in this niche market, with the off-road race scene suddenly taking off in all corners of the globe. More specialist bikes like this 32bhp machine (with a long-stroke 66mm x 72mm configuration) would follow as the years passed.

Interestingly, while US imports of British and Italian bikes had halved in 1968 compared to the previous year (and sales from other minor players had also dropped, too), Japanese imports had held steady, actually increasing slightly. Despite attractive publicity from the likes of Triumph and BSA, things would just never be the same again for the UK manufacturers.

Whilst on the subject of Britain, the UK had replaced the B100P with the B120 in 1967 (only the name changed in reality), and introduced the AS50 and A100 to run alongside it, although the sportier AS100 and AC100 models were not made available to British buyers until 1970. Numerous A-series models came and went, although the tiddlers remained popular in Europe throughout the sixties and seventies.

The sixties off-road scene

Scrambling had been popular in Europe for decades, and had caught on in the States, too, creating something of a trials bike boom in America. In reality, though, the sport was still a minor pastime until the sixties. By the second half of the decade, mud-plugging had gained international coverage in major publications, leaving manufacturers no choice but to treat it as another arm in which they had to compete to stay abreast of rivals in the hope of selling more machines – machines that became increasingly specialised as the 1960s progressed.

Suzuki had been involved in off-road racing since the sport's earliest days in the Land of the Rising Sun. Kazuo Kubo and Yamaha exponent Seiichi Suzuki (old friends, both involved in the bike trade through family connections) were quickly spotted by the Hamamatsu maker, just as the sport was evolving in Japan. Eventually, they brought other members they'd grown up with in their local Jyohoku Riders club into the team, giving Suzuki a strong line-up from the off. No less than 30 bikes of 50cc, 125cc and 250cc capacity were supplied by the factory, but they were almost standard production machines at this time, giving the lads little chance of winning.

Japanese advertising from the spring of 1961. The scrambling boom was already starting to take hold ...

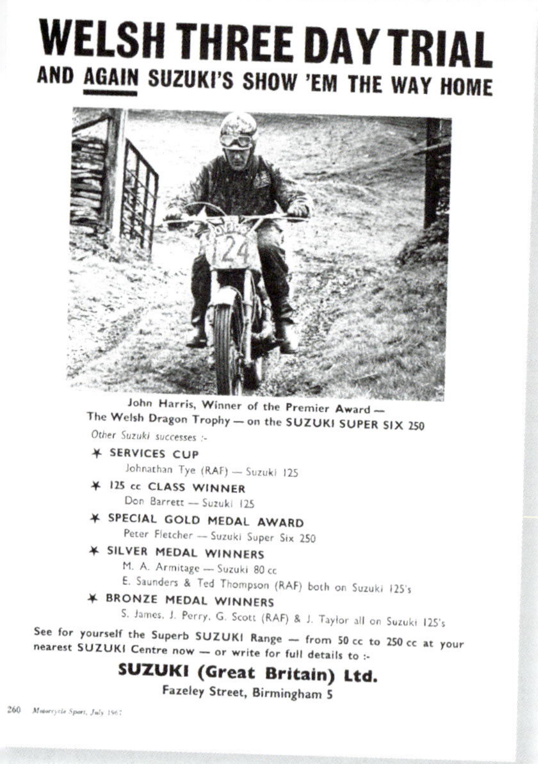

SUZUKI MOTORCYCLES: THE CLASSIC TWO-STROKE ERA

A UK advert from 1967 detailing the T20's success in off-road competition. More specialised bikes were also being prepared in Britain at this time, using the B100 as a base model.

Adverts for Pentalube Oil – one from 1969, and the other from the following year. The image change says it all regarding the scrambling boom in Japan.

Notwithstanding, perseverance and a good deal of learning on the job allowed Suzuki's new two-port single to run away with the 1964 All-Japan Motocross race, claiming first, second and third in the 125cc category. This was one of the two big scrambling events in Japan, with the popularity of the sport reaching new heights, spawning all manner of heroes that would later become household names, such as Nissan's Kazuyoshi Hoshino and Moto Kitano, for instance.

A string of early domestic victories led to Suzuki considering sending Kazuo Kubo to Europe to compete in the 250cc category of the World Motocross Championship in 1965 (a class introduced by the FIM to augment the existing 500cc one in 1962), with a full works programme cited for 1966. Kubo was duly joined by Matsuhisa Kojima to campaign the RH66 and RH67, but, after an unsuccessful sortie, the team came to the inevitable conclusion that more development was needed.

With input from the highly-experienced Olle Pettersson (a new signing for 1968), the RH68 was far more successful, being lighter, with the single-cylinder (70mm x 64mm) piston-port unit delivering at least 30bhp, and a single exhaust instead of dual pipes. Pettersson did well with it in 1968 until he was injured whilst racing, but at least the bike was improved thanks to his input (not to mention the rapid responses of R&D head Takeharu Okano), in much the same way as Degner had enhanced the road racing machines. Despite having to finish the season without Pettersson, Suzuki was a reasonable third at the end of the year, giving a glimmer of hope for the motocross campaign, which now took the place of the cancelled Grand Prix road race one.

The RH68 was actually made available for sale, helping

Olle Pettersson flying high with the RH69. From now on, a full-blooded effort would be made to try and capture the world motocross title.

Yokohama was cashing in on the boom, too, offering all manner of off-road and dual-purpose knobby tyres. Yokohama was also advertising in US and European magazines at the time, while Dunlop, Pirelli, Continental and Avon were pushing their own block-pattern rubber.

budding enthusiasts on the domestic front. Taichi Yoshimura was an excellent example of Suzuki's homebred champs, winning the 125cc Japanese championship in 1967, and both the 125cc and 250cc crowns in 1970; Kinjiro Yajima was another (125cc champion in 1969 and 1971). In April 1969, Suzuki notched up 125cc and 250cc class wins in the motocross Japan GP race, adding to the bulging trophy cabinet.

On the world championship front, Pettersson signed with Suzuki again for 1969, using the RH69, which was 11kg (24lb) lighter and equipped with a new short-stroke (70mm x 64mm, as opposed to 66mm x 73mm) engine. Pettersson finished third at the end of the year, with Suzuki second in the maker's title chase. Interestingly, the pair of CZ riders that had finished ahead of the Swede were signed by Suzuki for 1970, giving a good idea of just how important the scrambling scene had become to the Japanese manufacturer by this time ...

Two very different images of the Suzuki brand in Japan, with the new for '69 Super Mini at one end of the scale, and a rorty road burner at the other.

The highlight of the 1968 Tokyo Show was almost certainly Honda's legendary four-cylinder CB750, although Suzuki displayed its new 315cc T350, which was put on sale immediately in the States as the $792 'Rebel' and was eventually offered in Japan during April 1969. It pointed the way towards a fresh styling theme also adopted on the T500 and T250 in due course, with a fully-painted Montesa- and Bultaco-inspired fuel tank (which Yamaha then used on its 1968 line), a quilted seat, and redesigned handlebars.

As it happens, the first Suzuki to hit the marketplace in Japan with a chrome-free fuel tank wasn't the T250, T350 or T500 but the new 86,000 yen Wolf 90 – an 89cc parallel-twin, which also made its debut at the Tokyo Show, but was released alongside the company's latest 50cc moped in January 1969.

The lightweight Wolf 90 (code T90) was an attractive bike, taking the AC-series theme a stage further with an even sportier appearance made possible through a tubular 'tri-form' frame. The front was basically similar to the AC90, but the headlight was almost round, with twin gauges above – something quite special for this class, although the tachometer was actually an option on the earliest machines, along with raised handlebars. The long, low fuel tank extended forward to give the machine a lighter impression, with the saddle kicked up at the back, sat atop a chrome mudguard. There were very few fairings, and a minimalistic chain guard. The distinctive black extensions fitted on the upswept exhausts of the early bikes could be removed, by the way, leaving straight chromed pipes exiting either side of the chromed rear shocks.

The air-cooled two-stroke two-cylinder engine was positioned almost horizontally in the frame, with alloy heads and an alloy crankcase sandwiching the cast iron barrels. Naturally, CCI lubrication was included as part

The T350 starring on probably the strangest piece of promotional material ever produced – a record called *Go Suzuki!* by Henry Drennan.

SUZUKI MOTORCYCLES: THE CLASSIC TWO-STROKE ERA

of the package, although traditional piston-port induction was employed, and combined with a pair of downdraught carbs and a 7.3:1 c/r to give the 89cc (38mm x 39.6mm) unit 10.5bhp at 9000rpm, along with 6.7lb/ft of torque. The 98kg (216lb) T90 came with a close-ratio five-speed gearbox, allowing a top speed of 69mph (110kph), although quite a few contemporary reports stated that while the race-inspired styling was attractive, the riding position wasn't particularly comfortable for long distances with the standard handlebars.

The Wolf was sold as the T125 'Stinger' in America (and the UK, for that matter). The engine was bored and stroked out to 43mm x 43mm to give exactly 125cc if we round off the decimal point. With twin Mikuni MD18 carburettors and a 7.3:1 compression ratio, the unit delivered 15bhp at 8500rpm through a five-speed transmission. As on the Japanese 89cc model, 2.50-18 tyres were used up front, with 2.75-18s replacing the T90's 2.50-18s at the rear, plus the same SLS drum brakes employed at both ends, which were said to work well by users. For about $470, it was an excellent all-rounder, and duly joined the domestic line-up in the spring of 1969 as the 138,000 yen Wolf 125. Oddly, the Japanese T125 fuel tank was different to the US one (which was actually the same as the early T90 one – 1970 models gained a stripe), having a slightly bigger capacity and revised kneepads, although this tank was adopted for all markets on the T125-II of late-1970 vintage. Incidentally, the T125 code could be used as the long-running model originally based on the Seltwin had fallen by the wayside by this time.

The spring of '69 was a busy time for the Suzuki PR men – even busier than usual. March 1969 saw the release of the 193,000 yen Hustler 250 (TS250) – a more specialised off-roader that came with Candy Sophia Green paintwork and took the place of the short-lived TC250 in Japan, which was much closer to a road bike that could handle tougher work if necessary.

Domestic advert dated January 1969 for the Wolf 90.

A rather different view of the Wolf 90 afforded by a contemporary catalogue cover. The tiny 'Suzuki CCI' badge was on the offside box underneath the leading edge of the saddle.

Flyer for the domestic version of the Wolf 125, with its unique fuel tank – export models used the same version as that adopted on the Wolf 90.

THE LATE SIXTIES

Nonetheless, the Hustler 250 was a sign of the times, following fashion and making the most of the scrambling boom that was by then in full swing. It was powered by a single-cylinder all-alloy 246cc (70mm x 64mm) engine, which with a 6.6:1 c/r, VM28SC carburetion, and piston-port induction, developed 18.5bhp at 6000rpm, along with 17lb/ft of torque 1000rpm lower down the rev-range. It came with a five-speed gearbox to allow riders to make the most of the power available on all surfaces.

The specialised nature of the 127kg (279lb) bike could be found in the styling cues and spec sheet, with the tubular cradle frame playing host to long-travel front forks with a huge clearance between the 3.25-19 knobby tyre and front mudguard. The thin headlight was removable, allowing weight to be saved in competition, and the exhaust sat very high, just underneath the flip-top seat that allowed quick and easy maintenance. A fatter 4.00-18 tyre was mounted on the smaller rim at the back, located by three-way adjustable shocks. Lighting, though, complied with all road laws, making the Hustler a practical proposition for enthusiasts stuck for space or enough cash for two bikes, and for those who could afford it, a tuning kit was available taking power up to 30bhp.

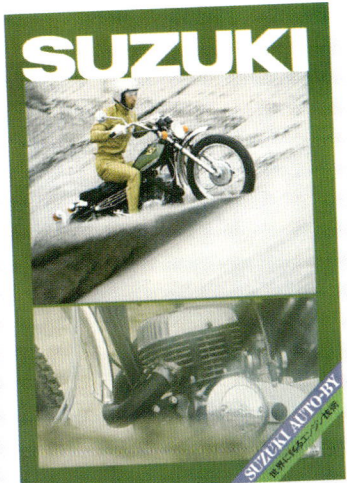

The TC120 was a smaller brother for the TS250, based on the model originally only sold in the USA.

The Scrambler TC120 was brought into the domestic line-up at the same time, the 118,000 yen machine basically being an updated version of the KT120 'Trail' with its revolutionary Posi-Select transmission. The transformation from KT to TC comprised a T350-style fuel tank (also found on the Hustler 250) and a quilted seat to bring the model in line with its contemporaries. In the States, where the bike's birth took place, the 118cc TC120 was known as the 'Cat'.

At last, in the closing days of April 1969, the 315cc T350 made it into Japanese dealerships, priced at 195,000 yen. The signature fuel tank (white with red stripes, or blue with white ones) and quilted saddle hid a stronger frame employed on the T350 and revised T250 (the T250-II), which looked much the same apart from the engine size

Promotional paperwork for the new TS250, aka the Hustler 250. This is the first version, with Candy Sophia Green paint and a narrow tank stripe.

The 1969 versions of the T250, T350 and T500.

SUZUKI MOTORCYCLES: THE CLASSIC TWO-STROKE ERA

Japanese advertising for Suzuki's 'big stuff' from the end of 1969.

A rather cute advert from the summer of 1969 for the Super Mini 50, obviously aimed at the fairer sex …

badge tacked onto the side covers. Oddly, the 1969 US 250 had a different fuel tank, which helped distinguish the pair Stateside, but only added to the confusion in retrospect!

The T350's piston-port twin was based on the 247cc unit, previously bored out to give the export-only 305 line, and bored out by another millimetre this time around (now 61mm x 54mm) to give a 315cc displacement. With a 12V battery and coil electrics, the engine was listed with a maximum of 33.5bhp at 8000rpm, but had a broad band of power delivery, put down to the road via a six-speed transmission and a combination of 3.00-18 and 3.25-18 rubber.

The 187,000 yen T250-II continued with its 30.5bhp engine and six-speed gearbox, with the styling changes being the main thing on this model. The all-chrome forks and new light (with revised paired-up gauges above) gave the bike a much leaner look, shared with the 350cc newcomer and the updated T500-II. The latter had already been on sale in America for several months, but the 47bhp machine didn't hit Japanese showrooms until the August of 1969, priced at 268,000 yen.

Meanwhile, the AS50 (described by *Auto-By* as a bike with "true sporting character for experienced riders, despite its engine size"), AC50, AS90 and AC90 had been allowed to continue unchanged going into the domestic 1969 season, although the 50cc models were phased out at the end of the year, as a new Scrambler AC50 took their place at the start of 1970. The AC90 lasted until mid-1969, with the AS90 version not that far behind.

On the moped side, the lightweight Super Mini 50 (later simply the Mini 50) shopping bike was launched in 1969 and listed for almost a decade, but it was the F50 (aka Super Free 50, or just Free 50 later on), announced in January that year, that was of far more interest to us. Apart from the fresher styling compared to the U-series, why would a 49.9cc (41mm x 37.8mm) moped hold such interest? Well, this was the first Suzuki to feature

THE LATE SIXTIES

現金正価 ¥63,000
　　　　¥70,000 (セル竹)

An early F50 moped, this being a Free 50, with slightly different badging compared to the original.

The K125, as it looked in the early part of 1969.

reed-valve induction, helping to improve low-speed response and smoothness, as well as enhancing fuel efficiency. This 4.5bhp machine was available in standard or deluxe guise (with a self-starter option adding a 'D' suffix to the model code), and was quickly joined by the F70 (confusingly listed as the Super Free 80 in catalogues) in April, which employed the older U70-type frame matched with a new 76cc single-cylinder engine.

The K50G (64,000 yen) and K50DG (71,000 yen with a self-starter) replaced existing K50 grades in September 1969.

The K50G of 1969 vintage, which came with a new engine and redesigned fuel tank. The updated K90 (or K90-2 officially) looked very similar at first glance, but, apart from cosmetics brought about by the G-package on the 50cc model, the exhaust dropped straight down before heading towards the back of the K90 bike.

These inherited the reed-valve induction engine from the F50, and were readily recognised by their new fuel tank design, chrome front

American advertising for the T500-II, or Suzuki Titan. This piece appeared in the June 1969 US edition of *Playboy*.

93

SUZUKI MOTORCYCLES: THE CLASSIC TWO-STROKE ERA

forks, separate rear mudguard, and a more modern seat and luggage rack. At the same time, while the K125 went untouched, the K90 received some engine tweaks and inherited the K50G's tank, front forks and rear mudguard to brighten it up. The revamped K90 was priced at 76,000 yen, or 83,000 yen in self-starting K90D guise, while the kickstart only K125 continued to be listed at its old price of 135,000 yen.

The timing was perfect, for 1969 saw another boom on 50cc bike sales in Japan. Better roads (allied with greater congestion) helped boost 125cc and over sales, too, and this helped Suzuki – now registered with 12,000,000,000 yen in capital – record a staggering 110,000,000,000 yen in sales for the year. Blessed with good sales again both at home and abroad (sales had been growing yearly in America, but exploded in 1969 thanks to dual-purpose bikes), a new factory for motorcycles, built at Toyama, was completed on October 3, 1969 (handling production of the F50 initially, and the K50, K90, F70, F90, A50, A70 and A100, plus selected parts for Suzuki's triples from 1970 onwards), and in the following month, the Osuka plant was opened at Kakegawa to deal with the company's aluminium casting operations.

For the record, an American advert from

The AC100 'Wolf' for America's 1969 season.

The TC120 'Cat' from the same year.

The T125 'Stinger.' Note the twin gauges.

The T350 'Rebel' as sold in the US in 1969.

Oddity corner #1. A Swedish advert for the 1969 season, although most of the bikes have already been superseded in the home market. The same was true in the UK, where older models were still listed many years beyond their finish date back home.

Italian advertising for the T500-II.

THE LATE SIXTIES

1969 showed the $244 AS50 'Maverick' (available in Redondo Blue), $374 AC100 'Wolf' (Mesa Orange), $460 TC120 'Cat' (Aspen Yellow or Mesa Orange), $471 T125 'Stinger' (Roman Red), $692 T250 X-6R 'Hustler' (Morro Green or Mesa Orange), $782 TS250 'Savage', which was closely related to the RH68 (Roman Red or Monterey Green), $749 T350 'Rebel' (Cape Ivory or Redondo Blue), and the $980 T500-II 'Titan' (Colorado Gold or Mesa Orange). During the early part of the year, the US dealers were also offering the T200, TC250, T305 and TC305, but all were either dropped or superseded as the season progressed.

Oddity corner #2. The 98cc AC100 and AS100 were sometimes known as the ACC100 and ASS100 in export markets.

1960s production

For ease of reference, the numbers are broken down into bikes with an engine capacity of up to 50cc, 51-125cc, 126-250cc, and 251cc and over. At this time, all would have been two-stroke machines.

	Up to 50cc	51cc to 125cc	126cc to 250cc	251cc +	Total
1960	123,153	46,201	11,683	-	181,037
1961	99,104	63,411	4485	-	167,000
1962	73,055	112,805	3843	-	189,703
1963	138,012	168,598	3912	-	310,522
1964	127,522	229,767	3262	-	360,551
1965	118,104	212,512	18,243	-	348,859
1966	220,546	231,748	36,313	-	488,607
1967	176,744	170,902	16,679	4102	368,427
1968	190,784	166,574	11,641	10,490	379,489
1969	205,945	164,451	21,878	9329	401,603

At the start of the sixties, just over 3,000,000 bikes were registered in Japan, rising to almost three times that figure by the end of the decade. However, while ownership and the number of bikes registered in use kept increasing, makers had to continue hunting for market niches, for seeing as the old Japanese stuff was built tough, the percentage of older bikes included within those figures would be increasing year-on-year, too.

As it happens, as the seventies came along, with more folks turning towards four-wheeled transport, the number of motorcycles in use stayed constant at around the 8,500,000 to

Michio Ichino at the wheel of the FL500 racer, which was put on display at the 1969 Tokyo Show. The inset shows the three-cylinder Fronte-based engine used to power the machine. Suzuki just couldn't resist the lure of racing …

9,000,000 mark, before finally breaking the 10,000,000 barrier in 1978 – trends more or less reflected in Suzuki's production. With our theory on more and more older bikes being in the mix each year brought into the equation, one can see that manufacturers had no time to rest on their laurels. Honda's production numbers had pretty much stagnated since the mid-1960s, and Yamaha, riding high on its recent racing success and strong exports, had now overtaken Suzuki as Japan's second-largest bike maker. There was a lot at stake as we entered the sizzling seventies …

95

SUZUKI MOTORCYCLES: THE CLASSIC TWO-STROKE ERA

Road bike evolution

The Suzuki motorcycle range is complex, and often confusing. This simplified table, following the evolution of each two-stroke model covered in this chapter, should hopefully allow things to become a lot clearer.

Model	1965	1966	1967	1968	1969	1970
Suzuki 50 M15 (50cc single)	M15	M15-2	K50	K50	K50G	
Suzuki 50 M15D (50cc single)	M15D	M15D-2	K50D	K50D	K50DG	
Suzuki Sport 50 (50cc single)	M12	M12-2	KS50	AS50		
Suzuki AC50 (50cc single)				AC50	AC50	AC50
Suzuki 52 M16 (52cc single)	M16					
Suzuki A70 (69cc single)		A70	A70			
Suzuki 80 K10 (79cc single)	K10	K10-2				
Suzuki 80 K10D (79cc single)	K10D	K10D-2				
Suzuki Sport 80 (79cc single)	K11	K11-2				
Suzuki A90 (86cc single)			A90	AS90	AS90	AS90
Suzuki AC90 (86cc single)			AC90	AC90	AC90	AC90
Suzuki K90 (86cc single)			K90	K90	K90	K90
Suzuki Wolf T90 (89cc twin)					T90	T90
Suzuki A100 (98cc single)			A100			
Suzuki B100 (118cc single)	B100	B120	B120			
Suzuki TC120 (118cc single)					TC120	TC120

96

THE LATE SIXTIES

Model	1965	1966	1967	1968	1969	1970
Suzuki 125SL (123cc single)	SL					
Suzuki 125 S10 (123cc single)	S10		K125			
Suzuki S30 (124cc twin)	S30 / S30-2		T125			
Suzuki Sport 125 (124cc twin)	S31					
Suzuki Wolf T125 (125cc twin)					T125	
Suzuki T200 (196cc twin)			T200			
Suzuki TC200 (196cc twin)			TC200			
Suzuki Hustler 250 (246cc single)					TS250	
Suzuki 250 T10 (247cc twin)	T10 / T20	T21	T250			
Suzuki TC250 (247cc twin)			TC250			
Suzuki T350 (315cc twin)					T350	
Suzuki T500 (492cc twin)				T500		

Note: Pure mopeds and models made specifically for export are not included in this table, although they are all covered within the text.

www.veloce.co.uk / www.velocebooks.com
All current books • New book news • Special offers • Gift vouchers

97

5 The Sizzling Seventies

Suzuki celebrated its 50th anniversary on March 15, 1970 with a special ceremony at Hamamatsu, and separate events held at all the other factories. Who would have thought, back in 1920, that a tiny loom maker could evolve into such a huge concern within just five decades?

With plenty to celebrate, more gatherings held to help commemorate this landmark occasion followed in April and May, with Michio Suzuki and Shunzo Suzuki in attendance, as well as dignitaries from Toyota and other companies, plus a large number of representatives from foreign countries, for the firm was now a truly global player. Indeed, May 1970 saw Suzuki sign a technical co-operation agreement with a company in Indonesia, leading to parts production there four years later, and ultimately formation of a joint venture. Similar things happened in the Philippines, Malaysia and Pakistan. On the same kind of subject, while exports had averaged around 125,000 units per year in the 1965 to 1969 period, with trade in the US picking up, the number shot up to 224,000 units in 1970; Suzuki was selling its products in over 100 countries by this time.

The product list was also growing. With Japan's national average wage now standing at 825,000 yen (almost double what it was five years earlier), people had more money to spend on leisure pursuits – a fact backed up by a new, two-storey showroom in Tokyo's trendy Shinjuku area, complete with old Colledas, a chopper bike (not road-legal in Japan), and a life-size effigy of Steve McQueen! There was no shortage of ideas surrounding the two-wheelers, the boat business was picking up slowly, and the car side was about to expand and be propelled into a new era.

During the spring of 1968, Osamu Suzuki (someone we talk about in the next chapter) had suggested building a unique, Jeep-type vehicle based on the *Kei* platform – an idea that ultimately led to the development and marketing of the iconic Jimny LJ10 four-wheel drive model. The Jimny would still be in production well into the 21st century, having hardly changed over the decades since its official introduction in April 1970.

A few months later, in November, the boxy 360cc Fronte 71 went on sale, duly joined by the Giugiaro-designed Fronte Coupe at the tail-end of 1971. The Fronte line would develop at quite a pace from now on, but, when all is said and done, it was the bikes that kept the Suzuki brand name in the limelight …

Part of the celebrations to mark the 50th year of the company. The V-sign was used internally as the symbol of a plan to move forward, building on achievement.

Suzuki boats and a selection of engines to power them on display at an event in Nagoya. Some of the promotional material for this side of the business was very workmanlike, while some of it was akin to a Bond film poster.

THE SIZZLING SEVENTIES

manufacturer can react to trends and booms due to their relative simplicity, with potential build numbers justifying investment.

While the 1969 Tokyo Show display had been quite stunning, designed to resemble a Stone Age cave with bikes and engines strewn around it, the stand was also lacking anything really new. As far as Suzuki was concerned, the big change for 1970 came on January 26, when the 69,000 yen Scrambler AC50-II took the place of the four AC and AS grades in the catalogue. In reality, other than a few detail changes, such as new front and rear lights, along with bolder graphics on the reshaped fuel tank and side covers (the black and white coachline on the flanks of the tank included the Suzuki name, while chequered flag motifs abounded), it looked much the same as its namesake from the previous year, with a pressed-steel frame. Mechanically, it was the same, too, with the 6bhp engine carried over, albeit with a black exhaust to match that of the bigger Hustler 250, and a few improved safety features. In keeping with the motocross image, a factory sports kit was available to allow those who wanted to race at weekends do so at a competitive level, with the engine pulling almost half as much power again as the standard unit. On the colouring side, Candy Orange was listed first, alongside a lime green used on the Wolf, with blue and red added soon after.

The Hustler 250 duly followed the lead set by the newcomer, inheriting a new stripe on the fuel tank with the Suzuki name inside by the time spring arrived, although Candy Sophia Green (Monterey Green abroad) was still the only colour available at this time. More importantly for users, the TS250-II, as it was now known, was put on a diet resulting in a weight reduction of over 10kg (22lb).

The original Jimny 4WD model, introduced in April 1970. The LJ10 evolved into the LJ20 in mid-1972, powered by a water-cooled rather than an air-cooled engine. It was still a two-stroke unit, though, and a revised grille was one of the few other changes. The Jimny range was duly expanded with different body and seating arrangements, with LHD versions helping open up fresh export markets.

The 1970 line-up

Flicking through pages of contemporary magazines from the various continents, it's striking how fashionable an industry the motorcycle trade was. One maker would release something, with an interesting styling angle, and five minutes later, a competitor would have a similar offering with the latest shapes and graphics. The beauty of motorcycles, of course, is the speed with which a

The Fronte Coupé, illustrated in a 1974 Japanese advert.

An AC50-II in red. Unlike the export versions of the bike, the domestic models all came with a rack over the rear lights.

SUZUKI MOTORCYCLES: THE CLASSIC TWO-STROKE ERA

Officially replacing the T90 Wolf and TC120 in the domestic line-up (the T90 was kept in the catalogues alongside the newcomer for a little while, whilst the T125 Wolf limped on into the spring of 1971, although both remained available beyond that if one knew the right dealer), the Hustler 90 (TS90) was announced on February 25, 1970, with the "emphasis on racy, motocross styling, harmoniously combined

The AC50-II engine, as seen in the parts catalogue.

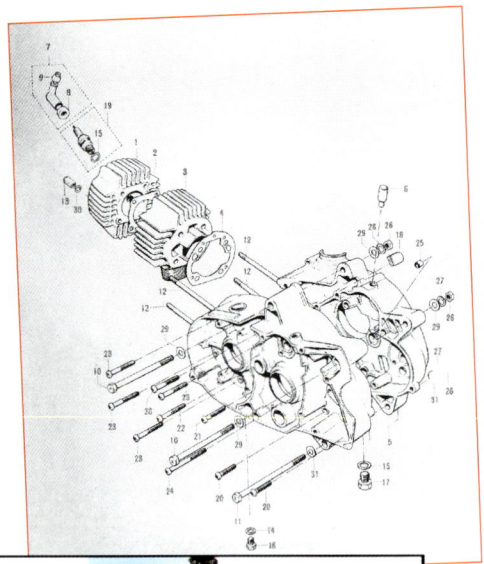

Flyer for the 1970 version of the Hustler 250.

Catalogue page from late 1970 showing the original Hustler 90, plus the Hustler 50 and Hustler 125 models that eventually went on sale in January 1971.

The sports bikes as they looked at the end of 1970, including a late version of the Wolf 90, and a special interloper that wouldn't be launched for some time to come. The last of the Wolf breed had black exhaust pipes, incidentally.

Cover and centre spread from the 1970 TS250-II catalogue, with the cover designer using a new Hustler 90 for the background, identified by the slightly different tank graphics and the fact that the exhaust is on the nearside rather than the offside.

Flyer for the T350-II, with revised graphics on the fuel tank. The red stripe on the tyres were a fad from the time, available on larger bikes as a striking alternative to all-black or the traditional but rather more staid whitewall rubber.

The T500-III, with a luggage rack placed on top of the fuel tank.

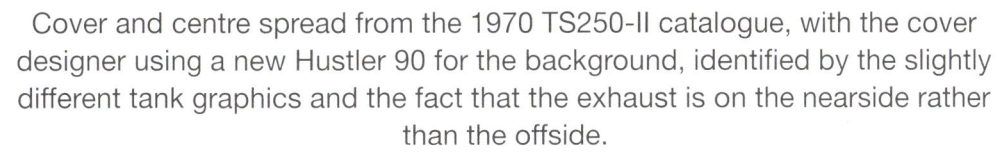

with street legal equipment." This was a sign of the times, with the scrambler boom in full swing, but it was a lot more than a cosmetic gloss-over, as the rivalry between Suzuki, Yamaha and Kawasaki was hotting up in this arena.

The TS90 featured a new tubular double-cradle frame, a fuel tank aping that of its bigger brother, albeit with graphics like those of the AC50 (it would be a few months before the TS250 got the same type of stripe with integrated lettering), plus a folding seat. Chrome forks were used at the front, with a clear single gauge above (separated from the Wolf-style lighting), and exposed chrome springs specified for the rear. The TS90 employed body-coloured mudguards, as opposed to silver ones on the AC50, which covered knobby 2.75-18 tyres.

The two-stroke, single-cylinder engine was also new, with an alloy head and cast iron barrel, disc rotary-valve induction and an upswept exhaust system. With a 47mm bore and 51.8mm stroke combining to give an 89cc displacement, the kickstart unit delivered 10bhp at 8000rpm and a very usable, broad torque band. A five-speed gearbox was standard, with

SUZUKI MOTORCYCLES: THE CLASSIC TWO-STROKE ERA

Japanese advertising from the tail-end of 1970 for the Super Free 90. The badging under the saddle was changed in 1972.

The 'business' bikes as they looked at the end of the 1970 season, with the K125-2 sporting its new fuel tank design. This 138,000 yen 10.5bhp model tipped the scales at 114kg (251lb). The snowmobile was another line the company was trying …

Below and right: The amazing 15-page spread used to announce the 1970 Suzuki range in America.

competition parts available for weekend warriors.

Before moving on, it should be noted that the last of the Wolf 90s gained a new fuel tank with a stripe and black exhausts (with removable chrome ends). This arrangement was also adopted on the Wolf 125, with the T125-II designation being used for the face-lifted model, which officially ran until early 1971 (at least as a catalogue model, although both Wolf models were still in the October price lists as it happens), or late 1971 in export markets. As for the other T-series models, the T250-II became the T250-III in 1970, while the T350 became the T350-II, and the T500-II became the T500-III. The main thing on these bigger T-class bikes was revised graphics on the tank and side covers for this season,

102

THE SIZZLING SEVENTIES

although the 500cc model also gained a luggage rack on top of the petrol tank.

Things were becoming complicated on the moped front, but some of the innovations are important for our story, so we have to follow progress regardless of whether we want to or not! The Super Free 50 continued, but the Super Free 80 was replaced by the Super Free 70 with the latest body and a 6.2bhp reed-valve engine in May 1970. Three months earlier, at the start of February, the Super Free 90 (F90) had been launched, also with a reed-valve engine. This unit pumped out 7.5bhp, but was mounted in a longer frame compared to the other pair of bikes in this series. To add to the confusion, the Super Free designation was dropped, giving birth to Free 50, Free 70 and Free 90 in early 1971, although the bikes themselves were unchanged. As it happens, the F90 was dropped in 1974, but it did at least lend its powerplant to the K-series.

SUZUKI MOTORCYCLES: THE CLASSIC TWO-STROKE ERA

UK advertising from August 1970, with older models still enjoying their share of the spotlight.

The K50G was carried over, although the K90 gained the F90's 88cc (50mm x 45mm) 7.5bhp engine, which was less powerful than the old unit (almost 1bhp down) but significantly cleaner and a lot more fuel-efficient. At the same time, the K125 (now officially known as the K125-2, or Mark II) gained a new fuel tank as the season progressed, closer in profile to that of the larger T-series tanks, along with front and rear side markers and revised badging, taking the price of this long-running machine up to 138,000 yen.

The Americans were desperate to get their hands on Suzuki scramblers, and advertising from the time reflected this. "This year, fly Suzuki," said one piece, with eight bikes jumping a ridge, or "There are only ten bikes built to take on the country. Suzuki has them all." Speed was also a big theme, with the T350 and T500 matched against muscle cars and beating them all in the standing-quarter stakes. The promotional budget was now massive in the States, the 15 pages taken in the April 1970 edition of *Cycle World* standing as testament to this fact – Harley-Davidson and BSA took a couple each in the same issue, for instance, showing where the money was, and the undoubted importance the Hamamatsu firm placed on the US market.

Key models for America in 1970 included the AC50 'Maverick', priced at $265, and the TS90 'Honcho'. The TS90 quickly spawned the TC90 'Blazer', which was even more of an off-road machine, with chunkier tyres, an engine guard and greater clearance for the front mudguard. At $374, it was only $5 cheaper than the 'Honcho' – enough of a saving to fill the fuel tank at least!

The TC120 and TC125 continued, along with the TS250 'Savage', and the traditional T250, T350 and T500 lines. The T500 could still turn heads, though, and impress magazine testers, too.

After trying an $899 T500-III, *Cycle World* declared: "Dollar for horsepower, money for performance, Suzuki's 500 is formidable … Bending corners on the T500 is a thrill to be experienced." Indeed, the Japanese Police Force were also enthralled by the beast, ordering 80 for Tokyo to run alongside the 650cc Kawasakis and 750cc Hondas already on patrol duty. The company later introduced a GT750 '*shiro-bi*' at the 1971 Tokyo Show, spawning more orders from the boys in blue.

Meanwhile, in the UK, the April 1970 price list had the U50 at £103, the AS50 'Sports' at £109, the A100 at £150, the B100P at £167, the T200 'Invader' at £239, the T250 Mark II 'Hustler' at £338, and the T500 Mark II at £448. Obviously, a lot of the mix was made up of older stock, as the domestic and US markets had moved on an awful lot since these models were introduced. The author has seen other foreign model lists from the time, and the same thing is true, with older models dominating. While this only adds to the general confusion and mystery surrounding early Suzukis, it does at least give a good idea of what was available when and where.

A new generation

Suzuki's much-heralded 750cc water-cooled triple made its debut at the 1970 Tokyo Show, which opened at the end of October. Journalist Yukio Kuroda stated at the time: "The new 750 is designed to lure the attention of riders who might otherwise be inclined to choose a Mach III or a Honda 750 Four. And if Suzuki prices the 750 right smack between the aforementioned behemoths, it will be like turning loose a wolverine in a rabbit hutch."

As it happens, rumours about the three-cylinder Suzuki had been floating around the industry for some time. While Kawasaki beat Suzuki to the marketplace with its legendary H1 Mach III two-stroke triple, the loss of impact was minimal, and the engineering sound. For starters, a triple is better balanced than a twin (indeed, later publicity material even went so far as to say the balance was as good as that of a four-stroke six!), and the width of an inline arrangement isn't that much different to a V-twin, as the heads tend to stick out if the engine is mounted in one direction, while the other option tends to reduce cooling efficiency by a significant amount on the rearmost cylinder on air-cooled units. It was certainly more compact than a flat-twin,

THE SIZZLING SEVENTIES

with good cooling, and exhaust routing on the centre pot being the most difficult problem to overcome. That, of course, plus meeting the increasingly stringent emissions regulations.

In reality, while manufacturers in all fields of engineering were celebrating healthy order books in all of Japan's industrial bases, smog was becoming a worrying menace in the Land of the Rising Sun in the post-Tokyo Olympics era. When all is said and done, the rapid, unchecked industrial growth of the country was much like that of China and India in more recent times, with short-term profits and employment prioritised, and little thought given to air quality then or in the future. As such, with highly vocal calls from the government to clear up the skies (without any effort to keep traffic congestion down on its part), the engineering team began work on what would ultimately become the GT series at the end of Suzuki's racing campaign, with emissions clearance the first concern.

The 750cc prototype wasn't the only interesting machine at the show, though, as preparations were made to overhaul the entire line-up by the spring of 1971: apart from the odd model here and there, the old K-series and mopeds were about the only familiar faces left by that time. Even then, the K50G reverted to its traditional K50 moniker, although the bike itself was unchanged.

Perhaps not surprisingly, the scrambler range was expanded again, with a couple of pure competition models and a distinctive line of off-roaders and touring variations of the same bike created in the process. There were also some real oddities introduced in 1971, as makers wanted to cash in on the mini-bike boom personified by the Honda Monkey range. Suzuki had the Hopper MT50 and, later in the year, the VanVan RV90 – the VanVan would receive various body and engine options over the

Cover of the catalogue issued at the time of the 1970 Tokyo Show.

Flyer for the TS50, or Hustler 50 as it was commonly known.

The first press picture of the magnificent GT750. The colouring was unique to the show model as far as the domestic market was concerned.

The 1971 version of the TS90, which, apart from the colouring, wasn't all that different to the 1970 Hustler 90 in reality, although the Touring model launched alongside it was certainly a lot less rugged in appearance.

SUZUKI MOTORCYCLES: THE CLASSIC TWO-STROKE ERA

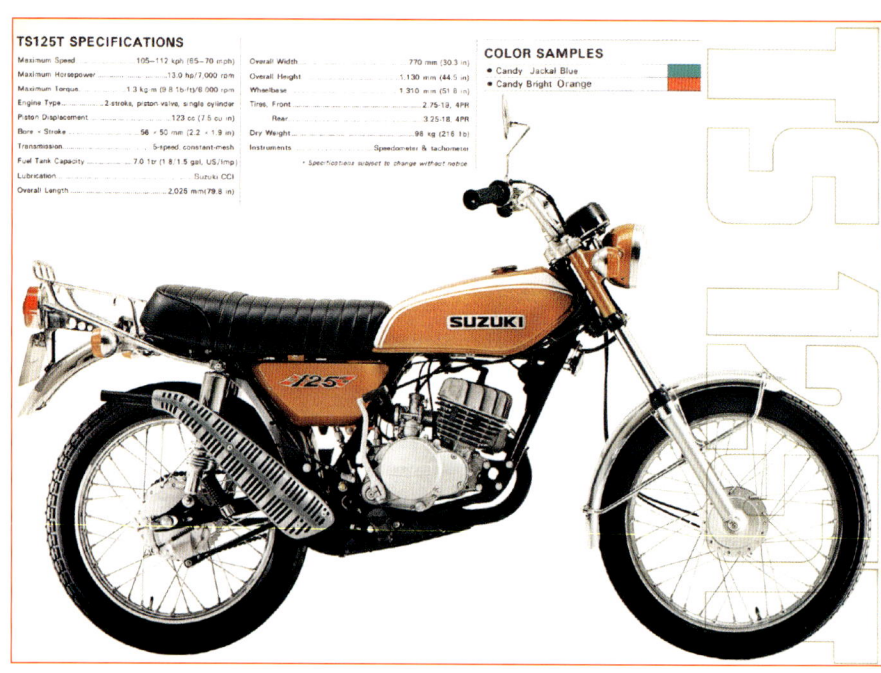

Spec sheet of the original TS90T, with the TS125T on the opposite side.

The TS185, released in Japan during the spring of 1971.

Brochure for the TS250-III, made for the 1971 bike season.

The 1971 GT250 in Chrome Orange.

coming years, becoming something of a cult model in the leisure category.

Anyway, back to normality. The AC50 was basically the same as the original model, apart from fresh decals on the side covers. It was the same situation with the TS90, although February 1971 saw a split in the catalogue, with the TS90 becoming the TS90T (the 'T' suffix standing for touring), as the Hustler 90 (strict TS90) moniker was now reserved for a pure scrambler costing 95,000 yen. As it happens, the five-speed TS50 was launched as a scrambler version of the AC50 at about the same time, costing 75,000 yen and available in the

106

THE SIZZLING SEVENTIES

Domestic advertising for the early GT range, with a GT250 illustrated.

Better views of the GT250, GT350 and GT500 of 1971.

same striking yellow and black as the 90cc off-roader, or red and white as an alternative; Candy Turquoise was listed later on.

Continuing the theme, the five-speed Hustler 125 (TS125), announced at the start of the year, was a pure scrambler with a single-cradle frame, duly spawning the TS125T in April, although the upswept exhaust couldn't mask the base model's intent. The piston-port 123cc single-cylinder engine for the Hustler 125 and TS125T was quite different to that used in the K-series, having a 56mm x 50mm bore and stroke, all-alloy construction, and delivering 13bhp at 7000rpm along with 9.4lb/ft of torque at 6000rpm. Rounding off the scrambler line, the Chrome Orange-painted Hustler 185 (TS185) was released in the spring of 1971, powered by a 183cc (64mm x 57mm) 18bhp single, and priced at 177,000 yen, while the 205,000 yen Hustler 250 gained a few extra horses (maximum power was now quoted as 22bhp) and a new red paint scheme to celebrate losing 9kg (20lb) after a successful diet plan.

The big two-stroke T-series machines were given a minor change on February 1, 1971 to respectively become the 197,000 yen GT250, the 205,000 yen GT350 and the 278,000 yen GT500 models, or at least in Japan, for America and Europe decided to keep the old designations until something more worthwhile and meaningful had been administered from the chaps in Hamamatsu. For the record, the bikes that carried the older T-series

Flyer for the GT350 at the time of its domestic launch.

107

SUZUKI MOTORCYCLES: THE CLASSIC TWO-STROKE ERA

The GT500 as it was sold in its first year on the Japanese marketplace.

Another Japanese advert, this one from just before the GT750 hit the market.

American advertising for the 1971 range.

Your ship just came in.

With 14 new Suzukis built to take on the country.

It's the greatest motorcycle cargo yet! Far and away the most outstanding bikes ever. With more power. With more features. With exciting new designs. Take a look. The wait is over. Your bike is right here.

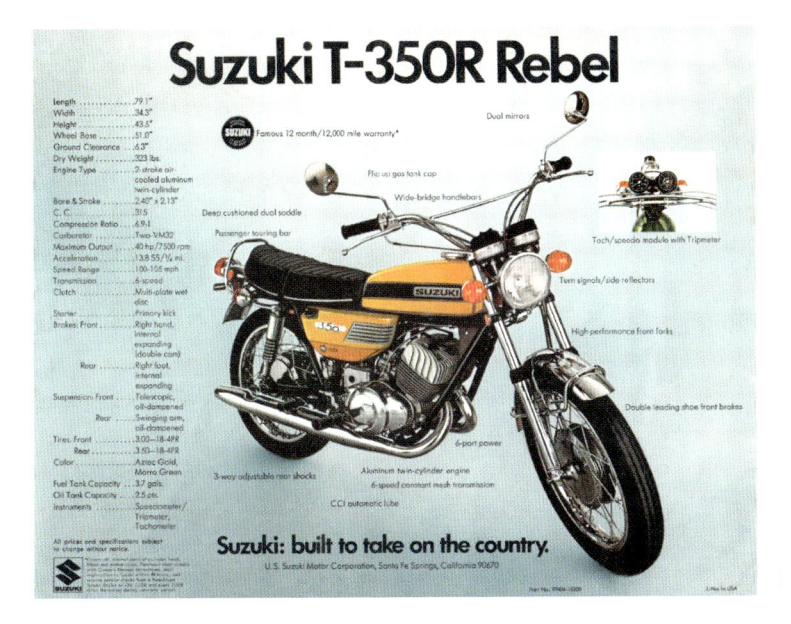

THE SIZZLING SEVENTIES

Specification sheet for the US T350 'Rebel,' with the T500 'Titan' on the opposite side. The 'R' suffix represents the 1971 season.

Another spec sheet from the same series, this one showing the TS250 'Savage' scrambler.

A rather tired-looking but nonetheless important leaflet from the UK, released at around this time. Note the Hustler 50 (TS50) carrying the TSS50 moniker, and the AC50 named as the ACC50; the TS90T and TS125T were familiar nameplates, though. Other bikes sold at this time included true 'export only' models, such as the A80, and older machines, too, like the B120.

numbers were generally recognised by an 'R' suffix, so the T500-III became the T500R, and so on. In reality, the importers abroad had a point, as the leading specs were the same across the board, and only fresh colour schemes with revised tank graphics and new side boxes set the 250cc and 350cc models apart from their predecessors; the 500cc grade changed even less. The main reason for the new moniker, of course, was to pave the way for the latest triple – the GT750, which was eventually officially released on the domestic marketplace in September 1971.

Meanwhile, the USA accounted for over half of all Suzuki exports from 1970 to 1972 (and interest in Japanese bikes in general was as strong as ever, for 400,000 more were imported in 1971 than the 925,000 figure posted in the previous year), so it made sense to focus on American market needs. For 1971, dual-purpose bikes were the main line, in keeping with demand, with the TS50 'Gaucho', TS90 'Honcho' (the equivalent of the TS90T at home), TC90 'Blazer' (closer to the contemporary TS90 in Japan), TC120 'Cat', T125 'Stinger', TS125 'Duster', TS185

109

SUZUKI MOTORCYCLES: THE CLASSIC TWO-STROKE ERA

'Sierra' and TS250 'Savage' listed alongside the T250 'Hustler' (described in the contemporary press as "an excellent machine for the novice and expert alike"), T350 'Rebel' and T500 'Titan'. Prices ranged from $294 for the 'Gaucho' up to $899 for the 'Titan'. For the record, America also listed the $239 F50 'Cutlass' moped, the MT50 'Trailhopper' and the $999 TM400 'Cyclone' motocross machine. As with all the other machines sold in the States in 1971, an 'R' suffix was applied to the model code to distinguish them from earlier versions.

It was fascinating to see how the company's US advertising campaign matured over the years, with 1971 making use of a stunning 32-page "special report presented by US Suzuki on the world of motorcycling" in some magazines. One will remember, not that many years earlier, that we were lucky to see a quarter-page ad for months on end! The supplement included pieces by competition stars Joël Robert and Ron Grant, and frankly put the efforts of others to shame.

Racing revival

As well as a number of privateers using ex-works bikes, the Suzuki name had been kept alive in European racing circles by a hardy band of enthusiasts, led by the likes of Eddie Crooks and Harry Thompson, as well as Suzuki GB, who also raced the T20 in the late-sixties. The success of the model in racing led to the development of the TR250, which was released in the UK in the latter part of 1967, alongside a TR50 tiddler.

Indeed, Suzuki GB ordered a batch of 20 of these MR43 race bikes (better known as the TR50, and definitely not to be confused with its namesake of the late-1990s) at this time,

The TR750 (XR11) of 1972 vintage.

equipped with an 8.5bhp 49cc single. Priced at £385 at the end of 1967, when they were made available to clients, the MR43 was an improved version of the MR41, but destined to remain a rarity – one of the reasons being that just £100 more secured a TR250 piston-port twin!

The 492cc (70mm x 64mm) Suzuki TR500 was released in the following year, powered by an air-cooled 63bhp twin that endowed the lightweight machine with a top speed of 135mph (216kph). These bikes did well in America, prompting the company to make a concerted effort to win the 1970 Daytona classic with a revised 500cc TR500 model. Jody Nicholas' race finished early with a faulty ignition, but Ron Grant rode an amazing race and should have won the 200-miler with ease. Unfortunately, the 70bhp Suzuki ran out of fuel on the last lap, and Geoff Perry ended up as the marque's top finisher on a 1969 machine in fifth place. It should also be noted that there was a Production class win on the Isle of Man for Frank Whiteway that year, while Frank Perris was third in the Senior TT, albeit eight minutes down on the winning MV.

With 71.5bhp on tap, the two-stroke TR500 came good in 1971, with a four-man team making the most of it in the States, and success in the world championship, too – success that was all the more remarkable given that the bike was a production-based model adapted for racing rather than a pure racer. While Giacomo Agostini ran away with the 500cc championship title aboard an MV Agusta, Keith Turner was second on a Suzuki-powered machine, followed home by Rob Bron. In addition, Jack Findlay had won the Ulster GP round in August, giving Suzuki more to celebrate.

Interestingly, this is where Barry Sheene enters the story, using an ex-works 125cc machine to almost capture the 1971 world title at the tender age of 21 (he finished eight points behind a works Derbi rider in the 125cc category). After a year with Yamahas, he returned to Suzuki power in 1973, with a TR500 at his disposal. Soon, there would be no looking back for either rider or maker.

The success

An interesting domestic dealer advert from 1973.

THE SIZZLING SEVENTIES

of 1971 allowed Suzuki to justify making the TR500-II for 1972, although the specifications were largely unchanged. Sadly, the results were nothing to write home about beyond a few scattered podium spots, and Stan Woods' win in the Production class on the Isle of Man would ultimately serve as the highlight of the season, as the newly-introduced TR750 had failed to shine at Daytona, despite the 100bhp machines undoubtedly being the fastest bikes on the track.

With the TR500-III of 1973, Suzuki introduced water-cooling for the 73bhp engine, and upgraded the braking system, as this was now a 157mph (251kph) machine. Jack Findlay duly won the Isle of Man Senior TT with one, but could only finish fifth in the world championship. At least there was more success in the FIM Formula 750

Original press shots of the 1974 RG500.

A great piece of American advertising from the summer of 1973.

WHEN YOU'RE COOL, YOU'RE HOT.

Water-cooled Suzuki 750's have won two out of the first three AMA National Road Races this year.
On April 1, Paul Smart ran away from everybody at Dallas. June 3, Geoff Perry won Atlanta with a new track record of 94.467 mph.
Water-cooling gives us the hottest racing machine on the track. And gives you the coolest touring machine on the highway.
U.S. Suzuki Motor Corporation, Santa Fe Springs, California 90670.

A piece of UK advertising from November 1974, showing the success of Barry Sheene (and Stan Woods) on the 750cc Suzuki Team Castrol bikes during the 1974 season.

Castrol and Suzuki. Take winning to heart.

Castrol and Suzuki are 1974's great winning team. With the track record of both these high performers and the riding skills of Barry Sheene and Stan Woods, they have to be.
Suzuki-Team Castrol have notched up some impressive results against some of the toughest opposition.
Barry and Stan have won at just about every British circuit this year, including the Trans-Atlantic Match Race, the JPS Grand Prix and the Race of the Year.
With a track record like that it's not surprising that Suzuki recommend Castrol for their road machines.
Castrol have been at the heart of bikes for nearly 75 years. It's the great oil for any bike, on the road or on the track.
Now more than ever you need the high performer with heart. Castrol.

Now more than ever you need the high performer with heart.

SUZUKI MOTORCYCLES: THE CLASSIC TWO-STROKE ERA

Cup series, with Barry Sheene grabbing the title for Suzuki with a TR750 engine brought into the UK after its Stateside campaign.

It was the 500cc Grand Prix bikes that caught the headlines, however, with the FIM world championship classes consisting of 500cc, 350cc, 250cc, 125cc and 50cc categories. Suzuki knew the days of being competitive with the TR-series were over, and in 1974 introduced the legendary RG500, making full use of the fact that the FIM allowed a maximum of four cylinders on 500cc bikes.

Codenamed the XR14 and developed with incredible speed thanks to Guido Mandracchi doing the test-riding, the RG500 signalled that Suzuki was back in racing in a big way. This was basically a rebirth of the RZ65, but with its water-cooled square-four having a bore and stroke of 56mm x 50.5mm to give 497cc. With four carbs, it initially delivered 90bhp – enough to propel the six-speed 145kg (319lb) disc-braked machine up to 175mph (280kph). Unfortunately, a catalogue of teething troubles meant there were no wins to reward Suzuki's efforts in 1974, but at least 1975 would be kinder …

The GT750

The long-awaited launch of the water-cooled GT750 inline triple came on September 3, 1971. Naturally, the two-stroke engine was the key component in this new flagship model (interestingly, a four-stroke unit was never on the cards according to the engineers, only the cooling options and number of cylinders were mulled over for any length of time), having all-alloy construction with cast iron cylinder liners, piston-valve induction and four exhaust pipes (with the central pot having two smaller pipes, which were placed underneath the larger diameter ones for the outer pair of cylinders). The bore and stroke was set at 70mm x 64mm to give 738cc, and with 12V coil and battery electrics, a 6.7:1 c/r and three Mikuni

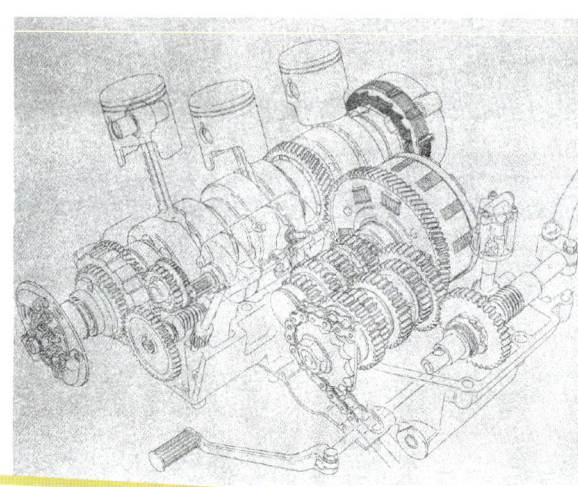

Inner workings of the GT750 engine. Interestingly, the early Japanese models (B-1 to B-3) had a split cylinder head, which was never used on export models, or the strict GT750 for that matter.

A typically flamboyant piece of Italian advertising introducing the GT750.

One of the very first Japanese adverts for the GT750 after domestic sales started; this was found in the November 1971 issue of *Motorcyclist*. By the way, while the GT750 was nicknamed the 'Water Buffalo' abroad, Japan enthusiasts called it the 'G-Nana' (with the Nana element meaning seven in English).

112

THE SIZZLING SEVENTIES

VM32 carburettors, the unit developed 67bhp at 6500rpm, plus 56lb/ft of torque at 5500rpm.

Seeing as a new technique had been applied to burn off extra oil and clean up exhaust smoke in the process (with the system given the SRIS moniker), there was a flurry of excitement and fresh research in the author's office surrounding the CCIS designation suddenly appearing in catalogues, but then the reality was rather an anti-climax after the realisation that an 'S' for 'System' had been added onto the end of the existing CCI nomenclature, and nothing more! Subsequently, all models duly picked up the CCIS automatic lubrication system at the tail-end of 1971, even though it was no different to the CCI of old, which explains why so little fanfare was made about the change. Ironically, the CCI badge continued to be used on the bikes themselves (or at least most of them), and even the export markets dropped the Posi-Force name in favour of CCI at this time. All very confusing, but then this is perhaps what we've come to expect …

The engine and five-speed transmission were mounted in a double cradle frame, with the front forks resembling those of the GT500, but with three gauges in a pack at the top of them rather than two (plus an electric starter on the right-hand side of the handlebars to augment the kickstart – something not seen on the regular bikes for some time), and the rear springs like those fitted to the smaller GT grades below a full-length saddle. The tank and side covers were unique to the 750cc machine, with the radiator shell (positioned between the front wheel and

Domestic range catalogue from late 1971, with a GT750 and the CCIS moniker on the cover. All illustrations were the same as those found in publicity material issued earlier in the year, albeit with a view from a different side of the bike in a few instances, and a different picture completely for the TM400. This particular TM400 has the 1972-style stripes on the tank, whereas the earliest bikes had a straight, heavyweight black line with the Suzuki name within; it was also painted yellow rather than red.

113

SUZUKI MOTORCYCLES: THE CLASSIC TWO-STROKE ERA

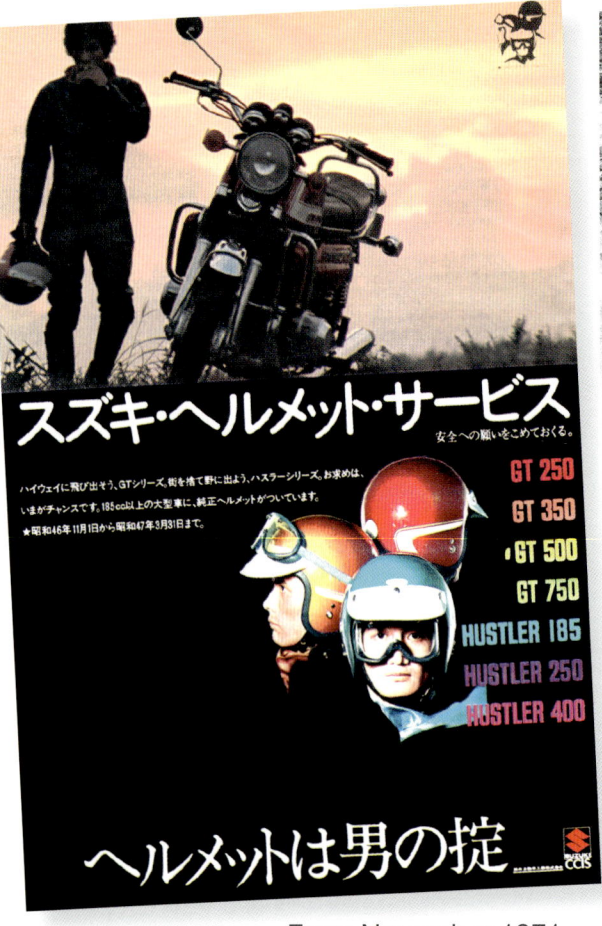

From November 1971 to April 1972, Suzuki offered the chance for owners of machines with engines of 185cc and over to order helmets with paint schemes and graphics to match their bikes.

The Toyokawa factory pictured in the early 1970s. The site surpassed the 1,000,000 mark for bike production in August 1974.

Aerial view of the Toyama Plant taken at around the same time.

A final Japanese GT750 advert, this piece dating from the end of 1971.

front of the engine) and virtually round headlight housing painted to match; the 3.25-19 and 4.00-18 tyres were covered by chrome mudguards that were also unique to the 750cc model. Drum brakes were fitted at both ends, with the rear brake still operated by the right foot, although there was no problem keeping the 235kg (517lb) machine – universally known by its Water Buffalo nickname – in check. Notwithstanding, the bigger bikes would soon inherit disc brakes, putting any doubts to rest once and for all.

It was certainly an impressive machine. *Cycle World* summed up by saying: "Suzuki's most pleasing combination, the GT750, is the most refined, and yet most awesome, two-stroke ever."

Bike & Rider joined in with: "Regardless of your first impressions, it's not until you spend some time on the road that [the bike's] true nature comes to light … After a while, one of the most impressive things about the engine is its broad torque range. Power comes on strongly from one end of the rev range to the other. The operation of the gearbox is smooth and positive. The ratios are well spaced, and well matched to the power characteristics of the engine.

"Winding through a twisting canyon brings out another side of the Suzuki. This is a machine that not only goes good, but stops and handles as well. Handling the GT750 around tight corners or fast sweeping bends is positive and sure. Steering is precise, and performance is predictable. Much of the credit for this must go to the design of the frame and suspension system.

"It is, in fact, difficult to find anything bad to say about the GT750. The Suzuki GT750 is a superbike by anyone's definition."

Priced at 385,000 yen (which would have secured six Mini 50s, plus a Hopper 50 thrown in on top!), the GT750 was built at the Toyokawa Plant – the old Nikko Sangyo works (an ex-press shop and foundry that used to supply parts for Suzuki), which opened in its new guise on the first day of October 1971. The Toyokawa Plant would be used for the production of medium-sized and bigger bikes in Aichi Prefecture, making the

THE SIZZLING SEVENTIES

GT250, Hustler 125, Hustler 400, VanVan RV125, and GT380 in due course. This allowed the Toyama works to concentrate on smaller motorcycles, while the head office factory was reorganised to handle engine components and machining, thus streamlining the Suzuki operation as a whole.

More new big stuff

While the GT750 was carried over into Japan's 1972 season, there was a mad burst of activity on the rest of the GT line-up, which really needs to be tackled with care. Starting with the GT380, we'll look at what happened to each of the GTs in turn until the autumn of 1972, when yet more changes were applied …

Shown as a reference model at the 1971 Tokyo Show, the GT380 triple was officially announced in Japan at the start of the new year, and put on sale at 245,000 yen very soon after, taking the place of the twin-cylinder GT350 in the process.

The basic styling was actually quite similar to the old model as it happens, but the strong double cradle frame was different, playing host to a brand new three-cylinder two-stroke engine with air cooling. The cooling system employed on the kickstart GT380 was actually quite interesting, carrying the Ram Air moniker, and introduced to enhance the cooling of the centre cylinder. A final check had been carried out on a racing bike, with excellent results, so it had already been proved in competition before it was released to the public.

The engine itself was of all-alloy construction with cast iron sleeves inside. It had piston valves, and a 54mm x 54mm bore and stroke to give 371cc. Three VM24 carbs were employed, and combined with a 7.2:1 compression ratio, this gave a maximum power output of 38bhp at 7500rpm, along with 27.5lb/ft of torque at 6500rpm.

While the exhaust system looks similar to the GT750 setup from the outside, with four pipes exiting out the back, it was actually quite different in its construction in order to make the most of the engine's smaller displacement. Incidentally, the oil filler for the CCIS lubrication system was hidden under the flip-up saddle on this model, allowing a neater appearance.

The GT380 came with a six-speed gearbox, with carefully chosen ratios to suit the engine's characteristics. Tipping the scales at only 183kg (403lb), this endowed the bike with a top speed of around the ton (160kph), which was kept in check by drums at both ends paired up with 3.00-19 tyres at the front, and 3.50-18 rubber at the rear.

The GT380 had a quite different paint scheme to that of the GT350 – indeed, it was unique amongst the GTs for a while. Colours included Candy Bright Red, Bright Blue Metallic and Grace Lime Metallic initially, and the new triple quickly

The sports bike section of the domestic range catalogue from the spring of 1972, showing the multitude of changes applied to the GT line at this time. The GT350 was still listed, but only to help dealers clear existing stocks, while the GT250 is shown in GT250B guise, with disc braking. Likewise, the GT380 is a 260,000 yen GT380B, although this early list still carries the strict 245,000 yen GT380 with drum brakes, again simply to allow dealers to move the last of their stock that much easier.

Part of the brochure introducing the original GT380.

115

SUZUKI MOTORCYCLES: THE CLASSIC TWO-STROKE ERA

Suzuki had racers Ron Grant and Jody Nicholas ride the new model for publicity shots, both wearing matching helmets colour-keyed to their mounts in the first catalogue, although they are seen with their regular headgear in this March 1972 advert.

established itself as the top seller in its over 250cc but under 400cc category.

The GT380 didn't keep that designation for long, however, as disc brakes were adopted up front in early April 1972, giving birth to the GT380B. Honda had led the way for the mainstream bike manufacturers in adopting disc brake technology for its two-wheelers, and the undoubted safety benefits prompted Suzuki to follow suit on its newcomer. Everything else stayed the same, except for the pricing, which went up by 15,000 yen when disc brakes became the norm.

At the same time as the GT380B was being introduced, the GT500 became the GT550 (or GT550B to be perfectly correct, although the GT550 Disc moniker was used in catalogues, so this would also be correct, as would GT380 Disc), with front disc brakes fitted from the off on this model in Japan. The rear braking system, by the way – as per the GT380B – continued to use a foot-operated drum.

Like the GT380, the GT550B was a triple with Ram Air cooling, but with a 61mm x 62mm bore and stroke, the displacement went up to 543cc. This increase boosted the power output, with 50bhp at 6500rpm being quoted in the catalogues, along with 40lb/ft of torque 500rpm lower down the rev-range. At 215kg (473lb), the disc/drum braking system teamed up with beefier 3.25-19 and 4.00-18 rubber was more than adequate to keep the 335,000 yen machine under control.

Despite having a significantly longer wheelbase (85mm or 3.3in. greater, and only a fraction shy of the GT750's wheelbase measurement), styling-wise, it looked much like the GT380, but the 550cc model's engine filled out the frame more, with a larger Ram Air arrangement, a GT750-style exhaust system was adopted, and the side boxes were different, too. Another item to note was the electric starter, restricted to the two bigger triples (ie. the GT550 and GT750 grades).

Original bikes came with a choice of Candy Gold, Napoli Blue or Candy Yellow Green paintwork, each having a black stripe across the upper section and trailing edge of the fuel tank. These latter two shades were also listed in the States. But, surprise, surprise, there's confusion in the camp again, caused this time by a domestic GT550B-2 that numbers only around 300 units according to the parts books, and not available elsewhere. This means the export GT550K is in fact the equivalent to the GT550B-3 in Japan, and even then the stripes are different! Indeed, we have to wait until the B-4 and M-series before we get a true match. Anyway, the GT550B-2 had a similar stripe to the original 550cc model, but the black and white graphics were changed around, so that off-white became the dominant colour with a black coachline. This was matched with Candy Gold, Olive Green or Deep Blue Metallic paint.

A month after the GT380 Disc and GT550 Disc

THE SIZZLING SEVENTIES

Press shot of the GT380B, with a brake disc fitted on the offside front. A drum brake was retained at the back.

The rare GT550B-2 model, with a negative stripe. Like the 750cc model, there was a police version built for Japanese law enforcement duty.

The original GT550 Disc, or GT550B-1.

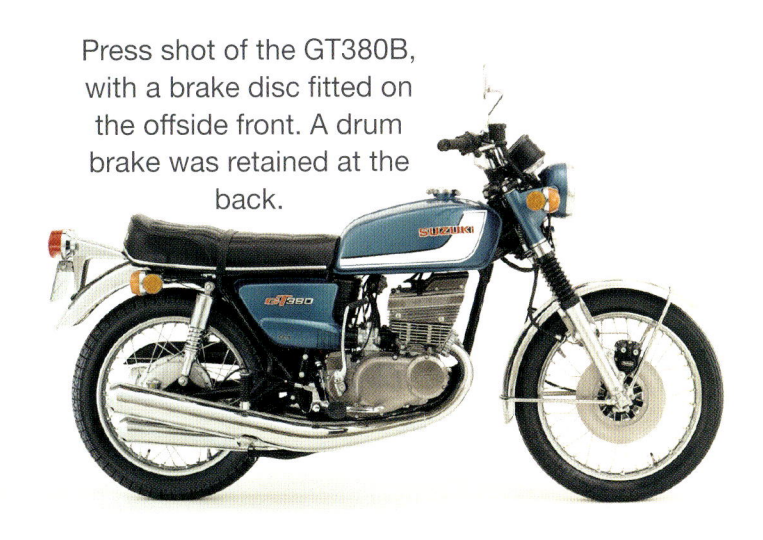

introductions, in May 1972 (the month in which the use of helmets became law in Japan on all roads for bikes with engines exceeding a 50cc limit), Suzuki announced a similar upgrade for the GT250 – disc brakes and different colouring and fuel tank graphics (like those of the GT550), along with the adoption of a Ram Air cooling system. While the power and torque outputs remained unchanged, as did the use of a six-speed transmission, this combination of revisions gave the bike a different impression altogether, even though the side boxes were the same as those found on its predecessor on this model.

In the meantime, other than the colours available, one would have been hard pushed to tell the difference between the original AC50-II and the one listed in 1972 and the early part of 1973 (and beyond in export markets, albeit with a simplified tank badge on the last of the breed). The TS90T and TS125T limped on virtually unchanged into the autumn of 1972, as a realignment of the Hustler range was in the wings, making these models redundant.

Notwithstanding, the Hustler 90, Hustler 125, Hustler 185 and Hustler 250 models were carried over into mid-1972 unchanged from their late-1971 counterparts, with only the Hustler 50 gaining some fresh paintwork, aping that of its American counterpart. It also bore a striking resemblance to the new TS400 model, as well as the TM pairing, albeit more arrow-shaped to follow the flat bottom of the fuel tank.

Within the TS400, TM400 and TM250 heavyweight group, the 40bhp TM400 was the oldest of the bunch, and the most expensive, listed at 250,000 yen (the TS400 was the cheapest, by the way, priced a couple of thousand yen less than the TM250). Announced in early 1971, this was a true motocross (MX) bike, that was for all intents and purposes a 500cc class works replica. Well, similar enough bearing in mind that it was priced for mere mortals rather than a factory competition budget.

In reality, the flagship of the TM-series is a little too

Brochure for the disc-braked GT250B-1, which sold for 212,000 yen, or put another way, 15,000 yen more than the strict GT250 with drums at both ends. Colours for this model included Bright Blue Metallic, Marble Scarlet and Grace Lime Metallic.

SUZUKI MOTORCYCLES: THE CLASSIC TWO-STROKE ERA

★単気筒400の味
TS400
標準現金価格233,000円
新発売
■最高出力34.0ps/6,000rpm ■最大トルク4.2kg-m/5,000rpm
■変速機5段リターン式 ■車両重量126kg(乾燥)

★世界のGPの栄光を君の腕で
TM250
標準現金価格235,000円
新発売
■最高出力31.0ps/7,300rpm ■最大トルク3.1kg-m/6,000rpm
■変速5段リターン式 ■車両重量102kg

★完璧なアドベンチャーモトクロッサー
TM400
標準現金価格250,000円
■最高出力40.0ps/6,500rpm ■最大トルク4.53kg-m/
■変速機5段リターン式 ■車両重量104.6kg(乾燥)

The big off-roaders as they looked in early 1972.

The original TS400 viewed from the opposite side to the brochure image. Like the GT380, a production-ready prototype of the TS400 had been on display at the 1971 Tokyo Show, giving punters a sneak preview well before the actual launch.

extreme to go crazy in these pages, as was the 31bhp TM250 launched alongside the TS400 on March 24, 1972. The TM250 used a tuned version of the Hustler 250 (TS250) unit, whereas the TS400 used a de-tuned version of the 396cc (82mm x 75mm) single used in the TM400. Except for the blacked-out alloy power-unit and exhaust profile, however, it was obvious that the TS400 belonged to the Hustler family, and indeed, other than the items mentioned, looked very much like the contemporary Hustler 250. With piston-port induction, a 6.7:1 compression ratio, a VM32 carb setup and breakerless electronic ignition (PEI in Suzuki speak), the 126kg (277lb) TS400 was good for 34bhp at 6000rpm, with drive taken through a five-speed transmission.

As for the so-called business bikes, some very minor changes were applied to the K-series models, although it took a dedicated follower of Suzuki lore to spot them, and things continued in a similar fashion until a thorough overhaul of the line, ultimately resulting in the loss of the famous chrome fuel tank. In the meantime, there were tiny detail changes

The K125-3 from 1972, with the 'Suzuki CCI' badge changed for a 'Suzuki 125' one, and the modified rear light bracket found on the contemporary K50 and K90 models. Like the other solo seat K-series bikes, changes were minimal after this (black plastic mirrors and engine emblems stand out as the most obvious things) until the traditional chrome fuel tank was finally dropped in the mid-1970s, although the 125cc model did gain leg guards as a standard fitting on the K125-4 variant.

THE SIZZLING SEVENTIES

here and there, but nothing to write home about beyond the K125 gaining leg guards in 1973.

The 1972 MY abroad

Looking at the first US brochures for the 1972 season bikes showed a basic similarity to the policy followed by Japan's marketing folks, which involved some fast mock-ups and an odd mix of new (as in pre-launch) and old machines on paper. Of course, it's never easy trying to cope with earlier introductions than those at home, season after season, to which the notoriously long lead times required by American magazines added further confusion (not to mention greater stress for the product planners), but there are times when it's as if we're looking at a parallel universe. Add in a type numbering system that's different to the one used in Japan, which doesn't use the useful model year code, but rather an almost endless variant indicator (and not found on the domestic catalogues, which are hardly ever dated anyway), plus a different frame number sequence on JDM versus export models, and even the author, with the benefit of being able to look back rather than try and see into the future, was forced into following each model's evolution on huge pieces of paper dotted with notes and small drawings of fuel tank designs from contemporary photos and parts books to pick the bones out of it all.

Anyway, there were a few things worth noting for the US 1972 season, including the loss of the T125, the TC120 (replaced by the TC125), and the F50. New models included the GT380, GT550, GT750, TS400, TM250 and RV90, although all the dual-purpose bikes received new fuel tank graphics that would ultimately be adopted in Japan, too, but not straight away – the TM400 was the first JDM model to adopt these stripes, followed by the Hustler 50, Hustler 400 and TM250.

Further to the notes made at the start of this section, naturally, one can be forgiven for thinking the first catalogue illustrations for the three GT models are not quite right, as the GT550J was not available until April 1972 in America, or

The K90 as it looked after a face-lift in early 1972. The updated K50 looked much the same, with both models gaining the side markers already fitted to the K125, new badging, a revised rear light assembly and a different luggage rack.

The water-cooled Suzuki GT750 featured on the cover of the American Bike & Rider magazine from March 1972.

French language version of the T350J brochure. The twins continued to be sold in several export markets, even though they had fallen by the wayside in the domestic line-up. The 'J' suffix indicates the 1972 MY. Only Suzuki could follow an 'R' with a 'J'!

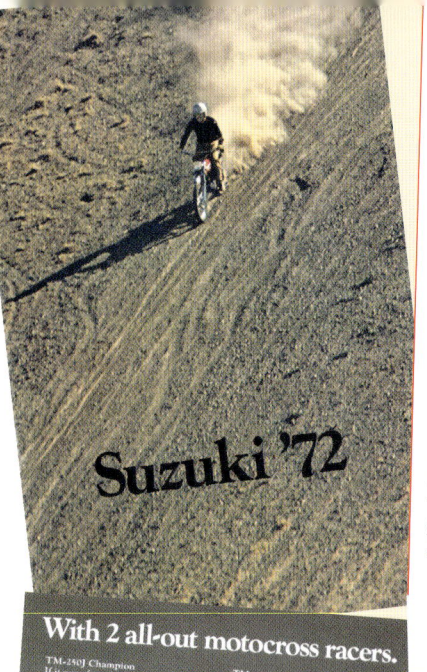

The 1972 season range brochure included in a number of US magazines.

THE SIZZLING SEVENTIES

Japan for that matter, but there, when it did hit the showrooms, it came with disc brakes from the off. So the author assumed that the bike in the early adverts was a prototype without discs, although consulting the parts book reveals that in fact the J-series export models were only ever fitted with drums, and that explains why it continued to be used in promotional material throughout the 1972 season; discs were duly introduced on the GT550K. The same is true of the GT380, with disc brakes coming with the start of the K-series, which is further proof that researchers cannot tie-up JDM and export model specifications as tidily as they would hope to. Sometimes America takes the lead, sometimes it's Japan …

The trials scene: 1970-1974

The winner and runner-up in the 1969 FIM World Motocross Championship, Joël Robert and Sylvain Geboers, were signed by Masazumi Ishikawa (Suzuki's team manager) for the 1970 season, the pair duly joining Olle Pettersson to create an all-star line-up. They were given the RH70, with improved low- and mid-range torque from the 246cc (70mm x 64mm) unit, as well as another round of weight reduction measures that took the bike's weight down to 80kg (176lb). Both newcomers were said to be very pleased with their new 32bhp five-speed mounts in early testing.

The faith shown in the RH70 was justified after Suzuki was deemed to have won the 1970 championship title by the eighth of 12 rounds. Robert won four races to take the 250cc riders' title, the Belgian having done so in 1964, 1968 and 1969 with CZ bikes. Robert, having scored 96, was followed home by Geboers on 94, and CZ rider Roger de Coster, who was stuck in the mid-70s; Pettersson was seventh on 42.

Suzuki also introduced the 367cc (80mm x 73mm) RN70 at this time, with 39bhp on tap and a four-speed gearbox, to compete in the 500cc class. This machine was on display at the 1970 Tokyo Show, and was priced at 250,000 yen in early 1971. There was a TM125 motocross machine announced in the autumn, too, with an alloy fuel tank and other weight-saving items. Its rotary-valve engine gave 20bhp at 9000rpm, although the FIM did not have a world level 125cc class, so Ishikawa concentrated on the 250cc and 500cc categories – the campaign in the bigger class being helped no end by the signing of Roger de Coster, who joined Robert, Geboers and Pettersson in the Suzuki works team.

Although De Coster had not had an amazing 500cc season in 1970, he won five of the 12 rounds for Suzuki in

An English language catalogue for the 1972 twin-cylinder T500J.

Italian advert for the 1972 T500. The SAIAD promotional pieces were always 'glam' in the extreme.

Launch advertising for the GT380 from the spring of 1972, when the bike was put on the UK market at almost exactly £500. This compares to £766 for the first of the GT750s, which was roughly the same as what was being asked for a Honda CB750 Four or a Kawasaki H2.

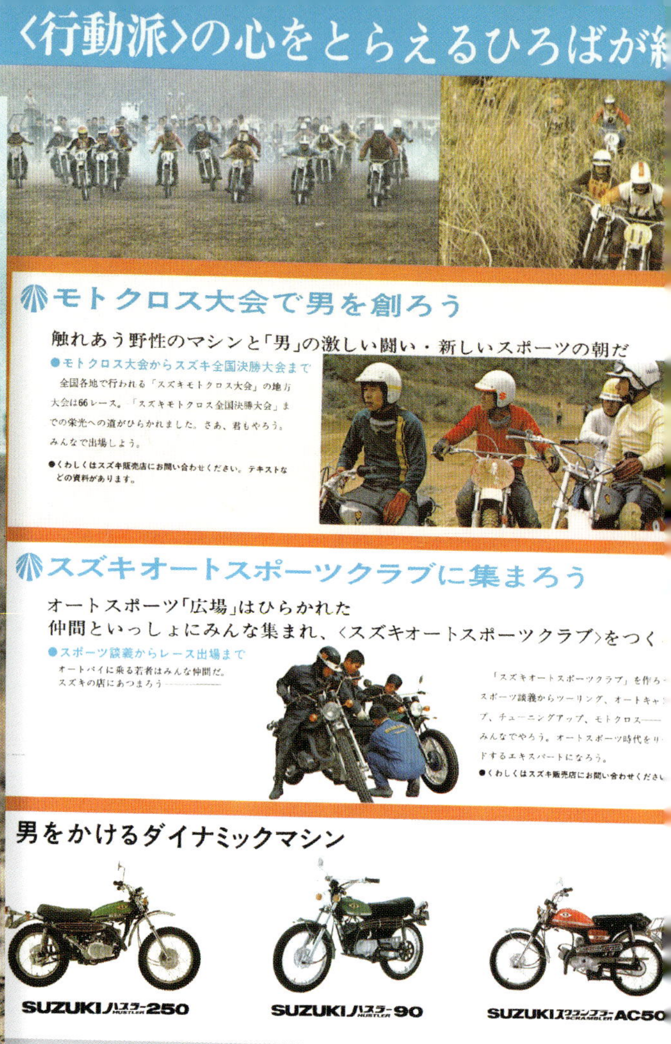

SUZUKI MOTORCYCLES: THE CLASSIC TWO-STROKE ERA

A newspaper sheet produced for the 1970 motocross season. Suzuki's commitment to the sport was obvious, going well beyond the simple sale of bikes, including a 75-round Suzuki-only championship. Note the tuning kits in the bottom right-hand corner.

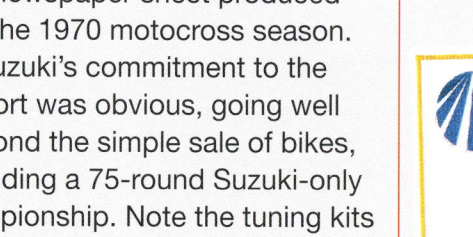

The all-important back page of the newspaper sheet, showing (top to bottom) Geboers, Robert and Pettersson having signed for Suzuki's 1970 campaign, along with a picture of the RH70.

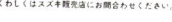

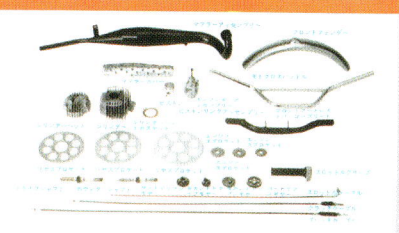

THE SIZZLING SEVENTIES

As well as a seemingly endless advertising campaign for the Hustler 250 in 1970, Suzuki also released this motocross-related piece showing the various Auto Land facilities owned by Suzuki to allow scrambler owners to enjoy their machines in a controlled environment.

1971, securing the 500cc crown for himself and his new masters, beating Maico and CZ to the title. Meanwhile, with no less than eight victories, Joël Robert retained his 250cc motocross title with ease, followed home by Geboers in third and Pettersson in fifth (the Suzuki runners were split by Husqvarna riders).

Yamaha had been doing well in the domestic scrambling scene, and joined the world championship in 1972, pushing the Hamamatsu rivalry to a whole new level, with Pettersson going to Kawasaki. De Coster dominated the 500cc class once

123

Making the most of the company's success in 1971, this panel took up an entire page in a road bike range brochure. Robert is on the left, with De Coster on the right.

Advertising celebrating Suzuki capturing the 1971 world motocross title.

A dealer advert from the summer of 1972 showing some of the goodies available for MX enthusiasts.

Suzuki's victorious bikes from 1972.

more, with Robert able to claim the 250cc category again as well, although Yamaha had certainly made it a much harder fight than the points in the final standings suggest. Geboers was third, incidently, but the 250cc class now had strong rivals in the shape of Montesa, CZ and Husqvarna, as well as the threat from Yamaha and Kawasaki.

To try and rein in Suzuki, with its vast budget making it difficult for the smaller concerns to compete on an equal footing, the FIM made a late rule change on minimum weights for 1973, perhaps reminding fans of the way the FIM tried to nobble Honda in the 1960s. Notwithstanding, De Coster scored his Suzuki hat-trick in 1973, narrowly beating Willy Bauer (Maico) in the 500cc title chase, although the Japanese maker had to settle for an also-ran position in the 250cc category, which now had KTM and Bultaco also vying for honours.

While Suzuki's management was still sulking about the FIM's antics in 1973, Gerrit Wolsink (a privately-entered Suzuki competitor from Holland) was signed as a works rider for 1974, lining up alongside De Coster to try and allow Suzuki to hold on to the 500cc title. Although the Suzuki lads did well towards the end of the season, the Belgian rider

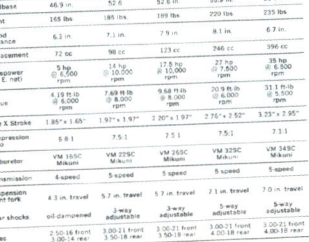

A four-page advert released in America at the end of 1973, with a fifth one added to rub salt into the wounds of competitors.

1973 season news

The big news for enthusiasts was the adoption of disc brakes on the GT750, and not just single discs as per the other GTs, but doubled up. This modification, which coincided with the use of a stronger frame and revised fuel tank graphics, was announced on October 21, 1972, in time for the 1973 season, and gave birth to the 395,000 yen GT750B, or GT750B-1 as it would become known in retrospect (an important point to remember as the story unfolds). All the other leading specifications were carried over from the original 'Water Buffalo,' however, so the engineering team was obviously pleased with the bike.

The launch timing could have been better from Suzuki's point of view, though, as Japan's Ministry of the Environment brought in stricter rules on emissions in December 1972, aping those of the Muskie Act in the States. It was a death knell for large two-stroke machines, or at the very least, a heavy flesh wound that would have to be tended to.

The company was also suffering from lower profit generation in America. For many years, the exchange rate between USD

was ultimately second to Heikki Mikkola's Husqvarna in 1974, with the Dutchman fourth. Sadly, Suzuki was still out in the wilderness in the 250cc class, Gaston Rahier being the marque's top finisher in a distant fifth, having won one of the 11 rounds; Goboers won one, too, but that was all there was to celebrate that year.

125

and JPY currency was fixed at 360 yen/$1, although President Richard Nixon abandoned the Bretton Woods System in 1971, and eventually a floating exchange rate system was introduced, changing everything. By the spring of 1973, the rate was around 260 yen per dollar, and although it slowly went in Japan's favour for a while after this, it hardly ever went above the 300 mark again. After the oil crisis and Nixon debacle, inflation followed in the States, combining with a severe fall in the value of the yen to make life even harder for Japanese exporters.

This double whammy helps explain why year after year of full model changes, that must have cost a small fortune to implement, most of what happened on the two-stroke front from now on was restricted to minor changes – often cosmetics and nothing more.

Meanwhile, the spring of 1973 saw the Free 50 become the FR50 (Birdie 50), readily identified by the modified styling underneath the saddle, which ran virtually unchanged into the 1990s. Sure, there were lighting revisions (with square light units being introduced later on), fresh graphics and so on, but the basic model was very much the same. Even the engine remained familiar, although later examples came with 4.2bhp instead of 4.5bhp, while the usual options – standard grade, deluxe and self-starter variants – were also continued.

At the same time, the Free 70 became the FR70 (Birdie 70), following the lead of the 50cc model. Again, the changes were minimal, with the 6.2bhp

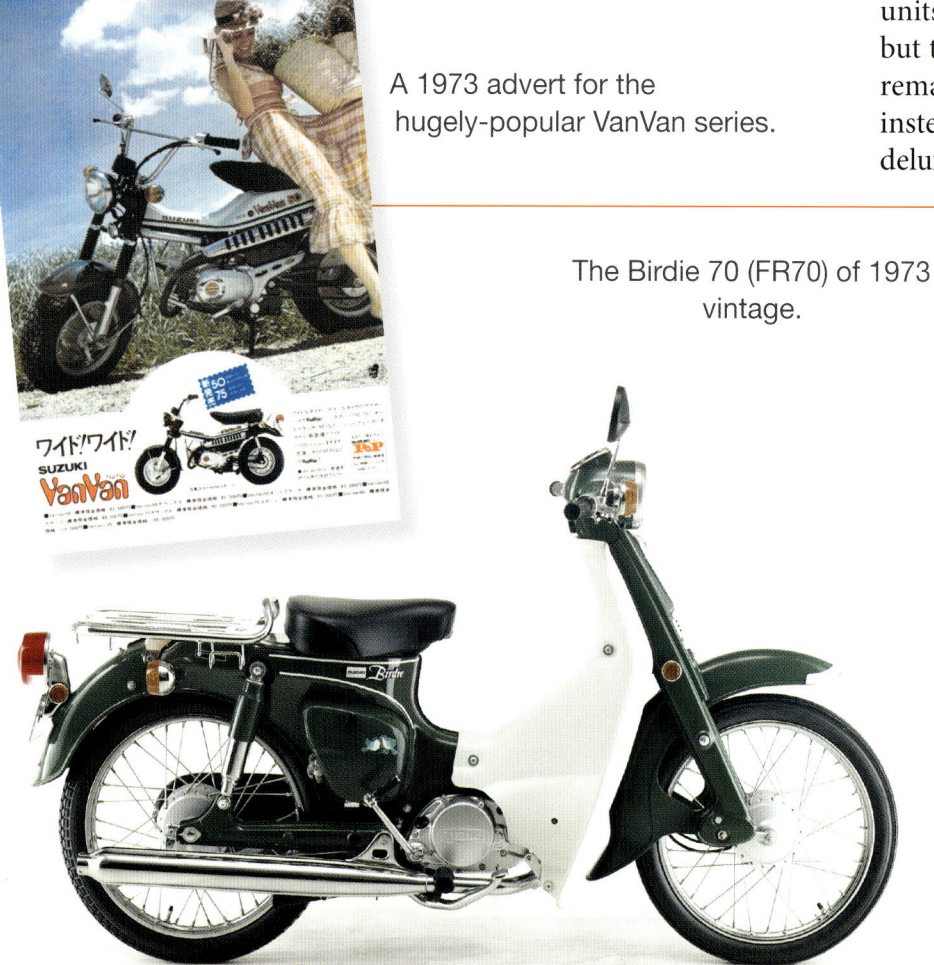

Japanese advert announcing the arrival of the GT750B.

Spec sheet for the GT750B, showing a weight increase of 17kg (37lb) compared to the strict GT750.

A 1973 advert for the hugely-popular VanVan series.

The Birdie 70 (FR70) of 1973 vintage.

Japanese advertising from the spring of 1973 showing the Hustler 250 (TS250-5) in the kind of environment in which it thrived.

THE SIZZLING SEVENTIES

69cc engine carried over. One will remember that the Birdie name had been used by Tohatsu in the past, but the company was no longer there to complain, of course ...

For the record, the Free 90 continued pretty much as before, keeping its name and F90 designation, although engine power was reduced from 7.5bhp to seven dead, despite the leading specs of the 88cc unit being unchanged. This 97,000 yen model (or 104,000 yen when equipped with a self-starter), disappeared from the catalogues before 1974 came to an end, however.

Other than this, the dropping of the TS185 and TM400, expansion of the VanVan line via new 50, 75 and 125 grades, the launch of the TS90MX and TM125, and the GT750 changes noted earlier in this section, the price list looked much the same going into the summer of 1973 as it had at the end of 1972.

That's not to say that the bikes looked the same, of course, with the introduction of the short-lived GT550B-2 in mid-1973, and a fresh tank design on the GT380 to give birth to the GT380B-2. While the GT250 was carried over, the Hustler 50 had gone through two more face-lifts (the TS50-2 had been similar to the 1972 US model, with the TS50-3 sporting a tank stripe pointing the other way, again following export market practice, while the 83,000 yen TS50-4 of spring 1973 was a preview of the 1974 season bike for the States) during this time. With lines moving as quickly as this, it's a perfect example of why there's so much confusion when one tries to follow changes on an annual basis.

The Hustler 90 had also gone through a series of cosmetic upgrades, having reached the TS90-4 stage by mid-1973, with stripes similar to the majority of 1973 MY export dual-purpose models, and the TS50-3 for that matter. By this time, the front mudguard had been raised, giving the 105,000 yen machine a more purposeful look, but otherwise the 10bhp tiddler was similar to its predecessors in terms of general styling.

The Hustler 125 had also been given a new stripe for the 1973 season, but it was changed almost immediately to one matching the contemporary TS90, as was the Hustler 250 and Hustler 400. Actually, the 1973 upgrade on the 250cc model was rather more far-reaching than a flashy decal, for the TS250-5 (there was no fourth variant for some reason) adopted an alloy front suspension and five-step rear-end, while the old-style thin headlight was dropped for a regular item.

The 1973 Hustler 400 (TS400-2), which was frankly a little 'too much' for novice riders. Tellingly, the power was dropped a fraction on US-bound bikes for the following season, and in Japan, too, a couple of years after that.

The GA50 was announced in July 1973.

Jitsujiro Suzuki was named as Suzuki's new President in May 1973.

127

SUZUKI MOTORCYCLES: THE CLASSIC TWO-STROKE ERA

The domestic Suzuki GT-series line-up as it looked in the summer of 1973, with the GA50-1, the GT250B-1, the GT380B-2, the GT550B-2, and GT750B-1.

While the TM400 was dropped from the regular catalogue in the spring of 1973, the TM250 was given a new tank stripe for the 1973 season, and joined in January that year by two fresh models of a similar nature – the Suzuki TS90MX, and the TM125.

Both of these newcomers were aimed squarely at competition types, lacking the equipment it takes to make them road legal, so we needn't say more than the TS90MX was powered by a single-cylinder unit borrowed from the Hustler 90, but tuned to give a far greater 16bhp output, while the TM125 engine was basically the TS125 unit, namely a 123cc (56mm x 50mm) single, but again supplied in a higher state of tune. Indeed, the TM125 was quoted as having 22bhp on tap, against just 13 horses for the Hustler.

There was actually another newcomer of note during this period, for on May 28, 1973, Jitsujiro Suzuki took over as President of the company, having been an executive for many years. Shunzo Suzuki (now named as Chairman) had left things in superb order, but bold plans were cited by the new man at the helm, including an epoch-making engine and a push in fresh areas of activity, such as a marine business (both two-stroke engines and boat hulls – not a bad idea when one sees how much water there is in the area surrounding the factory, as Suzuki was bound to attract local support, as Yamaha did), leisure machines like snowmobiles and jetskis, cycles, welfare equipment (Suzuki would later claim the number one spot in market share in the latter field), and even prefab housing.

Japanese advertising for the GA50, with the TM75 competition bike trying to muscle in on the act on the right-hand side. The TS90MX looked very similar to the TM75, so the TS designation seems a little out of place …

THE SIZZLING SEVENTIES

Jitsujiro Suzuki was also quite keen to revive the old company spirit through the formation of quality control (QC) circles, and at the same time, save energy and reduce costs – a lost wax casting process was one of the first cost-cutting introductions on the new man's watch. History tells us that his term wasn't particularly successful, however, with many ideas just too far ahead of their time, or scuppered by world events out of his control. At least there were leaps in Suzuki's technology that wouldn't have been possible under the steady but more conservative leadership of Shunzo Suzuki …

Anyway, Jitsujiro had hardly had a chance to warm his seat when the TM-series was expanded via a TM75 model, and the 89,000 yen GA50 was announced. Whilst the power-unit was exactly the same as the Hustler 50 engine, this was a far more sporting bike than the old AC50, with the front downtube being a good indicator of its purposeful nature, and was actually classed as part of the GT-series as such. This five-speed machine, with drum brakes at both ends, weighed in at just 82kg (180lb), so it was remarkably sprightly. It ran on 2.25-17 tyres up front, and 2.50-17 rubber at the rear.

Export markets for 1973

The 1973 Model Year was given the 'K' designation, so most of the export markets used a combination of the model code and a K suffix for identification. As such, the Americans had the GT185K, GT250K, GT380K, GT550K, GT750K, TC100K, TC125K, TS50K, TS100K, TS125K, TS185K, TS250K, TS400K, TM125K, TM250K and TM400K for the 1973 season, along with the T500K oldtimer, and MT50K, RV90K and RV125K playthings …

While Japan kept the Hustler 90 in its catalogue, the TS100 had replaced the TS90 in the States, keeping the 'Honcho' name, but adding a 97cc 11bhp engine into the equation. At the same time, the TC90 became the TC100 through the same power-unit swap, US buyers lost the old T250 and T350 grades, but gained a new GT185 'Adventurer' and GT250 'Hustler' to take their place. The smaller TM125 'Challenger' was another useful addition to the range, filling a gap in the smaller capacity line-up.

For the record, the GT250, GT380, GT550 and GT750 all came with disc brakes, while drums were the norm on all the other models. In addition, we should note here that the Canadian line-up was the same as that for the USA, but this was to be the last year when things tied-up so easily, for Suzuki Canada (a direct sales subsidiary) was formed in June 1973, meaning there were subtle differences in the line-up fielded by the two countries for the coming season.

Interestingly, in Europe, Suzuki had displayed a GT125 prototype at the 1972 Paris Salon, although it would be quite some time before a production model was made available. The GT250 was sold in Europe as a K-series model, however, with disc braking and the Ram Air cooling system, as was the GT185, which had the Ram Air head, but drum brakes at both ends.

The GT550B export model for 1973, being built at the Toyokawa factory, and then photographed in the studio. This tank decoration was never used in Japan.

Choice of Champions is King of the seventies for groovy guys.

Happiness is yours today with SUZUKI

The majority of an extremely useful 1973 MY (K-series) catalogue produced for export markets in general, rather than a specific country. Some models, such as the A-series and B120, were not sold in Japan or America, but were still available in a number of markets; the T500 was sold in the States, however, with this paintwork design, too, for the 1973 season. In addition, bikes like the GT185 had yet to find their way to Japanese dealerships, while the tanks on the GT250 and GT550 are different to the JDM versions, instead following the US-style pattern.

FUNSTERS — RV125, RV90, RV50, MT50

BUSINESS — B120, K125-II, K50, F50/70

SUZUKI: BUILT TO TAKE ON THE COUNTRY

MOTOCROSS & TRAILS

TS400 · TS250 · TS185 · TS125 · TS100 · TS50 · TC125 · TC100 · TM400 · TM250 · TM125

TOURING

GT750 · GT550 · GT380 · GT250 · GT185 · T500

SPORT

A100 · A80 · AC50 · A50-II

A European GT750K finished in Candy Gold, which had dark accents on the fuel tank. The Americans (and Canadians) had a real oddity in their line-up, with the red bike having an orange arrow design; the blue one was the same as the JDM version.

The unusual paintwork on the red GT750Ks shipped to the US, seen here on the cover of the long-running *Cycle World* magazine.

The GT250K, now with disc braking.

American advert from March 1973 for the TS185K.

An Italian advert for the GT380K that's interesting for a number of reasons. Italy actually had a unique 384cc GT380, the extra 13cc being achieved via a 55mm bore, in order to sell the bike in accordance with local regulations. As for the lady, nudes were appearing just about everywhere at the time, even gracing Motor Show exhibits. Most of those pushing the PC movement had yet to be born!

GT750 colour schemes

This serves not only as guide to the correct colours for each season, but also a handy reference for which export models tie-up with the domestic versions of this iconic bike. As usual, none of the numbers issued in Japan have any direct or useful meaning in other markets, and the "B-1 equals 1971, B-3 equals 1973" theory is certainly not correct, at least not throughout the entire run.

GT750 (strict), from September 1971: For Japan, Candy Bright Red (157), Candy Jackal Blue (195), Candy Yellow Ochre (253); tank graphics in black (019) and pure white (064), plus a black seat (403). America's 1972 MY J-series bikes had the same graphics, with Candy Jackal Blue and Candy Lavender as the paint options. Candy Yellow Ochre was listed as an alternative in certain European markets.

GT750B (or B-1), from October 1972: For Japan, Candy Yellow Green (289), Pearl Blue (707) and Pearl Red (708). There was a short-lived B-2 variant, with Flake Bright Red (745) replacing Pearl Red, and a dedicated stripe closer to the B-3 version but light in colour (the late 1973 B-2 is a real oddity, as the number is skipped in most of Suzuki's official paperwork). America's 1973 MY K-series bikes had the same basic graphics as the B-1 in the case of the Pearl Blue machine, although the US Pearl Red paint option (there were only two listed for the States) had a unique arrow-shaped stripe. Candy Gold was listed as an alternative in certain European markets.

GT750B-3, from January 1974: For Japan, Olive Green Metallic (738), Flake Blue (761), Flake Orange (762), and Deep Moss Green Metallic (782). America's 1974 MY L-series bikes had the same graphics, with Flake Blue and Flake Orange as the paint options. Other colours were available in European markets.

GT750B-4, from October 1974: For Japan, Olive Green Metallic (738), Flake Orange (762), and Jewel Grey Metallic (00A). America's 1975 MY M-series bikes had the same graphics, with Candy Gypsy Red and Jewel Grey Metallic as the paint options. Other colours were available in European markets.

GT750B-5, from May 1975: For Japan, Olive Green Metallic (738), Jewel Grey Metallic (00A), and Flake Orange 2 (01A). Please note, however, that while the grey hue is listed in the parts book, all the relevant Japanese catalogues show the green and orange shades only. America's 1976 MY A-series bikes had the same graphics, with Coronado Blue and Ontario Orange as the paint options; these changed to Gloss Black and Rosed Red Metallic for the 1977 MY B-series models, and came with a subtly modified coachline. Other colours were available in European markets.

Tough times ahead

Suzuki displayed a prototype of the RX5, a rotary-engined bike, at the 1973 Tokyo Show. This was an interesting development, leading on from Suzuki signing an agreement with NSU for rights to the Wankel RE unit at the end of November 1970. A proper RE team was put together soon after, leading to the first mock-ups being tested in summer of 1971. Hopes at this stage were to launch the bike in spring 1973, but there's no doubt that mastering the rotary, for all its charm and simplicity, is no easy matter, especially when Toyo Kogyo (known more commonly as Mazda) had patented so many aspects of the RE during its own lengthy development phase.

The rotary Suzuki – doubtless the epoch-making piece of engineering Jitsujiro Suzuki had hinted at during his induction speech – would ultimately make it into production, but the timing was off. Not only had the West German Hercules

Japanese advertising introducing the GT125.

SUZUKI MOTORCYCLES: THE CLASSIC TWO-STROKE ERA

The GT185, released on the domestic market at the start of 1974. The GT185 was unusual in that it had an electric starter – something generally reserved for the GT550 and GT750 grades at this time. Like the GT125, there were no gaiters on the front forks, giving the bike a particularly modern look.

The GT250B-2, also from the opening weeks of 1974.

W2000, powered by a Sachs RE, beaten Suzuki to the showrooms as the first rotary-engined bike, the company was being hit from all angles – the threat of emissions regulations hanging like an axe over certain model lines (this led to Suzuki forming a four-stroke development team in January 1974), falling profits from changes in exchange rates, and then, to cap it all, a major oil crisis following OPEC's decision to place an oil embargo on countries seen to be supporting Israel during the Yom Kippur War.

For a country like Japan, with few natural resources, this proved a real burden for manufacturers, so in order to store petrol stocks, the company set up the Suzuki Sekiyu oil concern. Materials started running low, so they were bought from anywhere possible, and what could be bought was generally more expensive, with the cost of aluminium up by 45 per cent, for instance, leaving no choice but to increase prices. There was a tyre shortage, leading the company to sell cars without a spare, and a quick reaction was needed to develop more economical machines – at a time, remember, when Suzuki was committed to a heavyweight rotary-engined cruiser. By the end of 1973, the cost of oil was 60 per cent up on the start of the year, which naturally hurt sales all round, and then an economic downturn in the aftermath of the fuel crisis only added to Suzuki's woes.

Still, the management and marketing teams fought on, and while there was an ultra-rare GT750B-2 released at the end of 1973, January 1974 saw the announcement of a uniform overhaul of the domestic GT series, including two new grades in the shape of the GT125 and GT185 to close the gap between the unchanged GA50 and the existing 250cc machine, and a number of largely cosmetic revisions for the GT250, GT380, GT550 and GT750 models.

While the GA50 was obviously a lightweight, the GT125 looked every bit a GT model. Listed with 16bhp at a heady 9500rpm, thanks to a 6.8:1 c/r and a pair of Mikuni VM18 carburettors for the piston-port induction system, it revived the old 125cc Wolf twin bore and stroke dimensions (43mm x 43mm), but the all-alloy engine looked completely different to its noble predecessor, with a toned-down version of the Ram Air system. This stylish five-speed machine was equipped with disc brakes up front, and 2.75-18 and 3.00-18 tyres. The 185,000 yen GT125 was a good way of expanding the domestic

The GT380B-3 launched at the beginning of 1974 at 300,000 yen. The GT550B-3 tank stripe was not the same, but it wasn't dissimilar. One can see the variations at the bottom of the contemporary GT125 advert, or the top of the GT750 one. The GT550 was priced at 85,000 yen more than the GT380, by the way.

THE SIZZLING SEVENTIES

The flagship 750cc model in GT750B-3 guise, from early 1974. It was priced at 438,000 yen by this time, and had lost the auxiliary cooling fan fitted to the earliest of the breed.

The Hustler 90 in TS90-5 guise.

range at limited cost, as was the other newcomer, but to an even greater extent with the 185cc model.

The 210,000 yen GT185 was also endowed with a unique powerplant as far as the JDM was concerned, although the model had been sold abroad in the previous season, albeit with drum brakes at both ends. By adding disc brakes at the front (as adopted on the export 1974 MY GT185L) and the obligatory fresh paintwork, of course, Suzuki now had a full line of GTs at a reasonable cost. The styling was very similar to the GT125, with the same cradle frame with the front downtube split low down, but a 184cc (49mm x 49mm) vertical twin was used as the source of motive power. With VM20 carbs and a 7.3:1 compression ratio, the Ram Air unit developed 21bhp at 7500rpm, along with 15lb/ft of torque. The tyres were the same as those specified for the smaller GT, and tipping the scales at just 129kg (284lb), this five-speed bike was capable of around 80mph (128kph).

Japanese advertising announcing the GT750B-3.

The 1974 Hustler 400 with TS400-3 colouring that eventually matched that of the other contemporary Hustler models – it seems like the TS400 was always a step behind the smaller Hustlers as far as the home market is concerned. Close inspection reveals a new frame and a fresh mudguard at the back, along with the adoption of a larger wheel shod with a 3.00-21 tyre up front.

The rather extreme but roadworthy 1974 RL250 trials machine. It was 20kg (44lb) lighter than the equivalent Hustler.

The 258,000 yen GT250B-2 was the same as the original GT250B save for a new paint job, although a gear indicator was added on the three triples, helping to justify their new designations (GT380B-3, GT550B-3 and GT750B-3) a little easier, as power and torque outputs remained similar to those quoted before. One feature the triples lost at this time was their front fork gaiters, bringing them into line with the two newcomers (this left only the GT250 with rubber boots, plus the GA50 if you want to include that as part of the GT series).

The Hustler range received some attention at the same time as the GTs were updated. While the TS50 continued unchanged, the TS90 became the TS90-5 thanks to some fresh colouring and a new rear mudguard. The same upgrades (including similar graphics) were applied to the TS125, giving birth to the TS125-4, and indeed, the TS250 as well. The Hustler 250 carried the TS250-6 designation after this face-lift, which put the majority of the Hustler line-up in touch with the 1974 export models. The remaining model, the TS400, was brought into line soon after, gaining new graphics and the TS400-3 designation along the way. Interestingly, during this face-lift phase, the 125cc, 250cc and 400cc models also gained a larger front wheel and tyre combination, making their appearance quite different from a number of angles, not just cosmetics.

While the TM line was treated to a new stripe or two, there was another deadly serious competition machine put on sale from April 1, 1974 – the 295,000 yen RL250 trials bike, with an RL250L version that was 15,000 yen cheaper but lacking road equipment in much the same way as the TM-series models did. This bike had actually been waiting in the wings for some time, as press previews had taken place in the previous year, but it was a fascinating addition to the catalogue, powered by a de-tuned, 17bhp version of the Hustler 250 lump.

The 1974 season abroad

Naturally, America continued to provide Suzuki with its biggest export market, with the 1974 models sent across the Pacific being given an 'L' suffix. Starting with the GT line-up, the GT185L looked a lot like the Japanese model introduced at the start of 1974. Indeed, the GT250L, GT380L and GT750L all followed a similar pattern, although the GT550L graphics were very slightly different, missing the upper tail found in the Japanese design, presumably to add a little distance from the 550cc model fielded abroad in the year before. There was no GA50 in the States, of course, or a GT125 for that matter, but the T500 continued, this year with a similar but heavier tank stripe that dropped further down at the front.

The dual-purpose models were also much the same as their counterparts in Japanese dealerships, with the TS50L, TS100L, TS125L, TS185L, TS250L and TS400L making up the range. Granted, the Hustler 185 had long since gone in the Land of the Rising Sun, and they

Super advert from Suzuki's American arm at the start of the 1974 season.

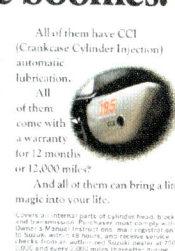

A four-page advert included in the February 1974 issue of America's *Cycle World*. The off-roaders basically looked similar to their JDM counterparts, although it took a while for the TS400 to catch up on its Stateside cousin. Note the larger front wheels used for the four bigger-displacement models compared to those employed in previous seasons.

had a TS90 (Hustler 90) rather than a TS100, but the similarities were there. One feels that Suzuki was finally starting to realise that standardisation can save a fortune!

The RL250 'Exacta' was added to the US range in due course as an excellent alternative to the Bultaco, along with an export only TM100 from April 1974, and joining the new TM75, the TM125, TM250 and TM400 MX machines. Looking through old magazines, it was obvious that Suzuki had cut its advertising budget quite dramatically, and the TC100, TC125 and the new TC185 appeared only once in the year as far as the author can make out, as did the RV90 and RV125 that rounded things off for Suzuki's American branch in the 1974 season.

Other markets still had their oddities, like the B120 and so on, and there was also a TS75 introduced during the year for certain European distributors, including the one in the UK. Perhaps the most interesting local variants came via SAIAD in Italy, however, continuing the Vallelunga and other exotic S and TT grades that appealed to those of a sporting bent …

Another two-pager from the same period; this piece showing the TC-series machines.

137

The US sports bike line-up for the 1974 season.

Italian advertising from early 1974. Most of the colouring was out-of-date in most markets, with only the GT380 being truly current. It's fascinating, though, to see the T500TT with drop handlebars and a racing seat, the GT550S with a locally-fitted solo sports saddle (plus a GT750S with similar treatment), and the Vallelunga – SAIAD's GT750-based creation with race-style bodywork and an engine tuned to pump out 81bhp.

US advert for the RV90 and RV125, a model line sold under the VanVan name in Japan.

Fabulous publicity material for the GT750L. Some foreign paperwork was quoting a slight reduction in power, from 67bhp to 65 for the flagship triple, although it remained at 67bhp back home. It could just be the conversion from Japanese PS to DIN or US SAE figures, of course, as this happens a lot in the car world.

THE SIZZLING SEVENTIES

Early 1970s production

For ease of reference, the numbers are broken down into bikes with an engine capacity of up to 50cc, 51-125cc, 126-250cc, and 251cc and over. At this time, all would have been two-stroke machines.

Year	Up to 50cc	51cc to 125cc	126cc to 250cc	251cc +	Total
1970	161,471	198,617	35,389	21,015	416,492
1971	151,389	235,301	82,711	72,655	542,056
1972	180,383	250,350	78,539	89,891	599,163
1973	187,902	321,413	92,309	53,539	655,163
1974	190,563	445,467	129,358	96,254	861,642

There was a sharp rise in the percentage of exports versus production at this time, with foreign sales (224,295 units) accounting for over half of production in 1970 – the first time this important figure had nudged past even the one-third mark, as domestic sales had always swallowed up the vast majority of bikes built. The trend duly continued, so that by 1974, no less than 609,557 of the 861,642 machines produced (around 70 per cent of them) found new homes abroad.

Incidentally, Suzuki nearly managed to reclaim the number two spot from Yamaha in 1974, but the gap would widen again, with Yamaha having an amazing year in 1977, almost catching up with Honda in the process.

Road bike evolution

The Suzuki motorcycle range is complex, and often confusing. This simplified table, following the evolution of each two-stroke model covered in this chapter, should hopefully allow things to become a lot clearer.

Model	1970	1971	1972	1973	1974	1975
Hustler 50 (50cc single)		TS50				
Scrambler AC50 (50cc single)	AC50					
Suzuki GA50 (50cc single)					GA50	
Suzuki K50 (50cc single)	K50G	K50				
Suzuki K90 (86cc single)	K90					
Hustler 90 (89cc single)	TS90					
Suzuki TS90T (89cc single)		TS90T				
Wolf T90 (89cc twin)	T90					
Suzuki TC120 (118cc single)	TC120					
Hustler 125 (123cc single)		TS125				

SUZUKI MOTORCYCLES: THE CLASSIC TWO-STROKE ERA

Model	1970	1971	1972	1973	1974	1975
Suzuki K125 (123cc single)	K125	K125	K125	K125	K125	K125
Suzuki TS125T (123cc single)		TS125T	TS125T	TS125T		
Suzuki GT125 (125cc twin)					GT125	GT125
Wolf T125 (125cc twin)	T125	T125				
Hustler 185 (183cc single)		TS185	TS185	TS185		
Suzuki GT185 (184cc twin)					GT185	GT185
Hustler 250 (246cc single)	TS250	TS250	TS250	TS250	TS250	TS250
Suzuki RL250 (246cc single)					RL250	RL250
Suzuki T250 (247cc twin)	T250	GT250	GT250B	GT250B	GT250B	GT250B
Suzuki T350 (315cc twin)	T350	GT350	GT350			
Suzuki GT380 (371cc triple)				GT380/B	GT380/B	GT380/B
Hustler TS400 (396cc single)				TS400	TS400	TS400
Suzuki T500 (492cc twin)	T500	GT500	GT500			
Suzuki GT550 (543cc triple)			GT550B	GT550B	GT550B	GT550B
Suzuki GT750 (738cc triple)			GT750	GT750B	GT750B	GT750B

Note: Four-stroke models, pure mopeds, playthings and bikes made specifically for export are not included in this table, although they are all covered within the text. Likewise, the TM-series, TS90MX and RH250 are too specialised as pure off-roaders, so they appear in the text only; the RL250 scrapes in due to the provision of road equipment.

6 End Of An Era

There was so much activity in the closing weeks of 1974, that it makes more sense to pick up the story afresh, treating this chapter as a 1975 season rather than beginning it on January 1 as we have, more or less, earlier on in the book. It will also help with spacing, as otherwise this section could be very short indeed compared with the last one, as the end was in sight for our beloved two-stroke machines, at least when looking at things from a 'classic' standpoint. Indeed, while two-stroke motorcycles continued in numerous shapes and forms, in reality, the 'classic' era more or less finishes as soon as the GS-series arrives …

1975 season changes

Probably the biggest news for the 1975 season was the release of the rotary-engined RE-5, although the model was built for export only, and was ultimately an unfortunate victim of the times – financial woes, stronger emission codes, and so on. This technical tour de force sadly only lasted a couple of years before being dropped. It should be noted that Yamaha had also had a go at creating a rotary bike, but gave up on the idea in the development stages.

In the meantime, there was a dramatic overhaul of the GT and Hustler ranges announced in October 1974 that saw almost all of the two main domestic lines given a face-lift. The few models that did escape revision this time around were generally updated in the spring of 1975 anyway, so it was a busy period for the chaps in Hamamatsu.

Starting with the GTs, it was the flagship model that received the bulk of attention. As well as the obligatory colour and graphics change, the engine and transmission was given a number of subtle revisions, not only to provide the bike with better cruising speeds, but also improve fuel consumption.

The GT750B-4 had modified port timing, new carburettors (from VM32 to SU32 versions), a higher compression ratio (according to the press release, although missed in the catalogues), and a new exhaust system, aping that of the GT380 (the GT550 continued with the old GT750-style setup, however), giving a higher pitched sound. More importantly, power went up to 70bhp at 6500rpm, with a fraction more torque delivered as a result, too. The gearing was changed slightly, with fourth and fifth brought closer together, but there were also longer legs on the final-drive ratio; a new clutch plate rounded off the changes.

A contemporary Japanese tester remarked: "The earlier bikes had a bigger 'wow factor' at regular Japanese road speeds, but the new bike is more refined, as well as faster at the top-end to suit European buyers." The new GT750 was duly clocked at 128mph (204kph), confirming the guy's feelings.

The GT550B remained in B-3 guise at this stage, although the

Powered by a Wankel rotary (inset), the export-only Suzuki RE-5 entered production on November 1, 1974. Despite Giugiaro styling and an undoubted technical appeal, the model was not a success due to bad launch timing.

SUZUKI MOTORCYCLES: THE CLASSIC TWO-STROKE ERA

Advertising for the GT and Hustler series, spotted in the December 1974 issue of a Japanese motorcycle magazine. Amazingly, the company missed the opportunity to say the GT flagship now had more power …

The GT750B-4, introduced in October 1974. The export version of the bike, the 1975 season's GT750M, looked exactly the same, with all colour variations having a similar tank stripe design.

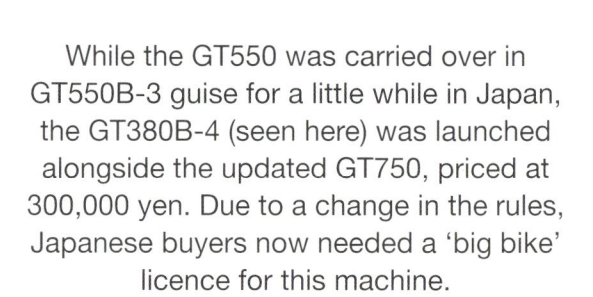

While the GT550 was carried over in GT550B-3 guise for a little while in Japan, the GT380B-4 (seen here) was launched alongside the updated GT750, priced at 300,000 yen. Due to a change in the rules, Japanese buyers now needed a 'big bike' licence for this machine.

GT380 became the GT380B-4 thanks to a cosmetic upgrade, with new tank coachlines combined with Candy Gypsy Red and Olive Green Metallic paintwork. Other than the choice of colours, it was the same story with the GT250 and GT185, with the stripe on the fuel tank being visually lighter on the new GT250B-3 and GT185B-2 versions, although the GT250 lost its rubber fork gaiters at last. Like the GT550, the GT125 and GA50 were unchanged, at least for the time being.

Remember, though, this is Suzuki we're talking about, so nothing can be taken for granted. At the start of the 1975 calendar year (CY, as opposed to MY), the GT550 and GT125 were brought into line. The latest GT550 (the B-4) had an extra 3bhp and classy coachlines on the fuel tank, while the GT125 (or GT125B-2) gained a new, albeit similar, stripe to go with its Maui Blue or Candy Tahiti Orange paintwork.

In the meantime, the Hustler range was updated for the 1975 season, in much the same way as the GT-series, with

END OF AN ERA

Catalogue page for the GT250B-3, which was the last of the GTs to rid itself of front fork boots (the GA50 was the only remaining road bike to sport them, and continued to do so until the end of its run). Colours included Candy Gold and Maui Blue Metallic.

The 1975 Model Year GT185, or GT185B-2. Although it may look similar to the GT250 shade, the gold used for this bike was Candy Tahiti Orange; Maui Blue was the other option.

The GT550B-4, which gained 3bhp and sold for 385,000 yen. With the national average wage standing at 1,875,000 yen in 1975 (more than double the figure for 1970), this has to be considered particularly reasonable.

The GT125B-2, the mildly updated version having been introduced at the start of 1975.

new catalogues printed in October 1974. Apart from revised side boxes that doubled as race number plates for the TS50, this face-lift was restricted to new stripes (a similar design for all models) for the Hustler 50 (now TS50-5), the Hustler 90 (TS90-6), the Hustler 125 (TS125-5) and Hustler 250 (TS250-7); the Hustler 400 was carried over unchanged.

March 1975 saw the 6bhp GA50 get some new fuel tank stripes to give birth to the GA50-2, and the launch of a new GT model – the GT100, or GT100B-1 if one feels the need to get technical.

The GT100 was very similar to the GT125 from a styling point of view, with dimensions that were within fractions of an inch compared to the 125cc twin. The main difference was the engine, which was completely different – a 97cc single (49mm x 51.8mm) borrowed from the TS100 and TC100 sold in America and some other export countries. With the compression ratio raised from 6.5 to 6.8:1, and equipped with a VM20SC carb, the two-stroke rotary valve unit developed 12bhp at 8000rpm when used in the GT application. In keeping with the GT image, it came with disc brakes at the front, although the tyres were perhaps a little on the weedy side, being a 2.50-18 and 2.75-18 combination.

Not long after, the GT750B-5 replaced the B-4 at the tail-end of spring 1975 without any fanfare whatsoever, being a purely cosmetic face-lift at first glance, although the gearing changes had been quietly reversed back to original specs on the JDM model, as they were doubtless better suited to the domestic road situation.

Things were moving on the dual-purpose bike side as well, with the Mini Cro 75 (CM75) being introduced on March 7, 1975, and followed by a Mini Cro 50 (CM50) three months later, on June 26. Respectively, these were basically a roadworthy version of the TM75, and a more serious Hustler 50 using the same frame. A 72cc (47mm x 42mm) VanVan 75 single was used in the CM75, while another familiar single-cylinder lump was employed in the CM50; at 5bhp, the 49cc unit was rated halfway between the version used in the Hustler 50 and VanVan 50.

During the Mini Cro introduction era, the TS400 inherited the same stripe as its contemporaries (becoming the

The 1975 MY Hustler 50.

Brochure image for the TS90-6, announced in October 1974.

Press photo of the TS125-5 for the 1975 season. Japanese buyers had a choice of silver with an orange stripe, or dark green with off-white graphics.

Publicity image showing the GT750B-5.

The five-speed GT100 as it appeared at the time of its launch. Colours for this 138,000 yen machine included Maui Blue Metallic and Colorado Orange Metallic.

The Hustler 250 featured on the cover of the 1975 MY dual-purpose bike catalogue, and the page dedicated to the model within the brochure.

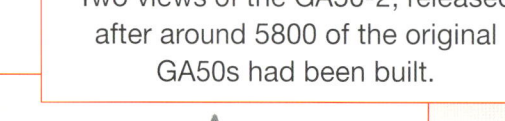

Two views of the GA50-2, released after around 5800 of the original GA50s had been built.

END OF AN ERA

The Mini Cro 75, which was priced at 100,000 yen. In reality, the Mini Cro 50 looked exactly the same, but lacked an engine size badge on the fuel tank. Colours included blue, orange, yellow and silver on the first of the breed. The 96,000 yen Mini Cro 50 Type II was introduced not long after the original 50cc variant, sporting a lower front mudguard (and the loss of the blue paint option), but the three Mini Cro models were duly sold alongside each other.

The Mini Cro and VanVan line-up in the summer of 1975.

The updated Hustler 90 (TS90-7) introduced in July 1975.

TS400-4), but it wouldn't stay current for long. Never being able to leave things be, yet more changes were made to the Hustler line on July 1, 1975, with the 135,000 yen TS90, 183,000 yen TS125 and 259,000 yen TS250 each receiving attention at this time.

Compared with the TS90-6, the latest TS90-7 gained a fuel tank design aping that of the Mini Cro series, but not much else it would seem. However, close inspection revealed a black headlight surround, new indicator light units and an extended front mudguard, so in many ways, it was a deeper face-lift than many we've seen so far.

The new TS125-6 was given the same treatment as its 90cc counterpart, but also gained a mysterious extra horse. According to the catalogue, power output increased to 14bhp, despite the 123cc unit having a slightly lower compression ratio.

The Hustler 250 (now in TS250-8 guise) was also upgraded in a similar fashion, and also gained some extra oomph, with 23bhp now on tap, even though the catalogue specs are the same as before with regard to the engine.

Within a matter of weeks, the Hustler 50 was brought into line, becoming the TS50-6. It was the same lighting and paintwork upgrade we'd witnessed on the bigger Hustlers (all except for the TS400, that is), although there was also a different chain guard adopted at this time for the tiddler.

After years of minimal change, the 'business' bikes were at last dragged into the modern era in 1975, with brand new painted fuel tanks to replace the old chrome ones. The 4.5bhp K50-8, the 7.5bhp K90-7 and 10.5bhp K125-5 were the first of this new breed, although all leading specifications – even weights and tyre sizes – were the same as those quoted a couple of years earlier. Indeed, had it not been for such a big change on the tanks, it would have been hard to spot much difference with the bikes fielded in the previous season.

145

The TS125-6 announced alongside the new TS90. Being able to see the two side-by-side allows us to spot the larger front wheel used on the Hustler 125s.

The latest Hustler 250 (TS250-8), which looked a lot more purposeful than its predecessors. Like the version before it, it tipped the scales at 115kg (253lb).

The TS50-6 from the summer of 1975.

The 1975 season abroad

The oil crisis had a lot to answer for. About 8500 people had been employed by Suzuki in 1970, rising to 10,500 in 1972. But by the mid-seventies, this figure had dropped back to under 9000, despite sales improving abroad. There was also a distinct cut in the advertising budget, and more sensible introductions on the various bikes to keep costs in check through greater standardisation across the various markets – something that makes the author's job much easier, and about time, too …

The Americans had a line-up that reflected the continuing off-road boom that even allowed Hodaka to keep selling in America, even though the brand was long gone as far as the Japanese market was concerned. The five TM models listed in the States have different tank decals to their Japanese counterparts, but were otherwise the same wherever model grades tied up (the TM75, TM100, TM125, TM250 and TM400 were marketed in the US); the RL250 'Exacta' was also the same, as were the RV90 and RV125. In addition to the TC100, TC125 and TC185 not sold in Japan, American enthusiasts received a TS line-up that looked very similar to the home market one, with the same stripe used on the newest October 1974 JDM Hustler models applied across the six-strong US range from the off.

As for the road bikes, while the rotary-engined RE5 made its way across the Pacific after the 1975 season got under way, becoming the sole machine not to be powered by a two-stroke engine in the process, the GT models again reflected home market upgrades. The GT185M was the same as the Japanese

The 'business' bikes were brought up-to-date with a major face-lift in 1975. While they still had a traditional look about them, the lack of chrome was obvious.

END OF AN ERA

The American range for the 1975 Model Year. These bikes were given the 'M' designation to distinguish them from machines offered in other seasons, with the same letter being adopted in Europe and other export markets.

B-2 variant, the GT250M the same as the B-3, the GT380M the same as the B-4, the GT550M the same as the B-4 that came late in Japan (and therefore didn't benefit from the power gain seen in the JDM model), and the GT750M was visually the same as the Japanese B-4. America also had the long-running T500, which was duly given fresh tank stripes for the new season.

US advertising for the GT550M. North America took 83,937 bikes in 1975, although the figure was set to increase, with Suzuki shipping no less than 113,753 units in the following year.

British flyer for the B120M. The B-series had been dropped in Japan a long time beforehand.

A UK advert from June 1975 for the T500M. The model sold in America looked very similar.

Racing in the late seventies

The 1974 campaign had been disappointing to say the least, but the RG500 was so new, so different to anything Suzuki had tried before, that perhaps the lack of early success was to be expected. After all, in top-flight racing, the learning curve is always a sharp one, and rarely overcome in a hurry. This did, however, delay the sale of the new bike to privateers, who had either the 80bhp TR500 or 116bhp TR750 to choose from in 1975. With Barry Sheene having secured a couple of world championship wins in 1975 (in Holland and Sweden) on the 100bhp machine, for 1976, Suzuki felt confident enough to drop both of the oldies in favour of an RG500 replica. This confidence would later prove to be justified, as Suzuki won nine of the ten qualifying rounds, with Tom Herron taking the flag in what would be the last Isle of Man classic to be included in the world championship calendar.

Coming back from an awful accident at Daytona in the early part of 1975, Barry Sheene took the 1976 title on his Team Heron Suzuki RG500 from the UK, winning five of the championship rounds in style. In fact, Suzuki riders took the first six places in the top 500cc category, driving home the dominance of their machines, which were by now pumping out almost 115bhp from a revised 54mm x 54mm configuration, first on Sheene's bike (code XR22), and then all the works racers soon after.

Sheene then won six of the rounds in the following year to

SUZUKI MOTORCYCLES: THE CLASSIC TWO-STROKE ERA

A signed photo from the author's collection, with Barry Sheene looking every bit the champion. The lad was also seen sitting on the same bike in Brut 33 adverts at this time.

retain his crown, and although he had to settle for second in 1978 and third place in 1979 (with Suzuki exponent Virginio Ferrari starting to come through with a fine second place), the duels between the Cockney lad and Kenny Roberts of Yamaha will forever be etched on the minds of race enthusiasts. Suzuki's interest – and effort – dropped off to a large extent when Sheene decided to leave Suzuki at the end of the 1979 season.

Notwithstanding, the XR34 version of the RG500 was knocking out 125bhp by 1980, having gained a completely new suspension by this time to make the bike easier to handle. While Roberts and Yamaha once again claimed the 500cc title, Suzuki riders Randy Mamola, Marco Lucchinelli, Franco Uncini, Graziano Rossi and Will Hartog filled the next five spots in the final season standings, helping to secure the manufacturers' crown with ease.

The RG500 Gamma followed in March 1981, and was heavily modified in 1982. In its final 1987 form, the type XR72, the bike was delivering no less than 140bhp! There was actually a road bike based on the racer built during

A rather funny advert released by Castrol in 1975.

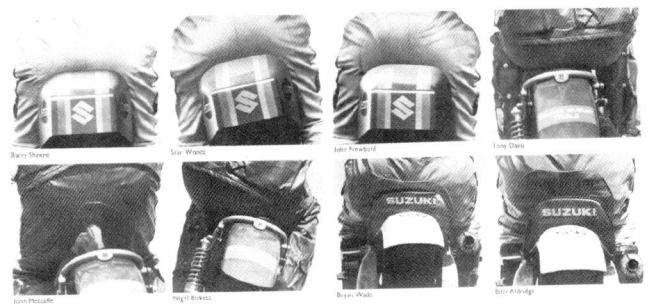

SAIAD, Suzuki's Italian distributor, had started building its own 500cc racing bikes as early as 1973. This is its race shop pictured in 1976, with four Suzuki Bimota SB1s in the background, and a pair of RG500s nearest the camera.

American rider Pat Hennen leading his Suzuki team-mate in early 1978. Sadly, Hennen had a bad accident at the Isle of Man not long after, prematurely ending a promising career. (Courtesy Wikimedia Commons/Smudge 9000)

END OF AN ERA

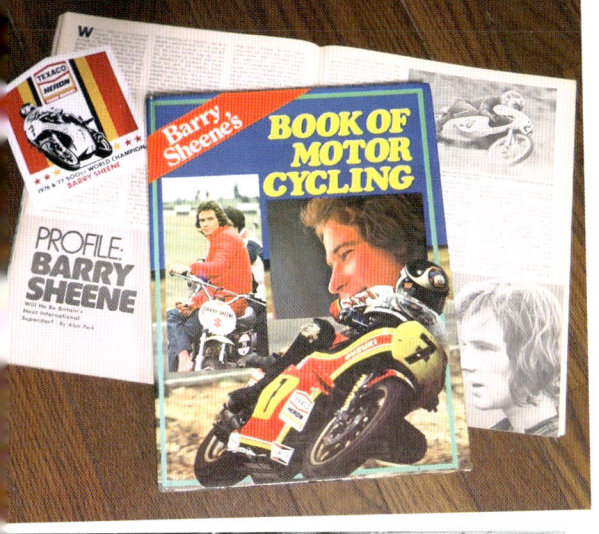

Childhood memories of a hero. Nice to be able to write about the guy at last, although I have touched on his exploits with Toyota in the past …

A still from the 1980 film, *Silver Dream Racer*, with Cristina Raines and Beau Bridges looking the part next to a Suzuki machine.

the mid-eighties, with 9284 RG500 Gammas produced between 1985 and 1987; during the same period, there were 6213 RG400 Gammas built as well.

Meanwhile, although no longer a championship round, the lure of the Isle of Man races would never go away, with its importance diminishing not one bit. Suzuki made the most of this promotional chance, scoring a remarkable run of consecutive 500cc Senior TT victories, with Phil Read declared the winner in 1977, Tom Herron in 1978, Mike Hailwood in 1979, Graeme Crosby in 1980, Mick Grant in 1981, Norman Brown in 1982, and Rob McElnea in 1983 and 1984. The two-stroke Suzukis had definitely left their mark on the racing world …

1976 news

As folks started putting up their new calendars, a few very minor changes were made to the domestic GT line-up for 1976. The GT125 became the GT125B-3 thanks to a lighter weight stripe on the tank and a fresh colour palette. Power and torque outputs remained the same, but at 196,000 yen, it was 11,000 yen more expensive than its predecessor. It was a similar story for the GT185B-3, which looked much the same as the B-2, but for different discs and slightly smaller indicators.

Even the price stayed the same on the GT550B-5, which had a modified coachline and a revised front mudguard but nothing more, and it was the same story with the GT380. The stripe was very similar on the GT380 as it happens, but for the record, the paint choices went from Olive Green Metallic and Joyful Maroon Metallic to Black and Forest Green Metallic on this model, which became the B-5 from early 1976.

Prices went up slightly on the TS50 and TS400, otherwise the Hustler range was the same as it was at the end of the 1975 season; the three Mini Cro machines, RL250, RM125, TM75 and TM125 were carried over as well, although the RH250 seemed to fall by the wayside. The moped line-up was much the same, and the 'business' bikes were continued as they were, but priced an average of 6000 yen higher than 1975.

The lack of major changes can be put down to two factors – one being the four-stroke GS range on the horizon, and the other being a new set of regulations regarding *Kei* cars that was introduced in January 1976. This saw the 360cc capacity limit replaced by a 550cc one, with hardly warning for the manufacturers, leading to a costly FMC scenario on a number of lines. Suzuki responded first with the Fronte 7S in June 1976, before ultimately overhauling the entire four-wheeler range in October 1977.

Notwithstanding, March 1976 brought with it the RM125-II

The GT750B page from a GT catalogue printed in early 1976. No changes to the domestic flagship model, but it's useful for reference. The water cooling made the machine quieter, by the way.

SUZUKI MOTORCYCLES: THE CLASSIC TWO-STROKE ERA

The GT125 was updated to become the GT125B-3 at the start of 1976. This brochure page from the time is extremely useful in that it explains something that troubled the author for hours – the first publicity shots had a tank coachline very close to the Suzuki badge, which seemed to move, and was impossible to find in a production model, only early catalogues. The bike illustrated on the left has the proper stripe!

to replace the original RM125, and the introduction of an RM250, which took the place vacated by the RH250. These were pure competition machines, however, lacking the equipment necessary to make them road legal, so there is no need to dwell on them, beyond putting them in their place in history.

The following month saw the FR70 replaced by the 95,000 yen and up FR80, and a face-lift of the FR50 line to go with it. There was very little to tell the new models from their predecessors in reality, other than different decals and a slight modification of the leg guards and front fascia under the headlight, although a glance at the spec sheets revealed the important part of the equation, with the FR70's 69cc engine being superseded by a two-stroke 79cc (49mm x 42mm) single-cylinder unit that gave 6.8bhp. Gaining square lights during a minor change at the end of the decade, ultimately, the FR80 would continue into the mid-1980s, while the FR50 made it into the nineties.

Meanwhile, the Mini 50 continued until the end of 1977 with a very mild face-lift, joined by the Landie FM50 family bike in May 1976. This long-running machine took the place of the Hopper in the line-up and was basically a cross between the Mini 50 and the VanVan, the latter available in RV50, RV75, RV90 and RV125 guise by this time, with more grades having been added at the start of the year. The RV50S was the last of the VanVan breed, incidentally, selling until 1987.

The GT185B-3. At 220,000 yen, it cost 10,000 yen more than before. Wonder how much that outfit cost? The mid-seventies was a groovy time …

At about the same time as the Landie arrived, prices increased by an average of 5000 yen on the VanVan and K-series models, as well as the GA50 and GT100, plus the smallest of the Hustlers; the RM250 got hit with a 10,000 yen hike. Interestingly, this is when the Hustler 400 moved up into TS400-6 guise (the company missed out the number five for some reason, which seems odd having used a four if patterns are anything to go by, but then Suzuki have a habit of throwing a spanner in the works, and it looks like there's a nine missing in

The GT380 was updated to GT380B-5 guise at the start of 1976.

END OF AN ERA

The GT550B-5, distinguished by a new, albeit similar, stripe on the fuel tank, and a front mudguard that lost its upper strut. Colours for the Japanese 1976 model included Olive Green Metallic and Peat Brown Metallic. Black, red and dark green hues were available in export markets.

the TS125 run, as well as a nine in all three of the K-series bikes!), its price going up to 290,000 yen in order to cover the use of a new carburettor setup and the adoption of expensive alloy wheel rims.

In the meantime, during the summer, the GT250 gained a 'big bike' front mudguard, a new, smoother side box design, and fresh indicators. Just as importantly, it lost the Ram Air Cooling system, and, combined with revised porting and a stronger bottom end, it duly became the GT250B-4 as a result. Despite arriving long after the 1976 MY began, this is actually the model the GT250A specification was based on.

The export markets adopted the letter 'A' to denote the 1976 season – a year in which no less than 647,000 units were shipped abroad. Although America was the largest single market, Europe took the most bikes as a continent, moving 109,053 motorcycles in 1975, followed by just over 140,000 in the next year.

The Hustler 400 finally caught up with the export market in the spring of 1976 with the release of the TS400-6.

The Birdie 80 (FR80) moped of 1976 vintage.

Advertising for the new Landie model. Another plaything, but one cannot blame Suzuki for following trends in order to survive.

The short-lived GT250B-4, minus the ribs on the side box, and later-style indicator lights and mudguard. This generation also dropped the Ram Air system, a modification that was applied to the GT250A models abroad.

Domestic advert from the tail-end of summer 1976 for the Mini Cro range, this being a Mini Cro 50 Type II, recognisable thanks to its low front mudguard.

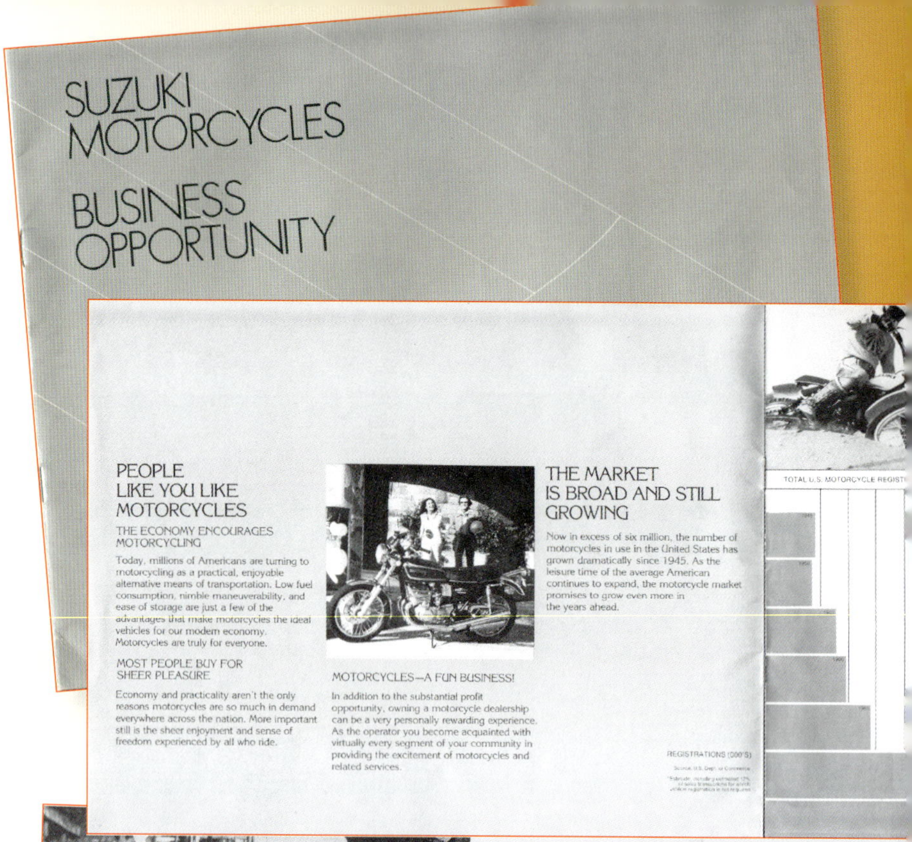

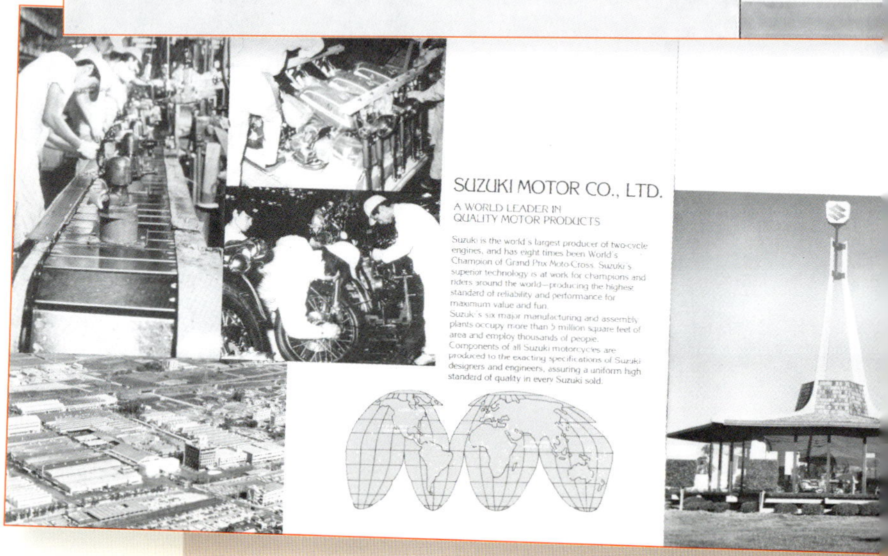

Advertising for the US 1976 season.

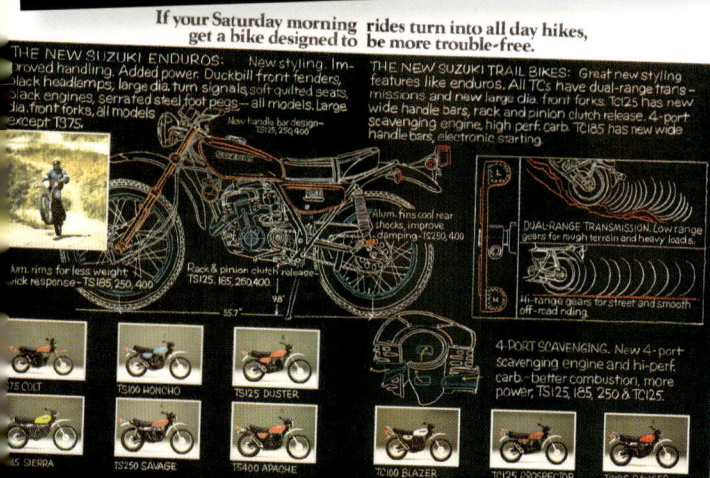

Compared to the staid but classy hues offered in Japan, buyers abroad were treated to a rather different impression of the GT550, available in Targa Red for export to North America. The GT550B-5 was known as the GT550A in the States.

An extremely rare 'business opportunity' brochure put together by Suzuki's US arm at this time.

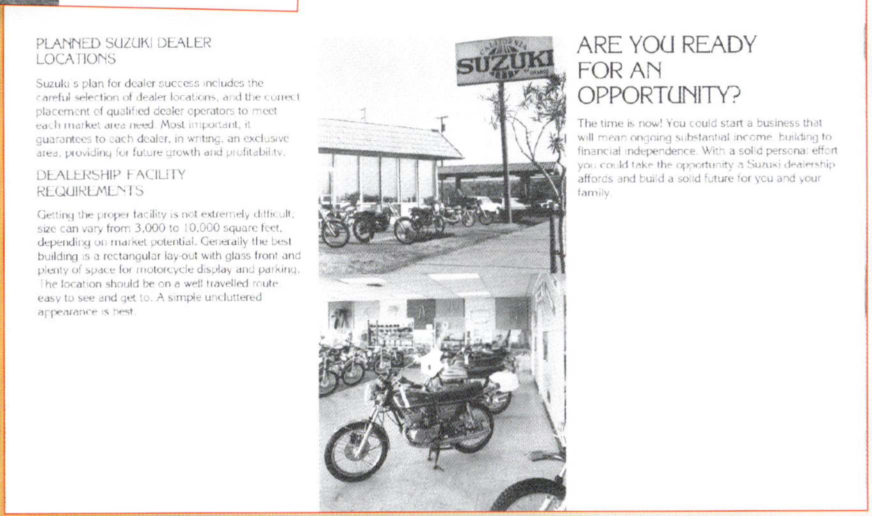

Anyway, Stateside sales were still considered the ones to chase, and Americans had a choice of six GTs for 1976, with the GT185A, GT250A, GT380A, GT550A and GT750A each conforming to Japanese specifications more or less (or at least as they stood once the year got under way, as the revised GT250 was particularly late in coming to Japan), but the sixth model was an unusual one – the $1295 GT500, which was basically a T500 with disc brakes added, a slightly modified 44bhp engine, and a few styling changes to make it fit into the GT range that much easier. The US line-up also tied up very nicely with the JDM range on the TS front (TS75A, TS100A, TS125A, TS185A, TS250A and TS400A) wherever grades coincided, and the American TC100, TC125 and TC185 models were brought into line with them this time around.

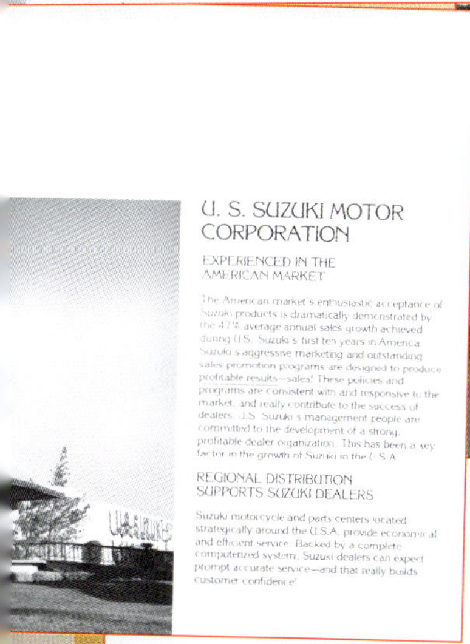

SUZUKI MOTORCYCLES: THE CLASSIC TWO-STROKE ERA

British advertising for the £529 GT250, this piece dated April 1976. It's easy to see the lack of a Ram Air box from this angle.

Barry Sheene doing a little promotional work with the GT750 for Heron Suzuki GB. He actually used one of these £999 motorcycles as a road bike for a while (the GT550 was £889 including VAT, for the record, and the GT380 £649). The UK distributor was also marketing the Dunstall GT750 at this time, incidentally, with glassfibre fairings and the option of alloy wheels.

Beginning of the end

Two decades had passed since Suzuki had fielded a four-stroke motorcycle, but the EPA in America and the equivalent body at home had forced the maker into a corner. Struggling with the latest emission codes, the Hamamatsu company had made the decision to swap over to cleaner four-stroke engines at the start of 1974, but only now, on the November 1, 1976, could the fruits of endless months of R&D be seen in the flesh in Japan.

The GS750 and GS400 were designed mainly for the US market, where the bikes became available in time for the 1977 MY, although the company was naturally a long way behind its rivals, such as the bigger Honda CB-series and 750cc Yamaha models, in terms of development time. This made the job for Suzuki's team, led by Hiroyuki Nakano and Yasuharu Fujii, all the harder, as this new line would have to fly the flag in the years to come, with no second chances.

This is naturally not the main topic of the book, but as landmark motorcycles that play an important part in the story, we have to at least take a look at the GS models. The first of the breed was a beautiful air-cooled DOHC four with a four-into-two exhaust. With a 748cc displacement, the all-alloy unit developed a healthy 68bhp, and was linked to a five-speed gearbox to provide a top speed of around 125mph (200kph).

The first GS750, introduced in November 1976 at 485,000 yen. Dual front discs were adopted at the front and the tank stripe was changed for the GS750-2, before the GS750Es came along with their distinctive alloys – alloy wheels for motorcycles were something that had started to become popular in the middle of the 1970s, especially in America.

The original GS400. The next version looked much the same, but gained coachlines on the fuel tank.

END OF AN ERA

The GS400 had the same bore but a shorter stroke and two less cylinders to give 398cc and 36bhp. This model was given a six-speed transmission to make the most of the horses available, and came with disc brakes at the front and drums at the rear. To keep the power in check, the original GS750 was given a single disc up front (a front pair of discs was adopted soon after), and – in a first for Suzuki – a disc at the back, too. It was an impressive machine on so many fronts.

As had happened with the two-stroke range, the four-stroke line developed quickly. A 549cc GS550, already being sold in the States a few months before, was added to the JDM line-up in June 1977, although many at Suzuki will remember that month for all the wrong reasons. Indeed, Shunzo Suzuki died on June 17, 1977, leaving the company with no Chairman, although Michio Suzuki continued as an honourary figurehead until his own death in October 1982.

A GS1000 was made available for export for the 1978 season, followed by a shaft-driven GS850G in October that year, that was also only ever sold abroad. The single-cylinder SP370 was an oddball, bringing four-stroke technology to the scrambler range and eventually replacing the TS400, but the GS line continued to evolve in the meantime, with the GS400E, GS550E and GS750E sprouting alloy wheels, and a GS400L with different seating and trim.

By the end of the 1970s, the GS750E had given way to the GS750G with shaft drive, and the GS550E had been replaced by a GS650G grade. These two ran alongside the old GS400, before being joined on January 1, 1980 by additional GSX250E, GSX400E and GSX750E models (as well as a GSX1100 for export, and the first of many in the GN line, sold in chopper form in Japan), the GSX moniker being used to showcase Suzuki's revolutionary four-valve per cylinder twin-swirl (TSCC) technology. The company had come a long way in a short space of time …

The trials scene, 1975 onwards

Roger de Coster was back to his winning ways in the 500cc category of the world championship, taking the flag at seven of the 12 meetings that made up the calendar that year. Team-mate Gerrit Wolsink won three of the remainder, which gave De Coster and Suzuki the 1975 rider and maker titles. Heikki Mikkola was second on a Husqvarna, with Wolsink third and Yamaha runners fourth and fifth. Fighting with the new RH250-II, Joël Robert and Willy Bauer (who took the place of Sylvain Geboers for 1975) put on a reasonable show, although the best Suzuki could muster in the 250cc category was a single

Catalogue image from the start of the 1975 season showing the contemporary TM series and the RH250, the latter being available as a pure off-the-shelf racer for 450,000 yen since the second half of 1974. The TS90MX, only introduced at the beginning of 1973, had already disappeared. The rider featured is homegrown hero Koji Masuda, by the way.

Another brochure image, this one from mid-1975, including the RM125 and RH250-II models announced in February that year. The RL was still available for trials enthusiasts, sold in road and off-road guise.

SUZUKI MOTORCYCLES: THE CLASSIC TWO-STROKE ERA

A 1977 Model Year RM250. Only the earliest versions of this bike had these front forks – a longer version, extending further down beyond the hub, was introduced soon after.

American advertising from the same period, appearing in a motorcycle magazine from December 1976.

This 1978 catalogue image shows that the TM range had gone, but the RM-series had been allowed to expand. Alongside these RM models, there were five dual-purpose Hustlers listed.

win and third place overall for Bauer; Robert finished the season in ninth.

De Coster won the 500cc title again in 1976, with Wolsink close behind and a country mile ahead of his Maico rivals. Between them, they won ten of the 12 rounds, although the 250cc campaign was as good as dead – Robert left for Puch, while Bauer went to the KTM team.

1977 was to be Mikkola's and Yamaha's year in the 500cc class, with De Coster and Wolsink having to settle for second and third, while the 250cc category was now KTM territory. The following year was much the same, as it happens, with De Coster dropping to third after an accident delayed his campaign. Everything changed in 1979, with Graham Noyce claiming the 500cc championship for Honda, but Wolsink had a decent season, winning four races to come second overall. There wasn't even a glimmer of hope in the 250cc class, though. Or at least it seemed that way …

In a surprise move, De Coster defected to Honda for 1980, with Wolsink going to Maico. Gérard Rond became Suzuki's best hope, finishing sixth in the 500cc category, but Georges Jobé won the 250cc title in impressive style. Jobé was runner-up to a Yamaha rider in 1981 and 1982, before claiming 250cc honours again in 1983. Ex-Kawasaki man Brad Lackey won the 500cc title in 1982, followed home by André Vromans. As well as breaking Honda's spell, this gave Suzuki an almost clear sweep of the championship that year, for there were now three titles at stake.

The FIM had introduced a 125cc class for 1975, which Suzuki duly dominated with the RA125. Indeed, the Japanese maker secured the 125cc world championship title each year between 1975 and 1984, which was a truly remarkable feat, as well as something of a godsend, making up for Suzuki's relative lack of success and silverware in the 250cc class during this period. Gaston Rahier won in 1975, 1976 and 1977, with Akira Watanabe claiming the crown in 1978. Harry Everts then won three times on the trot, with Eric Geboers (younger brother of Sylvain) taking the title in 1982 and 1983. The works effort finished at this point, but Italian Michele Rinaldi borrowed a factory machine in 1984, going on to win the title despite having missed the first three rounds of the championship. As it happens, this was to be Suzuki's last big victory on the motocross scene until the start of the 1990s.

END OF AN ERA

Cover of the catalogue for the 1977 GT and RG range, with a GT380 featured on the front.

Not quite the end!

Interestingly, at the time of the GS-series announcement, Japan was still fielding a full complement of two-stroke models. The GT750 limped on until the end of 1976, priced at 438,000 yen, and unchanged from 1975. The B-series (1977 MY) upgrades found abroad were never applied in Japan due to the imminent end of the model. Hence, there was never a GT750B-6, and, as such, the last GT750s sold in Japan were the equivalent to the A-series bikes sold in export markets. Another myth put to bed …

The GT550 was also left alone, as that, too, was dropped from the range at the end of 1976. However, with the exception of the GT100 initially, the other GTs were all updated at the time of the GS launch, and the GA50 was replaced by a new RG50 grade.

While the leading specifications were carried over, the GT380 became the GT380B-6 via a black finish on the headlight, upper fork area and side boxes (the latter, at least on lighter shades, as it looks like body colour was used with the dark green paint), fresh indicator and taillight designs, and yet another coachline change. Colours for 1977 included Olive Green Metallic and Candy Calypso Red in Japan.

Compared to the B-4 version, the new GT250B-5 had a bigger taillight, and black on the headlight, forks and side boxes to bring it in line with the latest GT380. Naturally, there was a fresh tank stripe, with paintwork coming in Olive Green Metallic and Marble Scarlet for 1977. There was also a slight increase in power, with 32bhp now available thanks to VM28 carbs replacing the old VM26s; there were no other changes on the spec sheet apart from a lower compression ratio, which went from 7.5 to 7.3:1 at this time.

Studio shot of the GT380B-6, which was priced at 310,000 yen.

The GT250 in GT250B-5 guise.

The 1977 GT185B-5. We get a good view of the Ram Air cooling fins from this angle.

Catalogue page for the GT125B-4. Colours available for 1977 included Candy Rose and Maui Blue Metallic.

The GT100B-2, which came in Maui Blue only, all the way through until it was discontinued in mid-1978.

The RG50, which took the place of the GA50 in the JDM line-up. It was, without doubt, sportier and more modern-looking than its predecessor.

As there was no B-4 variant in the GT185 line, the 1977 model is the GT185B-5. This came with the smaller indicators, larger brakelight, and the black treatment used on the bigger stuff, although the original front mudguard design was retained, as the struts were quite different to the larger bikes anyway, being the same as the smaller-capacity models. Interestingly, while the c/r was increased, like all the other main specifications, power remained unchanged at 21bhp; the only difference is that peak power and torque came in slightly lower down the rev-range compared to earlier engines. Priced at 225,000 yen, it came in Maui Blue Metallic or Candy Rose.

It was the same story with the GT125 – black painted areas, new lights, and fresh colours and stripes to give birth to the GT125B-4. The GT100, however, stayed the same for a while, finally being updated into GT100B-2 spec in the spring of 1977. With the GT100, the face-lift was restricted to new indicators and brakelight assembly, fresh paintwork/coachline options and black side boxes only. It wouldn't be around much longer anyway …

All-new, however, was the RG50. This had a new frame, which played host to a flatter fuel tank, and a solo seat sunk

First brochure page for the RG50. The next catalogue used all the same artwork, but the main image was now a black machine, with red, white and blue tanks illustrated above it.

The RL250-2, which looked virtually the same as the original. This highly-specialised bike would soon slip from the regular catalogues in Japan.

The original Mame-Tan 50 of 1977, which was based on the RG50.

Catalogue image for the Hustler 90, which was carried over from the previous season and would continue into 1978 unchanged, too. Even the colouring was the same.

The 1977 Hustler 125.

into a race-style fairing. Sportier mudguards at both ends, blacked-out areas of paintwork and a matt black headlight gave the machine a far more purposeful look than its predecessor. The RG50 used the same engine as the GA50, although it developed a fraction more power (6.3bhp) and had fatter tyres as a result. The 115,000 yen original came in red, white or blue, with black being added as another alternative later on.

The original RG50 was joined in January 1977 by a chopper version known as the Mame-Tan 50 (code OR50), powered by a de-tuned RG single developing 5.5bhp. Leading the way for this style of motorcycle in Japan, it gained a coveted Good Design Award, and was hugely popular when it first made its debut. It was duly sold in a number of export markets, too, becoming the OR50E after alloy wheels became the norm.

The 'business' bikes were the same as before, as were the mopeds and, more or less, the various crazy contraptions like the VanVan and Landie. This leaves us with the dual-purpose and scrambler range. Having followed the story thus far, one could be forgiven for expecting a major reshuffle, but things were surprisingly quiet in fact, which was perhaps a sign of the uncertain times as much as anything.

The off-road competition RM-series kept getting updated, while the RL250 had gained an extra horse and a fraction more torque thanks to the adoption of a reed valve induction system. The RL250 was joined by a bored-out RL325 version in certain export markets at this time, but this was never sold in Japan. The three Mini Cro variants continued as before, as did the Hustler 50 and Hustler 90, for the scrambler boom was at last starting to fade within the Land of the Rising Sun.

The Hustler 250 for the 1977 season, which carried the TS250-9 designation.

followed the same line of development, with more straight edges and a modified back-end. The TS400, on the other hand, was basically the same as the previous model, except for the adoption of a larger rear light assembly and a fresh colour palette. Indeed, time was running out for the Hustler 400, which disappeared from JDM catalogues in the early part of 1978.

Exchange rates

Prices have been quoted throughout the book, with Japanese yen being the most common. This table, showing the approximate amount of JPY each specified currency could buy during any given year, should help put things into perspective:

Year	USA $1-	UK £1-	German DM1-	French FF1-	Swiss SF1-
1955	360	1000	85	85	85
1960	360	1000	85	75	85
1965	360	1000	85	75	85
1970	360	865	85	65	85
1975	270	620	100	65	100
1980	220	485	110	50	120
1985	240	290	80	25	95

Export round-up

The American line-up changed completely for the 1977 season (duly given the B-series moniker), with the last of the RE-5s being joined by the GS750, the GS550 (at least from January 1977), the GS400, the TS400, a new TS250 and matching TS185, the RM370, RM250, RM125 and RM80 models, a PE250 enduro bike, and the RV90.

The TS400-7 version of the Hustler 400. This would be the final incarnation of this big scrambler, the last of the breed being sold in early 1978, although production ended at the end of 1977.

Although the pricing was carried over, Suzuki couldn't resist updating the bigger Hustlers, with the launch of revised versions of the Hustler 125 (the TS125-7), Hustler 250 (the TS250-9) and the Hustler 400 (the TS400-7).

While the engine and wheel sizes were carried over, the latest TS125 was in fact all-new, with modern styling making the most of the rerouted exhaust system, and a completely revised rear suspension. The TS250

160

END OF AN ERA

A fascinating catalogue showing the general range for the 1977 (B-series) models. Not all of them were available in all markets, not by a long way, but the sheer number of local variations (such as extended seats on the K50 and K125) and golden oldies is overwhelming. In some countries, therefore, the 'classic' era was still very much alive …

161

SUZUKI MOTORCYCLES: THE CLASSIC TWO-STROKE ERA

Amazingly, the triples continued for one last year, so we have a GT750B, a GT550B, a GT380B, and a GT500B – also basking in one final hurrah.

However, an advert in a May 1977 magazine stated that discounts were available on the remaining 1976 MY bikes, including the GT500A, which went from $1295 to $995 to clear stocks, which goes to show the extent of the range overhaul. One can only imagine how this affected sales of 1977 MY two-stroke machines. The final straw, proving that a new generation was taking over, was the launch of the so-called 'Dirt Scamp' range. Yes, the DS50, DS100 and DS185 had two-stroke engines, but they were a long way removed from the 'classic' models …

As it happens, the GT500 was still sold in quite a few places, including the UK, where the GT500B gained black side boxes like its US counterpart. Even Britain gave up on the oldtimer after that, but a number of European markets fielded a GT500C for 1978, with the side boxes back in body colour again. It was the same story with the triples, with the GT750 and GT550 fading away, with only the GT380 going into 1978; the last few were shifted in 1979.

The GT250 continued into 1978 in the UK, while the GT125C was actually an RG125 as far as Japan was concerned – something we'll

While Holland had a GT50P (which was basically an RG50E), for example, the Asian markets provided the greatest number of local variations. This brochure shows a GT125 made for Taiwan, complete with drum brakes at both ends. Incidentally, the 1978 MY range carried a 'C' designation, as one would expect following on from the 1977 'B' line-up, but the 1979 machines carried an 'N' code. Nothing is ever straightforward with Suzuki!

The GT750B, with a fresh front mudguard, now lacking the upper strut like the other triples, a black headlight surround, black side boxes (not easy to spot on this bike, of course), and a bigger taillight. This variation was never sold in Japan.

German catalogue for the GT380B – a true classic. Colours for the German 1977 model included blue, scarlet red and silver; same for the GT550B (albeit slightly different hues), while the GT750B came in blue, red or black.

END OF AN ERA

come to in a moment. The GT125 limped into 1979 alongside the GT185, which was available with alloy wheels. There was also a thoroughly modern GT250X7 sold in Europe, which was equivalent to the JDM RG250, and a new GT200 (and SB200N sister model) soon after; the GP100 and GP125 rounded off the renewal.

From a sales point of view, perhaps one has to stay quiet and admit defeat: North American sales had increased to around 180,000 units by 1978, and stayed that way until 1982 when sales eventually started falling off again. In Europe, too, sales hovered around the 120,000 mark for 1977 and 1978, and then there was a real boom, seeing imports rise to almost 200,000 units in 1980. After this, they fell off again, and in a big way in 1982, but considering the second oil shock had occurred in early 1979, one would expect sales to fall dramatically if a company wasn't doing something right …

End of the road

It's never easy to draw a line under an ongoing story, but it's fair to say that 1978 was the final 'classic' two-stroke year as far as the domestic market is concerned. The GT750 and GT550 had already gone in Japan. The last of the GT100s would be sold, while the GT250, GT185 and GT125 had all been replaced, leaving only the GT380 by the middle of the year.

Sure enough, the GT380B-7 was fielded as a final display of defiance. The side panels were brought back into body colour (the bike was initially available in Deep Burgundy Metallic and Candy Gypsy Red), and a new coachline graced the fuel tank.

Cover of a 1978 road bike catalogue, with only the GT100 and GT380 (seen here) representing their line, and the GT100 would be gone as soon as the final stocks were sold.

The 1978 GT380B-7 – the last triple, and the last of the traditional GT models as well.

The RG125. As with the GTs, the 185cc variant looked very similar.

163

SUZUKI MOTORCYCLES: THE CLASSIC TWO-STROKE ERA

Other than a new front mudguard and a revised disc brake system, Suzuki's engineers left things as they were, and who can blame them? The 169kg (372lb) triple would limp on to the end of 1979 with Olive Green Metallic added as a third colour option by that time, but that was to be the breed's last stand.

The RG line had been introduced via the RG50, which kept going (eventually gaining alloy wheels to create an RG50E offshoot), but the spring of 1978 witnessed the GT125 and GT185 transform, respectively, into the RG125 and RG185. There wasn't much difference from a mechanical point of view, but the styling had moved on a generation, borrowing design cues from its smaller-engined sibling, whilst also adding a touch of maturity that the RG50 lacked. There was also a new but sadly short-lived GP125, with softer lines and a 123cc single for motive power rather than a twin.

The GP125, which didn't last very long in the Japanese line-up.

The RG road bike range was completed, at least for the time being, when the GT250 was replaced by the RG250. This used a redesigned, lighter version of the old 247cc twin, its 30bhp being more than adequate, as the bike had shed a massive 20kg (44lb) compared to its predecessor. One has to pat Kiyoshi Kushiya and his team of engineers on the back for bikes like the RG250, but with its arrival, the classic era was well and truly over. In due course, the RG80E was added, and from March 1981, it was even possible to buy an RG500 racer off-the-shelf if you knew the right people.

The Hustler 50 in 1978 guise. Some export markets had similar but lighter weight tank graphics, while others had this JDM version combined with the tamer side box decals. The stripe seen here was also applied to the Japanese TS125 and TS250 at this time.

The Hustler 400 was basically gone, with only existing stocks available, and the Hustler 90 was unchanged (indeed, with a TS80 waiting down the line, it remained this way until the end of its run in 1981). At least the Hustler 50, Hustler 125 and Hustler 250 got new tank stripes in the spring of 1978, with these three models only treated to another set at the start of 1979. This move allowed them to tick over before the TS50, TS80, TS125 and TS250 made up a new, ultra-modern line of Hustlers from February 1981.

The TS125-8 of 1978 vintage. There was no number nine in this particular model sequence, so the 1979 version was the TS125-10.

The VanVan range still looked familiar, joined by a similar

END OF AN ERA

looking EPO in 1979, but the Mini Cro series had disappeared by now, and the RM line-up for competition work was revised on an annual basis. Of the other minor players, the Mame-Tan 50 range was expanded with new grades, including a short-lived 109,000 yen Mini-Tan 50 (OM50) dual-purpose bike from November 1977, which was supposed to be a new Mini Cro but failed completely due to a lack of focus on what users required.

There wasn't much happening on the moped side, with the modern Youdy range ultimately replacing the Mini 50 in March 1978, sold alongside the Landie – a bike with yet another dubious name. Numerous new scooters would swell the ranks over the coming years, many being promoted by heavyweight stars of stage and screen (the 1982 Love had Michael Jackson for its advertising campaign, for instance). The FR50 and FR80 were carried over, but would soon receive a square headlight, giving them a more modern appearance. The 'business' bikes, too, would soon have a fresh look, duly being updated in May 1978. This long-running line would just keep on going ...

If the K-series seemed like a permanent fixture, so did the man who became Suzuki's fourth President on June 28, 1978 – Osamu Suzuki. He'd been an executive of the company since the end of 1963, as it happens, concentrating on exports and sales, and was named President of the US arm in July 1966, so he was

The new 1979-style Hustler stripes seen on a TS250-11 (the 1978 version was the TS250-10). The same graphics were used for the Hustler 50, Hustler 125 and Hustler 250 that year. The next generation was more like a Stealth Bomber!

The K50 skipped nine in its numbering sequence, so the mid-1978 model received the K50-10 designation. The same coachlines and decals were applied to the K90 at this time, becoming the K90-8 as a result. Other changes included revised side boxes and a new seat.

The K125 gained its own tank stripes in the 1978 face-lift, as well as a new headlight, rear light and gauge pack, giving birth to the K125-6.

SUZUKI MOTORCYCLES: THE CLASSIC TWO-STROKE ERA

a very experienced businessman by the time he took up his new appointment.

His new policies included greater preparation for the waves caused by things like exchange rate shifts and fuel crises, putting greater emphasis on developing and fielding new products in established lines (which included cars and bikes) based on market research, and fighting harder to get new custom via highly competitive pricing brought about by cutting production costs wherever possible through efficiency and buying power.

Osamu Suzuki (centre, with a glass in his hand), fittingly pictured with a GT380, albeit from a somewhat different era.

Jitsujiro Suzuki became Chairman after this move, but it's fair to say Osamu Suzuki would be the one to leave a lasting impression. He would ultimately serve the company extremely well for decades, even after a business tie-up with GM and Isuzu in the summer of 1981.

Later production

For ease of reference, the numbers are broken down into bikes with an engine capacity of up to 50cc, 51-125cc, 126-250cc, and 251cc and over. All of the 1975 and most of the 1976 machines would have been two-stroke models, but after this date, the four-stroke bikes start to make their mark, with the two-stroke ultimately becoming something of a rarity after 1977. At least the numbers provide some useful information.

	Up to 50cc	51cc to 125cc	126cc to 250cc	251cc +	Total
1975	169,802	410,778	60,063	49,762	690,405
1976	241,562	483,074	59,599	85,812	870,047
1977	281,671	591,166	67,550	129,048	1,069,435
1978	346,407	454,925	77,201	140,532	1,019,065
1979	407,222	354,922	76,768	155,139	994,051
1980	592,035	493,705	121,826	229,605	1,437,171
1981	802,782	493,436	79,276	211,493	1,586,987
1982	678,156	417,694	80,337	121,133	1,297,320
1983	453,086	189,627	101,357	57,535	801,605
1984	469,520	252,495	95,040	77,863	894,918
1985	404,500	249,520	49,089	112,291	815,400

The percentage of bikes being exported fluctuated quite a lot at this time, being as high as 514,564 units (a peak of 75 per cent) in 1975, before falling off to around two-thirds of production for most of the late-1970s. During the tail-end of the seventies, South-East Asia was always the number one customer for Suzuki, although mainly smaller mopeds, with Europe second and North America third (sometimes the other way around); Africa and the Middle East were usually the next most important markets. As the eighties dawned, though, South America replaced the Middle East in the number five spot as foreign sales started to account for only around a half of production and, interestingly, by 1984, the home market was again the dominant force.

END OF AN ERA

The GT380 as it appeared in the 1979 catalogue. A glorious run of 'classic' two-stroke machines had come to an end …

The last catalogue in which the GT380 would appear, featuring an RG250E on the cover.

With annual Japanese bike production as a whole breaking the 5,000,000 mark for the first time in 1977, the number peaked at 7,412,000 in 1981 (when no less than 13,091,427 bikes were registered as being in use in Japan) before falling off to closer to 4,000,000 units a year just 36 months later. It must have been a nightmare for the management trying to plan ahead during such a volatile era, but Osamu Suzuki did a sterling job at the helm, guiding the good ship Suzuki through some treacherous waters. The one constant in all the upheaval was the largest maker continued to be Honda, with Yamaha next, Suzuki third, and Kawasaki fourth in line.

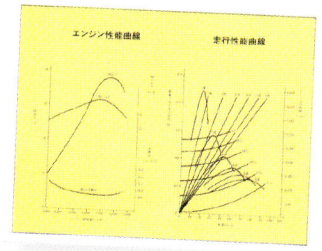

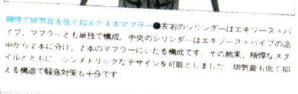

167

SUZUKI MOTORCYCLES: THE CLASSIC TWO-STROKE ERA

Road bike evolution

The Suzuki motorcycle range is complex, and often confusing. This simplified table, following the evolution of each two-stroke model covered in this chapter, should hopefully allow things to become a lot clearer.

Model	1975	1976	1977	1978	1979	1980
Hustler 50 (50cc single)	TS50	TS50	TS50	TS50	TS50	TS50
Suzuki GA50 (50cc single)	GA50	GA50	RG50	RG50	RG50	RG50
Suzuki K50 (50cc single)	K50	K50	K50	K50	K50	K50
Suzuki Mame-Tan (50cc single)			OR50	OR50	OR50	OR50
Suzuki Mini Cro 50 (50cc single)		CM50	CM50	CM50		
Suzuki Mini Cro 75 (72cc single)	CM75	CM75	CM75			
Suzuki Mini-Tan (50cc single)				OM50	OM50	
Suzuki K90 (88cc single)	K90	K90	K90	K90	K90	K90
Hustler 90 (89cc single)	TS90	TS90	TS90	TS90	TS90	TS90
Suzuki GT100 (97cc single)	GT100B	GT100B	GT100B	GT100B		
Hustler 125 (123cc single)	TS125	TS125	TS125	TS125	TS125	TS125
Suzuki GP125 (123cc single)				GP125	GP125	GP125
Suzuki K125 (123cc single)	K125	K125	K125	K125	K125	K125
Suzuki GT125 (125cc twin)	GT125B	GT125B	GT125B	RG125	RG125	RG125
Suzuki GT185 (184cc twin)	GT185B	GT185B	GT185B	RG185	RG185	RG185
Hustler 250 (246cc single)	TS250	TS250	TS250	TS250	TS250	TS250

END OF AN ERA

	1975	1976	1977	1978	1979	1980

Suzuki RL250 (246cc single)
RL250 ▬▬▬▬▬▬▬▬

Suzuki GT250 (247cc twin)
GT250B ▬▬▬▬▬▬ **RG250** ▬▬▬▬

Suzuki GT380 (371cc triple)
GT380B ▬▬▬▬▬▬▬▬▬▬▬▬

Hustler 400 (396cc single)
TS400 ▬▬▬▬▬▬▬

Suzuki GT550 (543cc triple)
GT550B ▬▬▬

Suzuki GT750 (738cc triple)
GT750B ▬▬▬

Note: Four-stroke models, pure mopeds, playthings and bikes made specifically for export are not included in this table, although they are all covered within the text. Likewise, the TM-series, TS90MX and RH250 are too specialised as pure off-roaders, so they appear in the text only; the RL250 scrapes in due to the provision of road equipment.

www.veloce.co.uk / www.velocebooks.com
All current books • New book news • Special offers • Gift vouchers

MORE FROM VELOCE ...

ENTHUSIAST'S RESTORATION MANUAL™

How to Restore Suzuki 2-Stroke Triples
GT350, GT550 & GT750 1971 to 1978

YOUR step-by-step colour illustrated guide to complete restoration

Ricky Burns

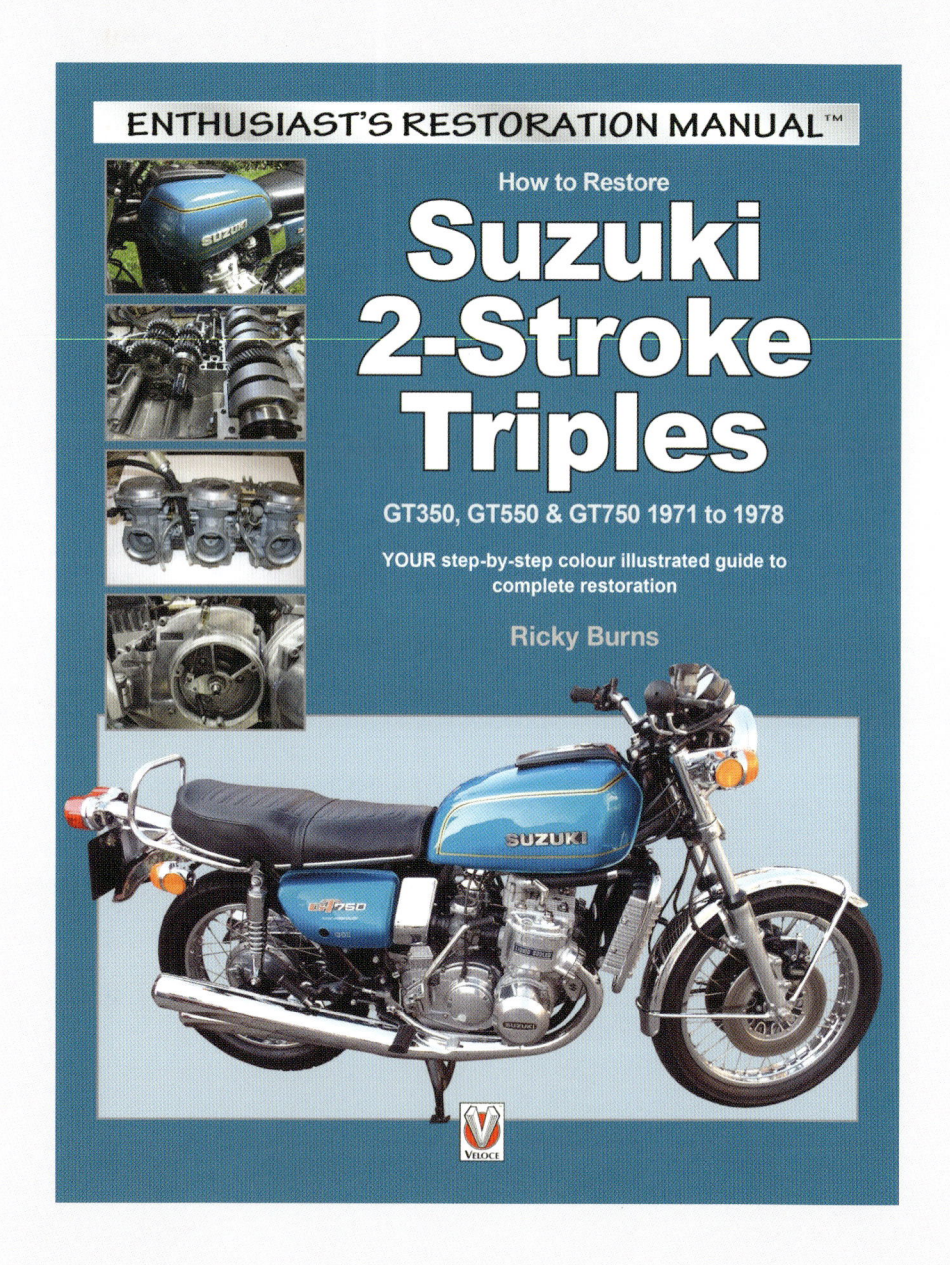

Whether it be an entry level GT380, or a ground-breaking water-cooled GT750, this step-by-step full restoration guide covers it, from dismantling, sourcing parts, spraying and decals, to polishing, safe setup and general maintenance. Even riding safely and storage are covered, making this a must-have guide for all Suzuki Triple enthusiasts.

ISBN: 978-1-845848-20-0
Paperback • 27x20.7cm • 176 pages • 586 colour pictures

**For more information and price details, visit our website at www.veloce.co.uk
email: info@veloce.co.uk
Tel: +44(0)1305 260068**

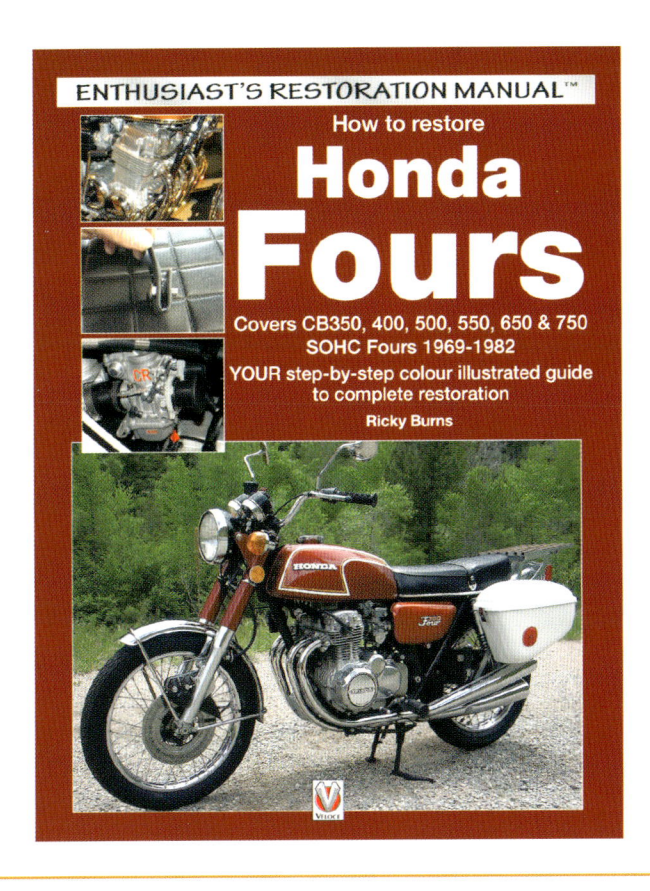

MORE FROM VELOCE ...

This book gives enthusiasts of the single overhead camshaft Honda Four a step-by-step guide to a full restoration. Whether it be the small but luxurious CB350/4 right through to the groundbreaking CB750/4. This guide covers dismantling the motorcycle and its components, restoring and sourcing parts, paint spraying, decals and polishing. The chapters cover, Engine, frame, forks, fuel, exhaust, seat, brakes, tyres, electrics, up to the rebuild and on to safe setup and general maintenance and finally onto riding safely and storage.

ISBN: 978-1-845847-46-3
Paperback • 27x20.7cm • 176 pages • 682 colour pictures

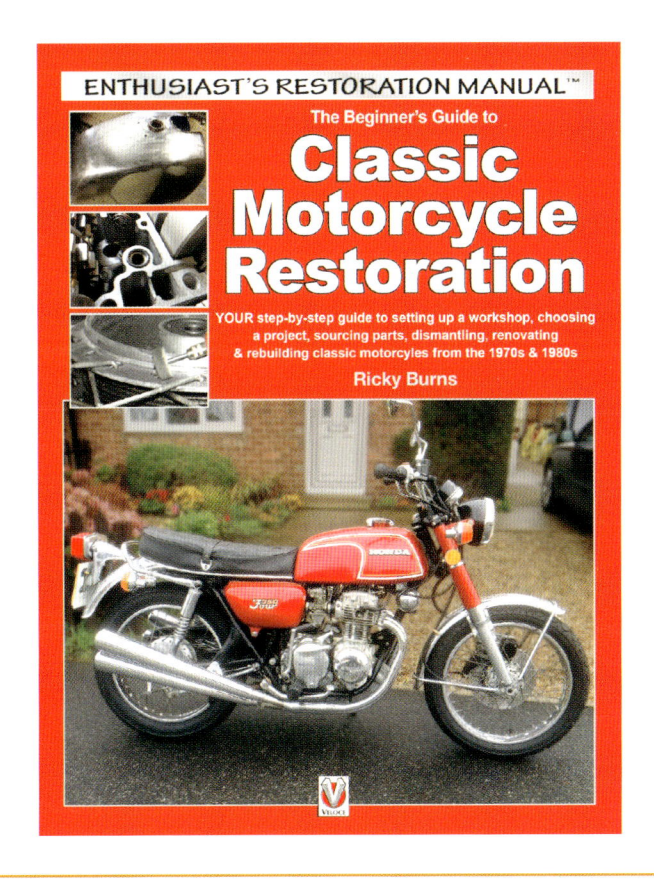

Seasoned motorcycle restorer Ricky Burns goes through each of the stages of a real-life restoration. Aimed at the total beginner but suitable for enthusiasts of all abilities, the reader is taken through each step in detail, and taught the techniques, tricks and tips used by experts. From choosing a project, setting up a workshop, and preparing a bike, to sourcing parts, dismantling, restoring and renovating, this book is the perfect guide for the classic motorcycle restorer.

ISBN: 978-1-845846-44-2
Paperback • 27x20.7cm • 144 pages • 594 pictures

For more information and price details, visit our website at www.veloce.co.uk
email: info@veloce.co.uk • Tel: +44(0)1305 260068

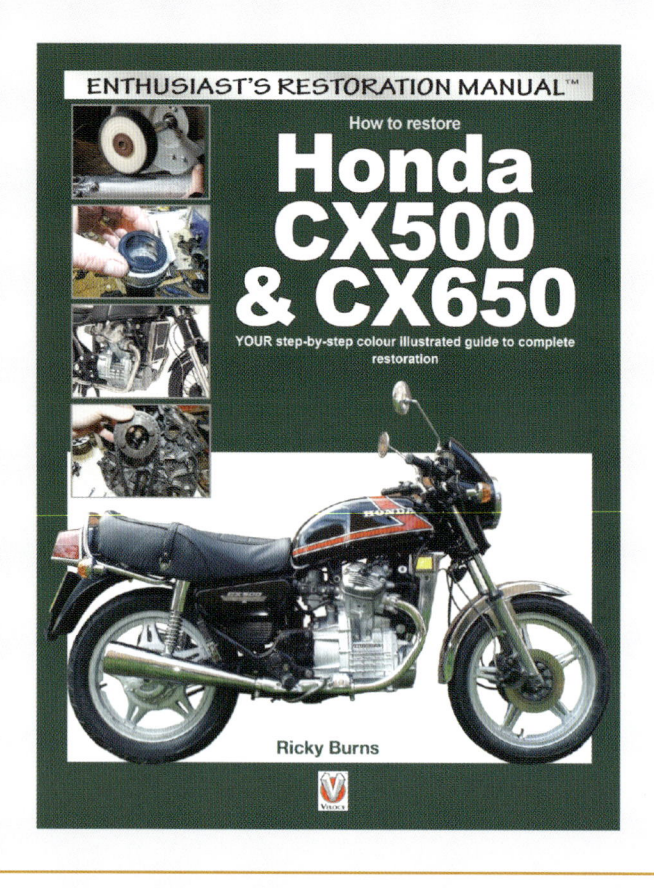

MORE FROM VELOCE ...

Whether a CX500, luxurious CS650 Silver Wing, or CX650 Turbo, this book provides a step-by-step guide to a full restoration. From dismantling, sourcing and restoring parts, to spray painting, decals and polishing. From the rebuild itself, to general maintenance and riding safety, this is the only restoration manual you'll need.

ISBN: 978-1-845847-73-9
Paperback • 27x20.7cm • 176 pages • 759 colour pictures

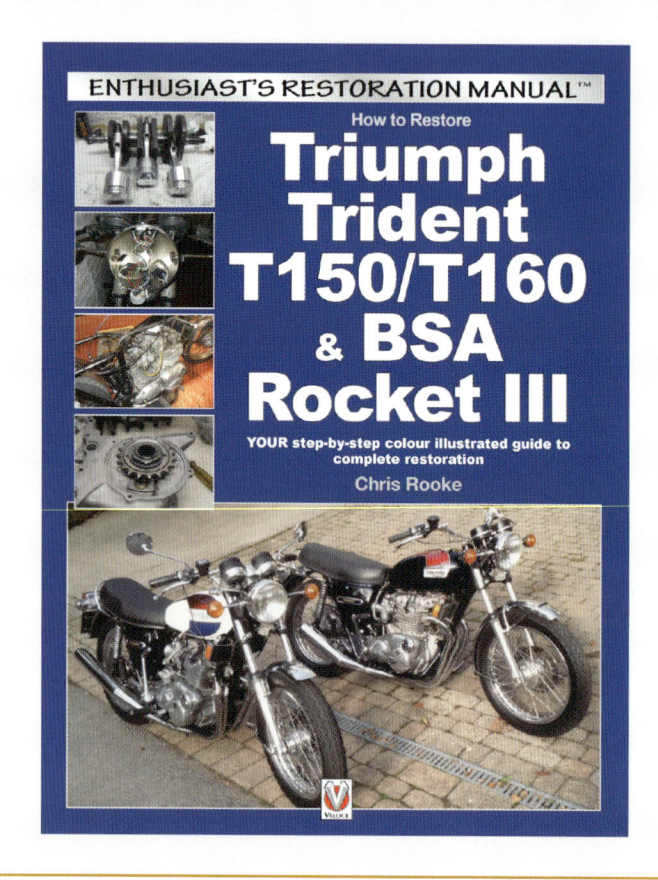

Completed at home by an enthusiastic DIY mechanic who has great experience rebuilding bikes, this book covers the complete restoration of a Triumph Trident T150V and a Triumph T160. Each and every aspect of the dismantling, refurbishment and reassembly of these classic bikes is covered in great detail, accompanied by a host of clear colour photos.

ISBN: 978-1-845848-82-8
Paperback • 27x20.7cm • 232 pages • 704 colour pictures

**For more information and price details, visit our website at www.veloce.co.uk
email: info@veloce.co.uk • Tel: +44(0)1305 260068**

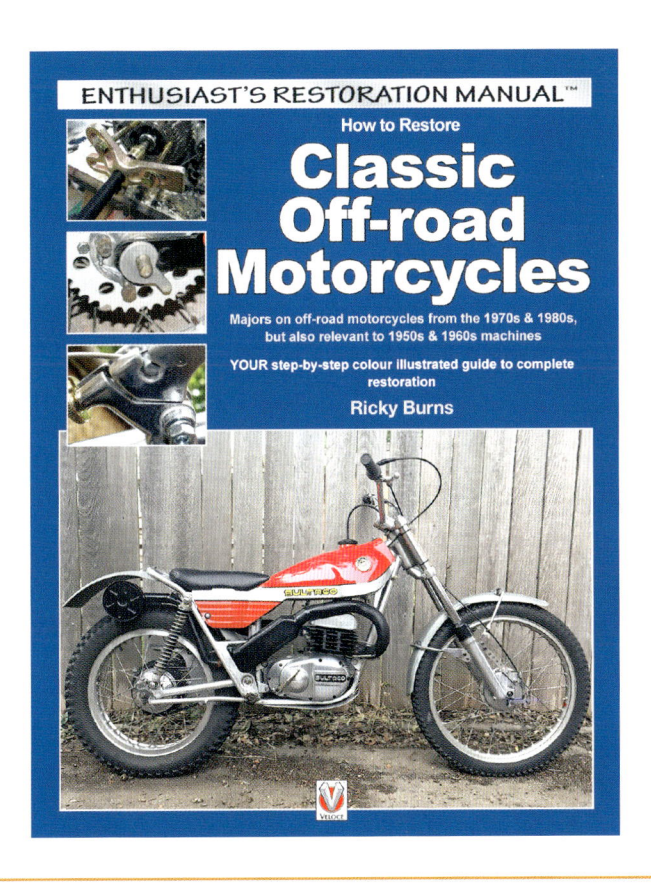

MORE FROM VELOCE ...

How to Restore Classic Off-road Motorcycles provides the classic off-road enthusiast with a step-by-step guide through a full restoration. Whether a post 1950 machine, or a more modern 80s twin shock, everything is covered in detail, from initial dismantling and parts sourcing to being ready to compete, including setup and maintenance.

ISBN: 978-1-845849-50-4
Paperback • 27x20.7cm • 160 pages • 488 colour pictures

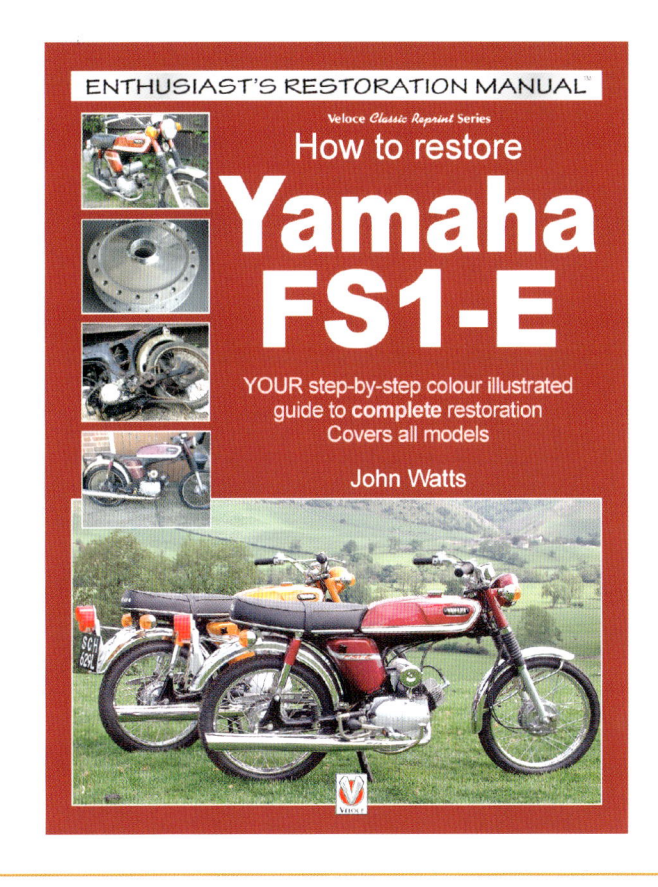

Most FS1-Es have not endured the test of time well, and very few good original examples exist. However, there are plenty of restorable machines around, and this book guides the do-it-yourself restorer through the minefield of finding a machine to restore and the pitfalls of a first restoration.

ISBN: 978-1-787112-50-6
Paperback • 27x20.7cm • 128 pages • 225 colour pictures

**For more information and price details, visit our website at www.veloce.co.uk
email: info@veloce.co.uk • Tel: +44(0)1305 260068**

Index

Adler 18, 20
Aermacchi 53
Agostini, Giacomo 110
Ahearn, Jack 55, 67
AJS 51, 80
Anderson, Hugh 40, 46, 47, 49, 50, 55, 56, 58, 67, 72, 73, 80
Anscheidt, Hans-Georg 72, 73, 80, 82, 85, 86
Argentine GP 48
Ariel 18
Associated Motor Cycles 51, 52
Austin 9
Auto Land 123
Auto-By 92
Avon 88

Bauer, Willy 124, 155, 156
Belgian GP 48, 49, 73, 82, 85
Berliner, Joseph 53
Berliner Motor Corp 53
Bianchi 53
Bike & Rider 114, 119
BMW 9, 18, 21
Brands Hatch 73, 78
Braun, Dieter 85, 86
Bridges, Beau 149
Bridgestone 53, 78
Bron, Rob 110
Brown, Norman 149
Brut 33 148
Bryans, Ralph 56, 73
BSA 18, 53, 87, 104
Buenos Aires 49, 50
Bultaco 89, 124, 137

C&N Enterprises 53
Cabton 18
Cadillac 22
Canadian GP 82
Canon 10
Castrol (Team Castrol) 111, 148
Citroën 14
Clermont-Ferrand 47
Cock, Frederick 17
Continental 88
Cosmopolitan Motors 53
Cotton 53
Crooks, Eddie 110
Crosby, Graeme 149
Cycle World 47, 49, 54, 55, 69, 78, 86, 87, 104, 114, 132, 137
CZ 89, 121, 123, 124
Czechoslovakian GP 67, 73, 81, 82

Davis, Walt 54
Day, Joseph 17
Daytona 49, 55, 56, 67, 110, 111, 147
De Coster, Roger 121, 123, 124, 155, 156
Degner, Ernst 40, 46, 47, 49, 50, 55, 58, 67, 72, 73, 80, 88
Derbi 47, 82, 110
DKW 15, 18
Drennan, Henry 89
Driver, Paddy 40
Ducati 53
Dunlop 88
Dunstall 154
Dutch TT 47, 49, 56, 67, 73, 82, 147

East German GP 49, 56, 67, 73, 82
EPA 154
Everts, Harry 156

Fay, Ray 39, 40
Ferrari, Virginio 148
FIM 42, 80, 85, 88, 111, 112, 121, 124, 156
Findlay, Jack 110-111
Finnish GP 49, 56, 67, 73, 82
French GP 40, 49, 56, 73, 80
Fuji Heavy Industries 10, 24, 42, 69
Fuji Speedway 73, 82
Fujii, Toshio 67
Fujii, Yasuharu 154
Fulton, Walt 54

Geboers, Eric 156
Geboers, Sylvain 121-125, 155
Gilera 49, 53
Giugiaro 98, 141
GM 166
Go Suzuki! 89
Graham, Stuart 80, 82, 85, 86
Grand Prix D'Endurance 73
Grant, Mick 149
Grant, Ron 110, 116
Greeves 53

Hailwood, Mike 65, 149
Harley-Davidson 18, 53, 69, 78, 104
Hartog, Will 148
Hashimoto, Shozo 54
Hennen, Pat 148
Hercules 134

174

INDEX

Heron (Team Heron) 147, 154
Herron, Tom 147, 149
Hirohito, Emperor 10
HMMA 13
Hockenheim 49, 73, 80
Hodaka 78, 146
Honda 8, 10-12, 14, 18, 21, 24, 31-33, 38-40, 42, 46, 47, 49, 50, 53-56, 58, 67, 69, 72, 73, 78, 80, 85, 89, 95, 104, 105, 116, 121, 124, 139, 154, 156, 167
Honda, Soichiro 8, 10, 14, 38
Hoshino, Kazuyoshi 88
Hosk 18
Husqvarna 123-125, 155

Ichino, Michio 39, 40, 47, 49, 67, 95
Imamura, Kotaro 8
Imatra Circuit 82
Indian 18
Ishikawa, Masazumi 121
Isle of Man TT 26, 34, 37-40, 46, 47, 49, 52, 56, 66, 67, 73, 80, 110, 111, 147-149
Isuzu 9, 166
Italian GP (Nations GP) 50, 58, 67, 73, 82, 85
Itoh, Mitsuo 39, 40, 47, 49, 55, 56, 67, 72, 73, 80, 82
Itoh, Yoshito 54
Ivy, Bill 73, 82

Jackson, Michael 165
Japan GP 50, 58, 67, 73, 80, 82, 85, 89
Jawa 53
Jobé, Georges 156
Johnson Motors Inc. 53

Kaaden, Walter 40
Kamen Rider 76
Kanebo 23
Katayama, Yoshimi 55, 58, 67, 72, 73, 80-82
Katayama, Yutaka 53
Kawasaki 29, 52-54, 69, 78, 82, 85, 101, 104, 121, 123, 124, 156, 167
Kawasaki, Hiroyuki 80, 82

Kay, Ken 51
Ken Kay Distributing Co. 53, 54
King, Alistair 40
Kitano, Moto 40, 88
Kojima, Matsuhisa 88
Koshino, Haruo 49, 67
Kreidler 42, 47, 72
KTM 124, 156
Kubo, Kazuo 87, 88
Kuroda, Yukio 104
Kushiya, Kiyoshi 164

Lackey, Brad 156
Lambretta 42, 53, 69
Lilac 18, 78
Lloyd 14
Lucchinelli, Marco 148

MacArthur, Gen. Douglas 10
Maico 53, 123, 124, 156
Mainichi Shimbun 14
Mamola, Randy 148
Mandracchi, Guido 112
Marusho 78
Maruyama, Yoshichika 11, 39
Masuda, Koji 155
Masuda, Sadao 40
Matchless 51, 53, 80
Matsumiya, Jimmy 39, 40
Matsumoto, Toshio 39, 40
Mazda (Toyo Kogyo) 15, 133
McCormack, Jack 54, 55
McElnea, Rob 149
McQueen, Steve 98
Meguro 10, 18, 21, 52
Mikkola, Heikki 125, 155
Mikuni 21, 29, 37, 64, 65, 71, 83, 90, 112
MITI 74
Mitsubishi 10, 42
Miyata 10, 18
Montesa 89, 124
Montjuic 67
Monza 50, 58, 67, 73, 85
Morishita, Isao 49, 55, 56
Mosport 82

Moss, Stirling 82
Moto Guzzi 29
Motobi 53
Motor Cycle 51, 79
Motor Cycling 37
Motorcycle Mechanics 50, 78
Motorcycle Sport 79
Mount Fuji Ascent Race 14
Mustang 54
MV Agusta 40, 47, 53, 110
MZ 40, 67, 82

Nakajima Aircraft Co 10
Nakano, Hiroyuki 154
New York Int Bike Show 87
Nicholas, Jody 110, 116
Nikko Sangyo 114
Nikon 10
Nissan (Datsun) 9, 53, 70, 88
Nixon, Richard 126
Norton 18, 40, 51, 53
Noyce, Graham 156
NSU 53, 133
Nürburgring 85

Okano, Takeharu 39, 40, 47, 88
OPEC 134
Otto, N.A. 16

Parilla 53
Paris Salon 129
Pentalube 88
Perris, Frank 47, 49, 50, 55, 66, 67, 72, 73, 80, 110
Perry, Geoff 110
Petry, Paul 40
Pettersson, Olle 88, 89, 121-123
Pirelli 88
Playboy 86, 93
Pointer 18, 53
Puch 69, 156

Rahier, Gaston 125, 156
Raines, Cristina 149
Read, Phil 80, 82, 149

Ridgway, Gen Matthew 10, 12
Rikuo 10
Rinaldi, Michele 156
Robb, Tommy 73, 80
Robert, Joël 110, 121-124, 155, 156
Roberts, Kenny 148
Rolls-Royce 52
Rond, Gérard 156
Rosengart 9
Rossi, Graziano 148

Saab 18
Sachs 53, 134
Sachsenring 67
SAIAD 121, 137, 138, 148
Sasaki, Toru 26
Schneider, Bert 49, 55, 57
Sheene, Barry 86, 110-112, 147, 148, 154
Shell 56
Shimizu, Masanao 82
Showa 10
Silver Dream Racer 149
Spa-Francorchamps 56, 67, 73
Spanish GP 40, 47, 49, 56, 67, 73, 80, 85
Steyr 53
Subaru 15, 42
Suzuka 46, 50, 58
Suzuki, Jitsujiro 127-129, 133, 166
Suzuki, Michio 8, 9, 11, 13, 14, 23, 98, 155
Suzuki, Osamu 98, 165-167
Suzuki, Saburo 9, 14
Suzuki, Seiichi 47, 87

Suzuki, Shunzo 11, 13, 15, 16, 18, 23, 24, 38-40, 43, 46, 47, 98, 128, 129, 155
Suzuki City 68
Suzuki Fun Center 68
Suzuki Jidosha Kogyo (SJK) 12, 13
Suzuki Loom Manu Co 9
Suzuki Loom Works 8
Suzuki Sekiyu 134
Swedish GP 147

Tanaka, Teisuke 55
Tanaka Kogyo 26
Taveri, Luigi 49, 58, 67, 73
Thompson, Harry 110
Tohatsu 18, 24, 46, 52, 127
Tokyo Show 28, 35, 36, 39, 43, 46, 49, 60, 63, 68, 69, 75, 82, 89, 95, 99, 104, 105, 115, 118, 121, 133
Tokyo University 16
Tokyo University of the Arts 25
Tomizuka, Kiyoshi 16
Tomos 42
Tosho 24
Toyoda, Eiji 10
Toyoda Automatic Loom Works 9, 11
Toyota 8-11, 98, 149
Triumph 20, 53, 87
Turner, Keith 110

Ulster GP 49, 56, 67, 73, 82, 110
Uncini, Franco 148
United States GP 55
USMC GP 49

Van Dongen, Cees 86
Velocette 69
Vespa 42, 69
Vincent, Chris 73
Volkswagen 14
Vromans, André 156

Watanabe, Akira 156
West German GP 40, 49, 56, 67, 73, 80, 85
West Valley Cycle Sales 53
White Motors 53
Whiteway, Frank 110
Wolsink, Gerrit 124, 155, 156
Woodman, Derek 67
Woods, Stan 111

Yajima, Kinjiro 89
Yamaguchi 32
Yamaha 8, 15, 18, 40, 42, 49, 53-55, 67, 69, 73, 78, 80, 82, 85, 87, 89, 95, 101, 110, 123, 124, 128, 139, 141, 148, 154-156, 167
Yamashita, Rinsaku 14
Yokohama 88
Yoshida, Shigeru 12
Yoshimura, Taichi 89

Zundapp 53, 83

The Suzuki Motor Company, its subsidiaries and products are mentioned throughout this book.

富士が認めた日本一
SUZUKI
-flyweight champion of the world
スズキ セルペット 80K
鈴木自動車工業株式会社
コレダ125SH
号125
適な乗心地……
125ST型　2サイクル125cc
コレダ／スーパーツーリング
COLLEDA SUPER TOURING
250TB
MOTOR CYCLE
3 SEPTEMBER 1964
MEET THE FLYWEIGHT CHAMPION OF THE WORLD
SUZUKI
WHICH SUZUKI IS FOR YOU?
SUZUKI
世界
エンジン技術の革命
スズキCCI
新機構スズキCCI方式
スズキが新しく開発した画期的直接給油方式。2ストロークエンジン特有の高度な性能を完璧に保証するメカニズムです。新鮮なオイルがコンロッド大端部に直接供給されるとともにシリンダーにも送られるので、エンジン内部の給油は理想的で耐久性も抜群です。
《画期的な直接給油方式》
●排気煙がでません
●生ガソリンが使えます
●エンジン回転部の耐久性が抜群です
●高速での連続走行が可能です
●カーボンがたまりません
●オイルのムダがなく経済的です
ガソリン
オイル
スズキ
RIDE A WORLD CHAMPION
—IT COSTS YOU LESS!
50cc. SUZUKI SPORTSMAN
SUZUKI MAINTAIN QUALITY AT ANY PRICE!
£95.11.0 TAX PAID H.P. AVAILABLE
SUZUKI
FLYWEIGHT CHAMPION OF THE WORLD
SUZUKI SPORTS
More gals per mile
SUZU